FROM WALDEN POND TO JURASSIC PARK

NEW AMERICANISTS ★ A SERIES EDITED BY DONALD E. PEASE

FROM WALDEN POND

TO JURASSIC PARK

ACTIVISM, CULTURE, & AMERICAN STUDIES ★ PAUL LAUTER

DUKE
UNIVERSITY
PRESS
DURHAM
AND LONDON
2001

© 2001 Duke University Press   All rights reserved

Printed in the United States of America on acid-free paper ♾

Typeset in Scala by Keystone Typesetting, Inc.

Library of Congress Cataloging-in-Publication Data

appear on the last printed page of this book.

FOR ANNIE

O my America! my new-found-land

My kingdom, safeliest when with one man mann'd,

My Mine of precious stones, My Empery,

How blest am I in this discovering thee!

—John Donne, "Elegy XIX"

CONTENTS

perhaps?

INTRODUCTION *"Whatever it is, I'm against it." Horsefeathers*

First, shopper, what this book is *not*. It is not a survey of the field called "American studies," though it contains information based on much observation of what American studies programs do, at home and overseas. It is not a chronicle of American studies, though I do occasionally pass myself off as a historian of moments in what some still call the American studies movement. It is not a set of examples that exhaust the assorted tactics American studies scholars use to examine the equally varied things we study—books, movies, paintings, posters, politics, circuses, classroom practices, catalogs, whaling ships, laws, and riffs. It is not, despite my best intentions, a political tract, though I hope on occasion that it speaks to or rather against the drift to unadorned greed and superficial moralism that mark this time, Buffett to Gingrich to Starr. It is not a memoir, though somewhat to my surprise, one of its first readers pointed to how many of the essays depart from and try to interpret personal experiences. If I've now painted myself into a negative corner, I need to strike a more positive note about what I'm trying to do in this book.

"I resist anything better than my own diversity." Walt Whitman

What does it mean, American studies? The first part of this book illustrates how varied the answers to that question can be. The objects of my study include movies like *Nashville* and *Jurassic Park*, social movements like the Nashville Agrarians and the nonviolent student protesters of the early 1960s, graduate school reading lists and course syllabi, contemporary policy papers on the financing of higher education . . . and my junior high school song book. And while my primary methods are those of close reading—once an English teacher, I suppose, always one—I have gathered my evidence from sources that would not likely have enchanted my 1950s New Critical mentors: *Variety*, Rand Corporation reports, movieland blurbs. I also argue that doing American studies is a kind of political act; no, not the sort one carries out in the voting booth, much less in the streets and on the parapets of the Pentagon. I don't identify our academic pursuits with insurrection. Neither, however, is what we do tame. It isn't only that inside the academy American studies is, as it has been for half a century, engaged in a conflict for resources, all the more intense in this time of strained educational budgets. In the larger world, American studies has never offered a peaceful collegiate abode.

"America why are your libraries full of tears?" Allen Ginsberg

In its academic phase—the last fifty years or so—American studies has been marked by a tension between its reigning ideologies, relatively progressive in their time, and the field's role in nurturing America's imperial aspirations, especially in the post–World War II period. But the agon of American Studies was hardly new news in 1950, for it extends back certainly as far as W. E. B. Du Bois's *The Souls of Black Folks* (1903) and José Martí's "Our America" (1891), and, if one sees them in this light, texts as historically distant as William Bradford's *Of Plymouth Plantation* (c. 1630–1650) and Thomas Jefferson's *Notes on the State of Virginia* (1785). Race and ethnicity have, of course, always been at the center of the paradox of American studies, from long before it was called that. How could it be otherwise when any serious study of the European presence on this continent needs always consider the racial record if it would not court evasion? So we ask how our field rubs up against, poaches on, sometimes embraces, sometimes avoids ethnic studies. And how we parade into the world where always, already, we are American, whatever our study. To such matters is part 2 devoted.

"I don't even like political poems." Lorna Dee Cervantes

The third part of the book returns to canon questions that have long taken up much of my own energies. Here I begin with a long essay about *The Heath Anthology of American Literature,* since it has become something of a touchstone for debates about cultural canons in this country. In fact, however, the real subject of this essay and the terrain of this part is modernism, or more precisely its conflicted constructions in the years during and since certain ideas of a modernist order became the dominant force of American literary culture. Our own exertions in producing the *Heath* provide but one instance of how an earlier view not just of the modernist canon, but of literary value, inhibited and complicated culturally progressive aspirations. The essays on Herman Melville and on Amy Lowell track ways in which their literary reputations rose, in the one case, and fell in the other in relation to certain developments in modernist thinking. Finally, I return, not surprisingly, to the work of my own mentors, against which, in certain respects, efforts like the *Heath,* my previous books, and this collection, too, are deployed. My intent has not so much been to kill the fathers—parricides all say that, of course—as to understand how those of us with a revisionist cultural agenda have used their ways of organizing cultural power, even as we contested the very grounds upon which they stood.

"I left the woods for as good a reason as I went there." H. D. Thoreau

But what of my title? Does it stake out anything but a catchy sound bite? I went to Walden, in fact, a bit over forty years ago, at about the time I was writing a review of then recent scholarship on Thoreau for *The New Leader.* It was 1959, and I was cheerfully (and accurately) predicting a political turn in our understanding of Thoreau, who seemed to me a prophet of the social movements just then gathering strength as blacks boycotted the Montgomery buses, Dr. Spock worried about fallout, and beatniks mocked the House Un-American Activities Committee in San Francisco. The review represented my engagement in a longer project, growing from my dissertation ("Emerson's Rhetoric"), which I imagined as a major academic tome on language and rhetoric (à la Kenneth Burke) in Emerson, Thoreau, and—down the road, my goal—Melville. I actually did complete a piece of the Thoreau section, in the form of an article, "Thoreau's Prophetic Testimony," for a 1962 issue of the *Massachusetts Review*. But by then life, or more precisely the Movement, had begun to intervene, and in 1963 I went to work for the American Friends Service Committee as director of peace studies. The study and practice of civil disobedience—as experience and politics—took over from the analysis of "Civil Disobedience" as text and theory. It would be two decades and more before I returned to American transcendentalism and then only by paths that led not so much from graduate school as from freedom school.

"Rigidity means death." Gloria Anzaldúa

Ironically, perhaps, as I was completing this book I was also finishing the introduction for an edition of *Walden* and "Civil Disobedience" in the New Riverside series, for which I'm the general editor. Going back to reread my 1962 Thoreau piece for the first time in at least a quarter century, I found to my astonishment that I had reproduced in my new introduction some of the very same language I had used when Thoreau was first helping lead me away from my academic New Critical training and into nonviolence. Perhaps that only proves that what goes around comes around, or how deeply the brain runs within its groove. But I actually think that the phrases I evoked at Walden forty years ago echo differently amongst the vines and beasts of today's Jurassic culture. For then I could assimilate Thoreau to Isaiah, to testify against nukes, racism, and complacency; whereas today he seems to me a more slippery and ironic fellow, playing out contradictions that appear not only in the woods, but in the study, the movie house, the classroom, and the bedroom. He's no less irritating or self-involved, queer as ever, smart as any grad student, but now I can learn from him something of what one needs to know to survive Jurassic culture. So my title acknowledges the inescapable trek of American studies from its ostensibly pastoral beginnings to a famous new role in the commodity jungle of Time-Warner, Disney, AOL, and Amazon.com. But the title also registers, I suppose, the curve of my own, peculiar career, which, having passed through Mississippi, Selma, the levitation of the Pentagon, the decline of the West, the fifty-sixth issue of *Radical Teacher*, the emergence of American studies in Vietnam, returns via Jurassic Park to the woods for as good a reason as I left there.

"I want to thank everybody who made this day necessary." Yogi Berra
Cleanth Brooks would be astonished to find himself directly following Yogi Berra, but the fact is that Mr. Brooks taught me well. Not only to read the ironies of juxtaposition closely, but—as the final part of this book suggests—how to organize intellectual workers. Perhaps, too, gentleman that he was, he conveyed to a callow Jewish kid from New York a certain small sense of grace—or, at any rate, sufficient to allow me to thank him even as I take issue with virtually all his judgments. Others have more directly had a hand in the shaping of this book—so many, in fact, that I can only apologize beforehand to those whose names I have managed to omit. They certainly include, first of all, the individuals who directly initiated or in one way and another helped edit one of the chapters: Jaap Verhuel, Hans Krabbendam, Rob Kroes, Donald Pease, Robyn Wiegman, Lucy Maddox, Hiroko Sato, Tatsuro Nomura, Ibu Puan Ellisafny, Sunarwoto, Ibu Dewi Murni, Subur War-doyo, Roland Hagenbüchle, Josef Raab, Yassen N. Zassoursky, Isaiah Smithson, Nancy Ruff, Kim Hastings, and, over and over, Cathy David-son. On no group of people have I drawn more than my colleagues on the editorial board of *The Heath Anthology of American Literature*: Rich-ard Yarborough, Juan Bruce-Novoa, Jackson Bryer, the late Elaine Hedges, Anne Jones, the late Amy Ling, Wendy Martin, Charles Molesworth, Carla Mulford, Raymund Paredes, Ivy Schweitzer, Linda Wagner-Martin, Andrew Wiget, and Sandra Zagarell. They and our colleagues Paul Smith, Randy Bass, and John Alberti have taught me more than they know, and a lot more than I can ever repay. On this project I must register particular thanks to Carla, Linda, Richard, and Sandy, without whose encouragement and responses, I would still be frittering away my time.

*"Bare lists of words are found suggestive to an
imaginative and excited mind."* R. W. Emerson
A great many individuals have helped me to think about the issues these essays address. Many were kind enough to share their responses

and thoughts at presentations I gave; others helped me recognize how people in very different venues might hear my remarks. The names of some, like the colleague at a United States Information Agency winter institute in Delaware who talked to me about *Jurassic Park* as a failed utopia, I am ashamed to say have faded from memory. But some, at least, I have managed to retain, and I hope they will regard a word here as a small gesture of appreciation for their generosity and as a symbol of what they have enabled me to write: thank you, Ibu Pia Alisjahbana, Dr. Burhanuddin Arafah, Estelle Baird, Hans Bak, Sergio Luiz Prado Bellei, Jesus Benito Sánchez, Paula Bennett, Dr. Melani Budianta, Selma Burkom, Johnnella Butler, Jan Cohn, Constance Coiner *(¡Presente!)*, Rob Corber, Michael Cowan, Kate Delaney, Jane C. Desmond, Micaela di Leonardo, Virginia Dominguez, Tim Drown, Emory Elliott, Ibu Estiati, SallyAnn Ferguson, Jeff Finlay, Shelley Fisher Fishkin, Dick Flacks, Phyllis Franklin, Doris Friedensohn, Peggy Gifford, Robert A. Gross, Wen-ching Ho, Rich Horwitz, Gordon Hutner, Heinz Ickstadt, Greg Jay, Anne Jones, André Kaenel, Carla Kaplan, Karen Kilcup, Andy Lakritz, Lee Yu-cheng, Günter Lenz, Hsien-hao Sebastian Liao, Shirley Lim, Ana Maria Manzanas Calvo, Jim Miller, Judy Moon, Marcy Knopf Newman, Gail Nomura, Dick Ohmann, Hassan Ouzzate, Carl Pedersen, Mikhail Pelipas, Margo Perkins, Jean Pfaelzer, Fred Pfeil, Marco Portales, Alvina Quintana, Chodidah (Toto) Rahardjo, Tim Reed, Dilvo Ristoff, Lillian Robinson, Paula Rothenberg, John Carlos Rowe, Richard Ruland, Claudia Sadowski-Smith, Eric Sandeen, Rita Schmidt, Shan Te-hsing, Judy Siegel, Dr. Doddy W. Sjahbuddin, Reynolds Smith, Bruce Spear, Hortense Spillers, John Stephens, Wesley Stewart, Stephen Sumida, Sun Mi Ra, Justine Tally, Rick Taylor, Ronald Thomas, Tamara Tsintsadze, Alexandr Vaschenko, Tatiana Venediktova, Joyce Warren, Don Q. Washington, Natalia Yakimenko, Janet Zandy.

"and a person for work that is real." Marge Piercy
Louis Kampf has had the misfortune to have virtually all of these essays forced upon him; nevertheless, with his usual good sense, he pronounced them appropriate for *Darwin University Studies*. For this—and a few hundred thousand other hints and indirections—a *b'ruchah*. Ann Fitzgerald, my fiercest critic and most indefatigable promoter, has been the seldom silent partner in this entire enterprise. It is a protocol

of this form to attribute one's virtues to one's partner; in this case it is simply true to say that not a paragraph in this book remains unimproved by her editorial hand, and much that I have come to look at, here and elsewhere on the turning earth, I have come to see through her curious and loving eyes. The words of thanks are elsewhere than on this page.

PART ONE ★ PRACTICING AMERICAN STUDIES

INTRODUCTION TO PART ONE These essays were written over a number of years and for very diverse situations. I have placed them in this sequence: the keynote talk at the 1997 meeting of the Netherlands American Studies Association in Middleburg; a talk at the first Dartmouth conference on the futures of American studies in 1997; the presidential address of the 1994 American Studies Association (ASA) convention in Nashville; the annual ASA president's speech at the 1995 Sendai meeting of the Japanese Association for American Studies; and an informal 1996 lecture on popular culture to a group of university teachers at Diponegoro University in Semarang, Central Java, Indonesia. They do, however, represent a common project: my own efforts to understand what it meant that I was "doing" American studies. Clearly, having been elected ASA president in 1992, and having been sent abroad to lecture about American studies, I was seen as an American studies person. But I have to confess that I really had no clear idea of what that might mean, apart from the fact that my scholarly work, largely focused on literary texts, concerned the United States. Of course, I had been writing "political" essays about the United States since the late 1950s, including one, as I recall, on Henry Kissinger and Norman Cousins. But it had only been in recent years that most—though obviously not all—literary folk had come to reject the sanctified divide between the "scholarly" and the "political," indeed, to acknowledge that the two categories might be deeply implicated with each other.

Crossing over into American studies, I found little resistance to the notion that the professional is the political. It was considerably more difficult, however, to locate some consensus about what Americanists generally thought we did, much less what the political project of American studies as a field could, or even should, be. Hence the enterprise to describe our labor. These essays represent the fruits of that effort—or, perhaps, the residue of the struggle. However that might be, I hope these can be helpful to others involved in what is, after all, a broad and common project of defining and redefining what it is we do under the name—itself increasingly contested—"American studies."

My basic contention throughout is that American studies as an academic discipline has developed a set of distinctive, somewhat eclectic, but logically connected methods for approaching its increasingly diverse subject matter. These essays attempt to describe and illustrate such methods. At the same time, I have tried to suggest methodological directions—for example, those of ethnography—in which I think American studies practitioners ought to be pushing in order to anchor our tendencies toward the cleverly speculative assertion and the abstruse theoretical design. I don't propose that these essays will resolve the field's methodological, much less its ideological, conflicts. But I think these pieces can prove to be useful contributions to what is and is likely to continue as an ongoing discussion.

CHAPTER ONE

RECONFIGURING ACADEMIC DISCIPLINES: THE EMERGENCE OF AMERICAN STUDIES

Few recent books have generated as much discussion as Daniel Goldhagen's *Hitler's Willing Executioners*. Reviewers have debated its evocation of "German exceptionalism," and historians have discussed the persuasiveness of the evidence it offers as well as the cogency of its explanatory framework. But one may also wish to ask about the role the book is playing in the United States today: what cultural work is it performing at a moment in which the Holocaust seems itself an ever larger presence on the American scene? This seems to me an absorbing, indeed major question. But I do not want to address it here. Rather, I wish to ask "where should such a question be studied within the academy?"

By "cultural work" I refer to the ways in which a book or other kind of "text"—a movie, a Supreme Court decision, an ad, an anthology, an international treaty, a material object—helps construct the frameworks, fashion the metaphors, create the very language by which people comprehend their experiences and think about their world. The question of the cultural work *Hitler's Willing Executioners* is performing today is not, then, a historical issue, strictly speaking; individual historians might venture answers, but most would maintain that it is rather more a matter for imaginative speculation than for the assessment of facts, logic, and alternative explanations—the historian's stock in trade. While the book is by any definition a "text," it remains unlikely grist even for the varied mills of English studies. A cultural anthropologist might take the issues on, but those who study the United States are rare, courses rarer, and their work has seldom "attained the scope of the concerns of cultural criticism."[1]

Are we then to conclude that this is a matter not for the academy but for that fabled hero, the Public Intellectual, or for more mundane Sunday morning TV pundits? That conclusion sells the academy short. More important, perhaps, it ignores the fact that the question of a text's cultural work is not one restricted to a few exceptional volumes like Goldhagen's. On the contrary, the issue arises with any human production—the movie *Jurassic Park*, for example, or the 1994 Republican "Contract with America"—that mobilizes creative imagery and artful details that resonate with force in the society. Nor do such issues emerge only with respect to contemporary works. The question of where and how one studies the cultural work of texts comes up as well with Melville's "Benito Cereno," the *Dred Scott* decision, the racist tract, *A Sociology for the South,* or the stitching of a Virginia sampler. So the question remains: where—and how—do we study not so much the texts themselves as what I have been calling the "cultural work" they perform? Where, moreover, do we ask how and why certain texts or objects come into existence in the particular historical landscapes of the United States?

The brief answer, I think, is in American studies.

My longer answer to these questions, to the problem of the academic divisions of knowledge, derives from what may be a distinctive experience of student capacities in graduate and advanced undergraduate courses, especially in American studies and in English, as well as in reviewing American studies programs. What is very striking to me are the differences among even—or perhaps particularly—stronger students in English, history, and American studies. Whether or not they do it well, English students seem drawn inexorably to close reading formats, even when these are inappropriate to an assignment. Most have seemed to me deaf to entreaties, demands, or even lessons in how to "contextualize" through anything but the vaguest references to "historical background." On the other hand, most history students seem to think it strange, at best, to focus on the textualization of concepts, on the specific linguistic constructions that give form to ideas, much less on the ways in which language and form can come implicitly to contradict, or at least call into question, the very arguments being made. They seem used to more generalized discussions of a writer's ideas, or to questions of how well or badly a scholar has marshaled evidence and worked out the logic of an argument. I am, to be sure, making large generalizations, and I would not try to insist upon them too unequivocally. But they do suggest that after all is said and done, literary and historical study continue, adequately or not, to maintain what were their earlier methodological emphases.

Such methods are, of course, quite relevant to the varied forms of study that have come to dominate American studies as it is practiced in the United States. But such traditional approaches, and the subject matters they effectively underwrite, simply do not begin to cover what is now being done in American studies. It was once the case that American studies amounted to a loose amalgam of history, literature, and art (HLA, to use the Harvard formulation). No more. In fact, I think, the return to more traditional methods and subjects now often urged upon English and history departments[2] needs to be understood as a response to newer forms of academic work pushing up between and within these older disciplines. I believe we are in the midst of a fundamental alteration in the academic division of what are sometimes termed the "human sciences."

How we divide academic knowledge is not altogether arbitrary, though it is deeply inflected by historical accidents. There is no necessary logic to the structure of English departments, for example, most of which are internally divided between literature and writing (and often further divided between "creative" and "remedial" writing), and many of which contain, or once did, areas like speech, film, and theater. Nor are these departmental divisions fixed, though the institutional structures in which they are embedded do persist, indeed tend to resist change. Still, as new ways of thinking about the world emerge, new disciplines like sociology and anthropology arise. Often such new areas of study develop within existing departments, from which, if they grow and flourish, they then separate as independent entities. But the place of such new programs in the academic system, their very right to exist, can long remain at contest. At my own institution, for example, anthropology emerged as a small independent department just three or four years ago. This is not surprising since much of the academy is conservative by design and exclusive in practice. Still, one cannot usefully pursue an inquisitional approach to new knowledge: one cannot exclude by fiat what intellectuals persist in asking about and what students find compelling.

Both intellectuals and students persistently ask about movies, *Jurassic Park* for instance (as I do later in this book). In a broadly constituted English department, one might approach it as yet one more "text," whose plot, characters, themes, and aesthetic tactics can fruitfully be analyzed in more or less traditional ways. But what if one wishes then to historicize this "text," addressing the conflict between its condemnation of commodifying dinosaurs and its real-life existence as one of the most successful commodifications of dinosaurs or, indeed, anything else in human history? Again, in light of the movie's thematic critique of technology applied to profit, how does one best study the origins, development, and use of the advanced technologies upon which the movie is so dependent? How does one explain the film's great audience appeal in the particular, post–Gulf War moment of its distribution and consumption; its role in salvaging the economic fortunes of the Matsushita Electric Industrial Corporation; or its function in the spreading internationalization of cultural production? Doesn't the pursuit of these historical, economic, marketing, even technological issues draw one away from any traditional discipline— even one as flexibly constituted as English—and into other, distinctly interdisciplinary fields, like film studies or, more often, American studies?

I point toward American studies in part because the annual convention of the American Studies Association and its journal, *American Quarterly,* have become venues of choice in the United States for many of those active in cultural studies and related areas concerned with mass culture, the media and its institutions, the politics of communications, academic conventions and discourses, and the like. At the same time, though the process has been less apparent, distinctive theoretical paradigms as well as objects of study have emerged within American studies. To compare the reading lists of introductory graduate courses in English, history, and American studies (one is appended to this chapter) is to observe three very distinct domains, within which practitioners are asking rather different, if related, questions. Such a course in American studies will include work by people located in English and history, as well as in anthropology, art, music, political science, and sociology departments. But what is more striking are the number of works which are very *unlikely* to be central to either introductory graduate history or English courses, books like—to cite just two from 1996—Richard Ohmann's *Selling Culture* and Rob Kroes's *If You've Seen One, You've Seen the Mall.*[3] Cixous, Culler, de Man, Derrida, Fish, Gilbert, Gubar, Hartman, Kristeva, Spillers, and Spivak continue to constitute meat and potatoes in literary criticism; work, that is, concerned predominantly with discourse, not history, and influenced by modes of philosophical speculation. A comparable American studies list would include Williams, Trachtenberg, Saldívar, Radway, Lowe, Lipsitz, Lenz, Hall, Denning, Carby, Anzaldúa.

Such core texts in American studies generally embody a number of distinctive methodological principles. One is embodied in Fredric Jameson's injunction "Always historicize," by which is generally meant focus less on the formal qualities and structures of a text or a material object and more on why it emerges as it does in its particular moment, how the forms of its production, distribution, and consumption materialize—what forces, social, economic, aesthetic, technological, have come together to produce this thing in this place at this time? The emphasis on historicizing texts extends to books in the field, including its "classics," works like Perry Miller's *Errand into the Wilderness* or Henry Nash Smith's *Virgin Land*, for example. These can be explored not only for their arguments but to understand why they emerged at a particular historical juncture and what were the roles they played in constructing an older, essentially cold war paradigm of American studies.[1] Just as scholars wish to understand the origins and the work of such texts, they likewise seek to grasp the functions of their own intellectual labor within the changing shape of American institutions, like the culture industries and the university. In this respect, the central concerns of American studies promote a kind of intense self-scrutiny among its practitioners, an effort to situate one's own practice and assumptions within American institutional life.

A second principle has to do with the fundamental importance of textuality, not just of the written sort but, as I have suggested, in the variety of forms people construct for the many purposes to which we devote ourselves. Textual form as such is of less concern here than the ways in which such forms express various relations of power, and also how texts themselves, like all cultural phenomena, shape and are shaped by the material conditions of everyday life. Moreover, like their colleagues in literary study, Americanists are interested in how language and form often reveal what an argument tends, indeed wishes, to veil, or how imagery and details reenforce or contradict a writer's ideas. An Americanist teaching certain founding documents, like Tom Paine's *Common Sense* or Hamilton's "Federalist no. 6," might call attention to the differing ways both employ gendered imagery to suggest what constitutes "manly" forms of behavior in the distinctive moments of these texts' creation.[5] One might point to how the language of the final sentence of Leo Marx's *The Machine in the Garden* opens a critique of the book's main argument about the centrality of American "high" culture to the sustenance of humane values.[6] Or to Priscilla Wald's intense scrutiny of the revisions of the Declaration of Independence or the terms used in the majority opinion of the *Dred Scott* case.[7] Similarly, Amy Kaplan roots a brilliant critique of how earlier forms of American studies had ignored American imperialism in her observation of how Perry Miller's brief African experience returns obsessively to Miller's account of the origins of his project to study America's "Errand into the Wilderness."[8]

In thus separating textuality from what is sometimes called "context,"[9] I run the risk of reinscribing the old literature/history dichotomy within the picture of American studies I am constructing. That division, as Donald Pease has pointed out, underwrote a more fundamental political separation of culture from politics in the forms of American studies that emerged after World War II.[10] It is important, therefore, to underline the ways in which current versions of American studies insist upon the political functions of textual forms, or, in Pease's words, "on literature as an agency within the political world."[11] Moreover, texts need to be seen as constituting but one element of what Lisa Lowe has described as "discourse": "I do not intend to limit *discourse* to only these particular textual forms; by *discourse,* I intend a rather extended meaning—a network that includes not only texts and cultural documents, but social practices, formal and informal laws, policies of inclusion and exclusion, and institutional forms of organization, for example, all of which constitute and regulate knowledge about the object of that discourse, Asian America."[12] I am not persuaded that "discourse" is the best term here, since as Lowe uses it, it encompasses the results not only of the close reading skills of literary critics, but also the practices of accumulating, classifying, evaluating, and interpreting empirical data central to the disciplines of the "human sciences," of economics, and of ethnography. Some Americanists do tend to emphasize the *reading* of cultural texts over the processes of tracking the economic or political work texts perform or the concentration of material factors that shape particular cultural moments and material objects. Indeed, current American studies practice can sometimes be criticized for restricting itself to the close and often clever readings of unusual "texts"—contracts, ads, legislation, organizational forms—detached from the worlds in which they perform their work.[13] My perception is that many, particularly younger Americanists are turning toward ethnographic investigation to root at least contemporary cultural speculations in material evidence. It may well be that ethnography will emerge as a new methodological force within the American studies mix, and that anthropologists who focus their work on the United States will be among the more active claimants for room in the American studies tent.

Third, American studies has increasingly become comparative and global in outlook,[14] often focusing on cultural, social, and geographic "borderlands,"[15] within which new multicultural personal and group identities are being constituted. Focusing, too, on the multiple interconnections between ethnicity and race as domestic social constructions and overseas communities from which Americans derive, and to which they display, degrees of affiliation. It is almost unnecessary to say that certain key categories of experience and analysis, particularly race, gender, class, sexuality, and disability, have become central to American studies discourse, as they have to most of the humanities and humane social sciences in the American academy, though as I point out in my third chapter, practitioners have been considerably less successful in focusing on "class" in the context of the United States than on others of these conceptions.[16] Scholars have also come to speak of a "postnational" American studies,[17] which may sound like a contradiction in terms, but which actually reflects one way in which the very globalization of American culture seems to require an increased local-ization of its study. Moving away from earlier methods—like the analy-sis of myths and symbols—which emphasized what was "exceptional" in American culture, today's scholars increasingly apply comparative tactics that illuminate what is continuous in the experience of Ameri-cans and of other people, what is hybrid, as well as what is uniquely American. In particular, American studies practitioners are interested in how aspects of American culture and politics, like ads, slogans, political ideas, organizational strategies are appropriated in different times and places by different people for differing ends—how, for ex-ample, Indonesian students adapt discussions of American elections to examine their own national politics, or, as Rob Kroes has shown in *If You've Seen One, You've Seen the Mall,* how Europeans deploy elements of American advertising toward somewhat different cultural goals.

A fourth principle, perhaps a bit less widely shared, has to do with the usefulness of Antonio Gramsci's ideas about "hegemony."[18] These provide what many find a useful framework for understanding how particular groups gain authority over political and cultural life in a state, how they respond to challenges from subordinated groups, how such subordinated groups themselves generate cultural and social au-thority, indeed how power is always contested, shifting, Protean.[19] Such ideas have been particularly influential in charting the dynamic interplay of race, gender, class, and other categories of identity in so multicultural a nation as the United States. Earlier metaphors of class or group combat—as in the Internationale, " 'Tis the final conflict, / Let each stand in his place"—were perhaps drawn from then prevailing ideas of warfare: armies confronting one another across relatively sta-ble lines of battle, critic-soldiers entrenched in intellectual strong-holds, exchanging learned shells across a front, and the like. The con-cept of hegemony reflects something of the character of guerrilla warfare, wherein the lines of combat, the distribution of power, even what precisely constitutes power continually shift, and to freeze into an altogether defined location is to court irrelevance, if not disaster.

Finally, a fifth point, American studies is part of the wave of inter-disciplinary programs that, particularly beginning in the late 1960s, gained a certain purchase in the American academy. It shares with history, as I have said, that focus upon "context," with literary study the devotion to the text, whatever it might be, with cultural anthropology a

functional way of reading texts and objects. American studies, however, consciously seeks the areas of intersection between the objects of
study of the various disciplines upon which it draws—between a literary text, *Uncle Tom's Cabin,* say, or "Benito Cereno," contemporary
sociological ideas about color and miscegenation, historical and legal
debates informing policy and legislation like the Fugitive Slave Act,
questions of citizenship and race embedded in American constitutional jurisprudence and manifest in a Supreme Court decision like
that in *Dred Scott,* the doctrines of evangelical Christianity, including
the tensions between the perfectionist ideology of abolitionist leaders
like William Lloyd Garrison and the more meliorative views of men
like Harriet Beecher Stowe's brother, Lyman Beecher, changing technologies of publishing and distribution (and travel) in the 1840s and
1850s, the iconography of fugitive slave posters, and the economics of
the slave trade and industrial capitalism, to name some of the most
obvious.

Interdisciplinarity is a source of the strength of American studies.
But looked at uncritically, as a kind of mantra, the concept of "interdisciplinarity" presents something of a problem. For it can be seen as
sustaining in normative roles the disciplinary arrangements of knowledge that prevail in most universities today. But disciplinary knowl-
edges are not grounded in nature. Rather, they are in significant measure ways of mapping authority and power over resources within the
greater education industry. They are not only that, to be sure, but to
assume their permanence or their epistemological innocence seems
to me a mistake both at the level of institutional politics and, as I have
been trying to suggest, in theoretical and methodological ways as well.
It may well be that the newer interdisciplinary programs as well as
some older ones, American studies, ethnic studies, women's studies,
lesbian and gay studies, the variety of area studies, cognitive science,
political economy, will thrive only by contesting for resources and
legitimacy with existing, monodisciplinary academic programs.[20] One
might, in fact, argue that interdisciplinary paradigms are to the traditional disciplines as queer paradigms are to the hegemony of hetero-
sexual norms.

One further problem with an unproblematized assumption about
the interdisciplinary character of American studies is that it may hide
the quite disciplinary premises from which most individual practi-

tioners actually work. The program, the department, the field, the project, may well be interdisciplinary by any measure; the practitioners may be something else again. As Claire Moses has put it, writing about another presumptively interdisciplinary area, women's studies: "We rarely acknowledge the disciplinarity of any of our work. We claim 'interdisciplinarity,' but it is often the case that interdisciplinarity in women's studies is rather like the 'universal' of Enlightenment discourse: seeming to be all-inclusive, our interdisciplinarity too often masks the predominance of one discipline over others."[21] That may help to explain some of the current tensions in the American studies world between those whose origins lie in literary studies and those of historical or social science extraction.[22] If that is the case, then American studies needs to be seen as a contested terrain whereon people with somewhat differing intellectual, or more properly disciplinary, loyalties struggle for authority.

All the same, these five characteristics—which I hope this book will in many respects illustrate—suggest how distinct American studies has become from history, English, art history, or anthropology—or, for that matter, from the other disciplines that constitute the older departmental structure of American colleges and universities. My methodological emphases are not the whole story, to be sure, especially because the current dynamics of American studies have brought sharply into view the relationships between certain interdisciplinary academic programs and communities variously marginalized in American society. Turning away from the fundamentally nationalist project that preoccupied Americanists in the post–World War II period, and learning from its peers in women's studies and in ethnic minority studies programs, American studies has increasingly sought to find—or, more properly, to construct—grounds upon which to connect its academic work with the needs to sustain humane values in an era distinguished by rising greed, chauvinism, and indifference. In the title of the 1997 American Studies Association convention, the issue has become "Going Public: Defining Public Culture(s) in the Americas."

That forms of cultural study have in the United States taken root within American studies is not simply a historical accident, though one could argue that it is coincidental. When cultural studies began to develop, it needed either, like women's studies, to create an academic home, or to find one within which it might flourish. Not having any ready-made constituency, and given the cutbacks that began to wrack higher education in the 1970s, the separatist route seemed chimerical. Popular culture venues were too narrow and fragmented. History departments were, on the whole, unreceptive, and while English as a national field was more open, fundamental stresses remained at the level of many departments, within which the very concept of historicizing led, for the most part, a shadowy existence and within which poststructuralist theory, with its philosophical implications and cachet, came to define the major departure from—or continuities with—the close-reading aesthetics of the New Criticism. American studies, however, seemed a reasonable abode: it had from its origins focused on cultural issues, it had outgrown the paradigms prevailing through the 1960s and was searching for new ones, it shared an interdisciplinary character, and there were significant connections between some of its most energetic practitioners and the British cultural studies school of Raymond Williams, Stuart Hall, and others.

There was, of course, a rudimentary contradiction: as Michael Denning has pointed out, the fundamental identity question traditionally asked by American studies—"What is American?"—is far narrower and perhaps less interesting than the questions asked by cultural studies; the identity question seems to lead inevitably toward what is unique, exceptional, whereas "the central questions [of cultural studies]—'what is culture?', 'what are its forms and how is it related to material production?'—formed a more productive theoretical agenda."[23] Yet, ironically perhaps, as the power of American-based capitalism has spread worldwide, as processes of globalization have brought elements of American culture to almost every corner of the world, and as components from many other cultures have come into and altered America—as, in short, the United States itself becomes more hybrid and international, the appropriateness of American studies as a home for the new intellectual work rooted in cultural studies becomes more logical.

As the advent of cultural studies has altered American studies, the reverse has been true as well. It would be a mistake to think about what I am describing as a popular culture glorification of *General Hospital*, Ice-T, and *I, Robot*. The new American studies encompasses a far wider set of "texts" and asks questions about them that students and colleagues in disciplines outside the older HIA framework find compelling. But it also asks similar questions of "high" cultural texts as well. This is an area of contemporary American studies work often misunderstood. Robert Berkhofer, for example, names a "recent trend" in theory "dehier-archicalization": "Such a trend is most evident in the erosion, even dissolution, of the scholarly and aesthetic boundaries dividing elite from popular cultures. Although it may be difficult to pinpoint when the Beatles became as legitimate to study as Beethoven, or *The Virginian* as *Moby-Dick*, or everyday objects as high art ones, American Studies was in its classic period already a leader in the trend."[24] Berkhofer's formulation can easily lead to the charge that American studies as an intellectual practice reduces, indeed degrades, traditional forms of high culture, valuing equally not just the Beatles and Beethoven but "What's Love Got to Do with It?" and "The Love Song of J. Alfred Prufrock." But the question of what is a legitimate *object of study* in no necessary or predictable way impinges upon how, in terms of aesthetics or continuing interest, one might *evaluate* creative productions. To be sure, listening closely to "Easy Livin' " or "A Little Help from My Friends" might increase one's valuation of such works—then again, it might not. What *is* at issue is Lionel Trilling's proposition that one best—or perhaps exclusively—comes to comprehend a culture by reading its "monuments of unaging intellect."[25] No doubt, one can come to understand some aspects of a culture in that way . . . and others not at all, as is so forcefully illustrated by what Trilling and his contemporaries chose *not* to write about (e.g., the meanings of slavery and racism for American culture and letters), or by the very titles *Virgin Land, Errand Into the Wilderness,* and *The Vital Center.*

What I am proposing here is finally not a rhetorical case for the charms of American studies, though I'd be willing to pursue that task. I am suggesting, rather, the inevitability of a significant realignment in how colleges and universities structure the humanities and humane social sciences. But, to apply my first principle, "Always historicize," why now and why in these forms? American studies has been around in its academic model for half a century, much longer in other versions. Why has a definitively separate identity begun to emerge only in the 1990s? A number of factors are, I think, in play, not all of which will comfort those of us active in American studies. First, the Right is probably right in pointing to something of a breakdown in the traditional disciplines: as new constituencies gained access to the university in the 1960s they raised questions about curricula parallel to those being asked in political arenas, such as "Where are the blacks? and "Where are the women?" Such canon questions through the 1970s and 1980s became particularly contentious, especially because demands for "new" areas of study conflicted in some degree with existing disciplinary structures in departments such as English (consider the name, just for starters) and to a lesser extent, perhaps in history. If one moved to fund a specialist in American Indian literatures (and necessarily cultures, perhaps religions) or in women's history, did that mean *not* replacing the resident Miltonist or the retiring medievalist? Work in American areas was easier to change: "American" was the new boy on the block, had only recently achieved a degree of legitimacy (American literature was regarded with some scorn even when I was in graduate school in the 1950s), and hadn't so hardened into academic categories. Even so, newer constituencies have often felt the response of traditional disciplines to their concerns to be inadequate, and thus have moved to establish a variety of forms of ethnic and women's studies or have seen American studies as a potential umbrella under which particular areas of work might flourish. Moreover, as poststructuralist theory undermined older forms of literary and art history formalisms, American studies, with its strongly historicizing tendencies and openness to socially inflected categories of analysis, like race and gender, took on a certain utility.

The end of the cold war has also, paradoxically, liberated American studies from at least some of the constraints under which it had operated. As an *academic* discipline, American studies came into being in the post–World War II era[26] as, in part, an expression of American nationalist objectives. For some, American studies offered an academic framework to carry out the kind of left-liberal program associated with the wartime Office of Strategic Services and significant tendencies in the early CIA—anticommunist, to be sure, but also antifascist and promotional of democratic, liberal values associated with the kind of coalition FDR had assembled.[27] For others, American studies offered a form of work, based in social and cultural analyses, distinct from the conservatively rooted, formalist approaches to texts characteristic of the New Criticism.[28] In the context of the cold war, American studies could thus be seen as constituting—and in my view was—something of an oppositional discipline, non-Marxist, of course, yet providing a critical (some have said "anti-American") approach to the study of American social and cultural institutions. The end of the cold war has presented some paradoxes: support for American studies by government and by major foundations has all but evaporated, but the discipline has spread. It no longer needs to be burdened with the fairly explicit nationalist agenda of the cold war years (though as I shall suggest in another chapter, that is only a half truth). At the same time, it has been invigorated by significant elements of Marxist thought (and Marxist thinkers),[29] now detached from the previously threatening specter of Soviet—that is, "foreign"—power and ideology. It may be the case that, once again, American studies is playing the role described by Michael Denning as "a substitute for a developed marxist culture."[30] Or it may be that it is one of the few games in town able to look consistently at and think freshly about the ugly contradictions in and the power and attractiveness of American social and cultural life. One thinks of Claude McKay's poem "America":

> Although she feeds me bread of bitterness,
> And sinks into my throat her tiger's tooth,
> Stealing my breath of life, I will confess
> I love this cultured hell that tests my youth!

Beyond that, the traditional functions of the academic enterprise have, as Bill Readings argued,[31] fundamentally eroded. Instead of transmitting a national culture, an enterprise to which departments like history and English were central, universities have come to enshrine "excellence," an empty signifier, as Readings points out, now usually filled with the ideology of the marketplace. As the traditional humanistic disciplines themselves are thus marginalized within the academy, loyalty to them erodes and therefore their ability to maintain discipline, as it were, even among practitioners. In fact, as universities have promoted forms of consumer culture among students, students have turned to areas of study which offer them that sine qua non of capitalist consumption habits, variety . . . as well as flexibility— qualities they tell us they see in majors like American studies.[32] More sinister, perhaps, for some administrators looking to reduce expenditures in now "nonessential" fields, American studies and other interdisciplinary areas offer opportunities for consolidation of resources: you can bring together forms of ethnic studies, literature, history, and the like under a single, presumably cheaper, roof. Moreover, as role differentiation among higher education institutions hardens, most universities feel little pressure to imitate those bastions of the traditional liberal arts, like the Ivy League universities, and sustain the older disciplines like English or history. In short, a gradual decrease in the centrality of conventional disciplines has been accompanied by an increase in the academic fungibility of American studies.

And not just "academic": I would not underestimate how cultural capital accumulated in American studies has from its beginnings been translatable into other goods and services, particularly overseas travel. To be sure, American studies has no corner on this particular market, but since overseas programs use the rubric "American studies" to cover a variety of academic practices, it has been possible for domestic Americanists to fit into overseas assignments sometimes quite tangential to their particular specializations. Thus the advent of literary Americanists in overseas politics classrooms. In any event, the benefits of associating oneself with American studies as a discipline have increased measurably in the scales of what counts in the academy.

In many colleges and universities, and in some secondary schools, I think a result of these changes will be newly independent American studies programs. The specific constitution of these will differ from one institution to another. In some, too, their names may be "cultural studies," "communications and society," "media theory," or even "America in the World." Whatever the precise rubric, such programs or departments will not only focus on social, political, and cultural issues involving the United States as such but will approach that content in the often eclectic but also distinctive methodologies that, I am arguing, distinguish American studies.

So far, I have written primarily about American studies as I see it being practiced *within* the United States. But American studies—or at least the name—has also been spreading overseas, even as American-based financial support for such work has declined, as U.S. government libraries and centers have closed, and as private foundations have shifted funding priorities. An overseas presence has long been important to the domestic prestige of American studies; the two, while separable, seem to echo back images of value. In this regard, domestic and overseas American studies programs represent not just intellectual but institutional components of each other.

Outside the United States, American studies often functionally constitutes one among a number of area studies programs. Though area studies conferences originating within the United States have seldom included American studies, overseas, Americanists usually participate in such meetings. To add to the distinction, disciplines in most universities outside the United States exercise greater academic hegemony than those within the United States. At least in the United States students do not enroll in rigidly delimited "faculties" from which one needs everything but a visa to exit. But in many places, American studies often amounts to a wholly owned subsidiary of a traditional discipline, like history or English, and these are heavily the fields within which American studies students actually labor. Thus work in American studies is less likely to take interdisciplinary form or by itself to challenge existing structures of knowledge. In many areas one remains not an Americanist but a historian or an economist who happens to study the United States. How stable such academic structures will be remains unclear. On the one hand, the title "American studies" seems to be a significant asset, though what is done under its head may appear rather like traditional American history, American-style empirical social science, or English (American mode) as a second language.

At the same time, however, students *learn* a great deal of what they believe—or think they know—about the United States from the media, from popular culture, and from related sources. My own experience suggests that a certain tension can thereby arise between what is studied and what is experienced of things American. Such conflicts may lead in time to more academic efforts to adopt the emphasis upon analyzing culture—its production, distribution, and reception—so fruitfully pursued today in many American studies programs in the United States. For such work offers opportunities to develop students' analytic abilities in relation to cultural productions—fiction, movies, ads, magazines—which are already of interest to them, and which are, moreover, one of the primary ways in which they actually encounter American power in their own space.

In this connection, Melani Budianta's Interroads (a discussion group on Georgetown University's Web site, *Crossroads*) comments in early 1997 on the University of Indonesia's American studies program may project one future for American studies overseas. The program in Jakarta begins with two courses designed to establish a "common ground for discussion" and to "develop skill in interdisciplinary analysis." The first course, "Contemporary American Society," looks closely at the ways in which American institutions and social issues actually operate, focusing on topics like race, ethnicity, family, poverty, the welfare state, and the press, and helping students begin to "understand the internal mechanisms of the US as a nation state." The second introductory course provides students with ways to look at the field of American studies itself, both historically and currently. Such courses, Budianta contends, are, on the one hand, shaped by the particular "cultural and political" conditions of Indonesian life, and, on the other, by the need for Indonesian students to understand concretely how American culture and politics affect Indonesian realities. The program carries forms of cultural study into its more advanced work: one of three second-level courses is called "American Texts," about which Budianta writes: "This . . . course studies how to use various kind of texts as material for cultural analysis. The class also discusses why certain texts become significant . . . [at] a certain historical and cultural juncture."[33] The other second-level courses are, traditionally, a survey of American history, and, atypically, an anthropological approach to American values. It seems to me that such a program is, on the one hand, responsive to the distinctive conditions of Indonesian society and politics, and, on the other, to the new directions in American studies in the United States that I have been trying to sketch. This is one meaning of the rubric I earlier proposed—that the globalization of American culture requires the localization of its study.

Another example is provided by the University of Houston. It illustrates how some programs and perspectives within the United States are responding—increasingly, I believe—to the implications of changing, perhaps often dissolving, borders, including those of nation states. The program at Houston was described by Steven Mintz in the same set of Interroads exchanges that Melani Budianta addressed. "The first question we asked," Mintz wrote, "was whether we should follow an existing model or instead try to create a program that would reflect the distinctive features of our border location and our student body. After a great deal of heated discussion, we decided that we should think about American studies in hemispheric terms and establish a program that would offer both interdisciplinary and multicultural perspectives on the United States and comparative perspectives on the peoples and cultures of the Americas."[34] Such a program illustrates that the kind of American studies I am describing is, like most other aspects of American culture, no longer a one-way proposition, from the United States outward. Rather, the impact of globalization here—including of the student body—is to reshape a program *within* the United States in a distinctively local fashion.

Both these programs, moreover, emphasize not American exceptionalism but difference in a comparative context. Houston's introductory course, for example, "The Americas: Identity, Culture, and Power," begins by examining "how very different experiences with colonialism gave rise to distinct countries, with different social structures and places in the global economy." The second part focuses on the diverse modernisms of the Americas, and the third on "issues of race, ethnicity, sexuality, and gender" as these have been constructed in our time.

Such courses are, to say the least of them, challenges to any—or all—of us. Mintz sees their team-taught introductory course as a means "to reeducate our faculty." I took, by teaching, an introductory graduate course in American studies in the fall of 1996 in which I am sure I spent many more hours than my students reading and rethinking a number of the texts to which I have alluded in this chapter.[35] One of my colleagues put it this way: "You are asking me to learn a new discipline. I'm not sure it is worth my while at this stage of my career." I agree with the first sentence, at least in part, but not with the implications of the second. For it seems to me that what is most exciting in American studies today is precisely what is troubling, reasonably so, to my colleague: that it is a new discipline, new in engaging America wherever it is found across the globe, and new in approaching the subject of America with a set of tools and methods fashioned to win its own space in the unruly world of the American academy.[36]

APPROACHES TO AMERICAN STUDIES[37]

Paul Lauter, Fall 1997

BOOKS

Henry Nash Smith, *Virgin Land*

Leo Marx, *The Machine in the Garden*

Annette Kolodny, *The Lay of the Land*

Alan Trachtenberg, *The Incorporation of America*

W. E. B. Du Bois, *The Souls of Black Folks*

David Roediger, *The Wages of Whiteness*

Richard Ohmann, *Selling Culture*

Michael Denning, *The Cultural Front*

George Sánchez, *Becoming Mexican American*

SYLLABUS

Readings are due on the date indicated. Please be aware (you will be soon if you're not already) that there is MUCH reading in this course.

SEPTEMBER 9   Readings:

Lawrence W. Levine, "William Shakespeare and the American People: A Study in Cultural Transformation," *The Unpredictable Past: Explorations in American Cultural History* (New York: Oxford University Press, 1993), pp. 139–171.

Paul J. DiMaggio, "Cultural Entrepreneurship in Nineteenth-Century Boston," *Nonprofit Enterprise in the Arts: Studies in Mission and Constraint* (New York: Oxford University Press, 1986), pp. 41–61.

Paul J. DiMaggio, "Cultural Entrepreneurship in Nineteenth-Century Boston, part II: The classification and framing of American Art," *Media, Culture and Society* 4 (1982): 303–322.

Janice Radway, "The Scandal of the Middlebrow: The Book-of-the-Month Club, Class Fracture, and Cultural Authority," *South Atlantic Quarterly* 89 (fall 1990): 703–736.

Optional: Jane Smiley, "Say It Ain't So, Huck," *Harper's Magazine* (January 1996): 61–67.

SEPTEMBER 16: *(We will attend a lecture by Tony Kushner at 7:30 P.M. in Austin Arts Center.)*   Readings:

Alan Sinfield, "Un-American Activities," *Cultural Politics—Queer Readings* (Philadelphia: University of Pennsylvania Press, 1994), pp. 40–59.

Reconfiguring Academic Disciplines ★ 29

Corber, "Masculinizing the American Dream: Discourses of
istance in the Cold War Era," *Homosexuality in Cold War Amer-
: Resistance and the Crisis of Masculinity* (Durham, N.C.: Duke
iversity Press, 1997), pp. 23–54.

laine Davis and Elizabeth Kennedy, "Oral History and the Study
of Sexuality in the Lesbian Community: Buffalo, New York, 1940–
1960," *Hidden from History: Reclaiming the Gay and Lesbian Past*, ed.
Martin Duberman, Martha Vicinus, and George Chauncey Jr. (New
York: New American Library, 1989), pp. 426–440.

Kate Adams, "Making the World Safe for the Missionary Position:
Images of the Lesbian in Post–World War II America," *Lesbian
Texts and Contexts: Radical Revisions*, ed. Karla Jay and Joanne Glas-
gow (New York: New York University Press, 1990), pp. 255–274.

David Bergman, "F. O. Matthiessen: The Critic as Homosexual,"
Gaiety Transfigured: Gay Self-Representation in American Literature
(Madison: University of Wisconsin Press, 1991), pp. 85–102.

Martin Duberman, " 'Writhing Bedfellows' in Antebellum South Carolina: Historical Interpretation and the Politics of Evidence," *About
Time: Exploring the Gay Past* (New York: Meridian, 1991), pp. 3–23.

SEPTEMBER 23   Readings:

Dwight Macdonald, "A Theory of Mass Culture," *Diogenes* 3 (summer
1953): 1–17.

Andrew Ross, "Containing Culture in the Cold War," *No Respect: Intellectuals and Popular Culture* (New York: Routledge, 1989), pp. 42–
64.

Anonymous, "Norman Holmes Pearson and the Origins of American
Studies," photocopy of unpublished article.

Leo Marx, "Text vs. Context" (1993), photocopy of unpublished article.

Eva Cockcroft, "Abstract Expressionism: Weapon of the Cold War,"
ArtForum 12 (June 1974): 39–41.

Optional: Paul Lauter, "Versions of Nashville; Visions of American
Studies," *American Quarterly* 47 (June 1995): 185–203.

SEPTEMBER 30   Readings:

Frederick Jackson Turner, "The Significance of the Frontier in American History," American Historical Association, *Annual Report*,
1893.

Perry Miller, "Preface" and "Errand into the Wilderness," from *Errand into the Wilderness* (Cambridge: Harvard University Press, 1956), pp. vii–ix, 1–15.

Henry Nash Smith, *Virgin Land* (Cambridge: Harvard University Press, 1950), pp. vii–xii, 3–34, 44–80, 102–154, 174–260.

Amy Kaplan, " 'Left Alone with America': The Absence of Empire in the Study of American Culture," ed. Amy Kaplan and Donald E. Pease, *The Cultures of U.S. Imperialism* (Durham: Duke University Press, 1993), pp. 3–21.

OCTOBER 7: *Beginning today, each of you (in groups) will be responsible for writing a critical paper focused on the reading for the day* and *for leading the initial class discussion. In your paper you should develop a critique of the book we are reading for the day. In order to do so, however, you will have to present, first, what the book's thesis is. Then you can go on to bring that thesis into question or otherwise to comment on it.* Readings:

Leo Marx, *The Machine in the Garden: Technology and the Pastoral Ideal in America* (New York: Oxford University Press, 1964).

Annette Kolodny, *The Lay of the Land: Metaphor as Experience and History in American Life and Letters* (Chapel Hill: University of North Carolina Press, 1975).

OCTOBER 14
No class: Reading week

OCTOBER 21   Reading:
Alan Trachtenberg, *The Incorporation of America: Culture and Society in the Gilded Age* (New York: Hill and Wang, 1982).

OCTOBER 28   Readings:
W. E. B. Du Bois, *The Souls of Black Folk.* (1903, any edition).

W. E. B. Du Bois, "The Souls of White Folks" and "The Damnation of Women" from *Darkwater: Voices from Within the Veil* (New York: Schochen, 1969; 1920), pp. 29–52, 163–186.

Richard Wright, "The Ethics of Living Jim Crow," *Uncle Tom's Children* (1940, any edition).

NOVEMBER 4   Readings:
David Roediger, *The Wages of Whiteness: Race and the Making of the American Working Class* (London: Verso, 1991).

George Lipsitz, "The Possessive Investment in Whiteness" with comments, *American Quarterly* 47 (September 1995): 369–466.

Ruth Frankenberg, "Questions of Culture and Belonging," *White Women, Race Matters: The Social Construction of Whiteness* (Minneapolis: University of Minnesota Press, 1993), pp. 191–235.

NOVEMBER 11 Readings:

Alan Trachtenberg, "Myth, History, and Literature in Virgin Land," *Prospects* 3 (1977): 125–133.

Michael Denning, " 'The Special American Conditions': Marxism and American Studies," *American Quarterly* 38 (1986): 356–380.

Robert Berkhofer Jr., "A New Context for a New American Studies?" *American Quarterly* 41 (1989): 588–613.

Joel Pfister, "The Americanization of Cultural Studies," *Yale Journal of Criticism* 4 (1991): 199–229.

Donald Pease, "New Americanists: Revisionist Interventions into the Canon," *Revisionary Interventions in the American Canon*, ed. Donald E. Pease (Durham: Duke University Press, 1994), pp. 1–37.

NOVEMBER 18 Reading:

Richard Ohmann, *Selling Culture: Magazines, Markets and Class at the Turn of the Century* (London: Verso, 1996).

NOVEMBER 25 Reading:

Michael Denning, *The Cultural Front* (London: Verso, 1996), parts 1 and 2, and selections from part 3.

DECEMBER 2 Readings:

Randolph Bourne, "Trans-National America," rpt. in *The Heath Anthology of American Literature*, vol. 2, 3rd ed. (Boston: Houghton Mifflin, 1998), pp. 1732–1743.

Thomas J. Ferraro, from *Ethnic Passages: Literary Immigrants in Twentieth-Century America* (Chicago: University of Chicago Press, 1993), pp. 1–52.

Priscilla Wald, "Terms of Assimilation: Legislating Subjectivity in the Emerging Nation," *The Cultures of U.S. Imperialism* (Durham: Duke University Press, 1993), pp. 59–84.

Lisa Lowe, "Heterogeneity, Homogeneity, Hybridity," *Diaspora* 1 (1991): 24–44.

David A. Hollinger, "How Wide the Circle of the 'We': American Intellectuals and the Problem of the Ethos since World War II," *American Historical Review* (April 1993): 317–337.

<small>DECEMBER 9</small>   Readings:

George Sánchez, *Becoming Mexican American: Ethnicity, Culture, and Identity in Chicano Los Angeles, 1900–1945* (New York: Oxford University Press, 1993).

Gloria Anzaldúa, from *Borderlands/La Frontera: The New Mestiza* (San Francisco: Spinsters/Aunt Lute, 1987).

<small>DECEMBER 11</small>   Readings:

Guillermo Gómez-Peña, "The Free Trade Art Agreement/El Tratado de Libre Cultura," *The New World Border* (San Francisco: City Lights, 1996), pp. 5–18.

Sonia Saldívar-Hull, "Feminism on the Border," *Criticism in the Borderlands: Studies in Chicano Literature, Culture and Ideology,* ed. Héctor Calderón and José David Saldívar (Durham: Duke University Press, 1991), pp. 203–220.

José David Saldívar, "Américo Paredes and Decolonization," *The Cultures of U.S. Imperialism* (Durham: Duke University Press, 1993), pp. 292–311.

Paul Lauter, "American Studies at the Borders: Identity and Discipline," photocopy of unpublished article.

Jane Desmond and Virginia R. Domínguez, "Resituating American Studies in a Critical Internationalism," *American Quarterly* 48 (September 1996): 475–490.

CHAPTER TWO

AMERICAN STUDIES, AMERICAN POLITICS, & THE REINVENTION OF CLASS

On May 28,1996, five or six thousand people gathered on the New Haven Green, across from Yale's Old Campus, the site of the university's commencement exercises. Many wore paper caps announcing their affiliation with locals of carpenters, warehousemen, miners, janitors, drug and hospital workers. They carried placards demanding that Yale University really negotiate with its clerical, dining hall, and custodial unions, and that it recognize GESO, the teaching assistants' union. Ralph Fassanella signed copies of his prints to raise money for a strike fund. Richard Trumka, secretary-treasurer of the AFL-CIO, demanded movement on the stalled negotiations. Representatives of Locals 34 and 35 asked why the second wealthiest university in the world's richest country, with an endowment then up to $4.7 billion, could not, or would not, provide ordinary workers in the nation's seventh poorest city with a living wage—not to speak of any reasonable share of local taxes. At a signal, the crowd formed into ranks and, led by Jesse Jackson and officials of the AFL-CIO, marched out onto Chapel Street from whence it proceeded to circle the Old Campus, wherein was taking place Yale's annual commencement. The walls did not fall, as we know.

Why memorialize this scene, even so briefly, and what has it to do with the future of American studies? Were I in a prophetic mode, I might claim that American studies has little future unless or until what that demonstration expressed marches fully into the Old Campus, Sterling Library, and most of all, the Hall of Graduate Studies and similar venues around the nation. But being of more moderate disposition, I wish only to remark that, at least for me, the future of American studies is inextricably bound up with the social forces that, in the recent history of the United States, inhabit the green, the streets, the kitchens and jails of New Haven and other cities and towns, but rarely their classrooms. Our problem as students of American studies is to understand why, to be sure; but more than that, in a well-known phrase, it is to change that reality.

Understanding the forces now reshaping American higher education is no easy task, and I will not pretend to draw a definitive picture. Contradictory policy proposals, shifting alliances, wide discrepancies between aspiration and reality abound. I will suggest, however, that a form of class analysis provides a peculiarly useful lens through which to interpret these forces. More important, perhaps, a class perspective may offer certain tools helpful to those desiring to analyze, contest and, it may be, to change the directions in which American higher education seems now to be moving.

The directions now being set for American higher education will mean the transformation of that institution. Are such transformations desirable? Or rather, as a class perspective leads me to ask, for whom might they be desired goals and for whom would they be problems, and why? We need to consider a quite varied set of recent and ongoing events in order to ask what, if any, patterns begin to emerge from them: the recent and unlamented culture wars; the Yale TA, clerical, and groundskeeper strikes; the efforts to eliminate or restrict tenure at places like Minnesota and the Arizona International Campus or to hire only to term contracts not to tenure lines; reports like that of the Council for Aid to Education, called *Breaking the Social Contract,* and that of a congressionally inspired National Commission on the Cost of Higher Education; the still more recent ending of affirmative action policies in Texas and California, and of student development courses at the four-year colleges of the City University of New York; the increasingly successful efforts to organize teaching assistants at the University of California campuses, and elsewhere. Are there discernable patterns in such miscellaneous data? Why might they make advocates of certain well-established ideas about higher education nervous? And, a preliminary but fundamental question, why fret at all about the futures of colleges and universities?

One might, after all, argue that the American academy has become little more than a training ground for consumption. Vartan Gregorian when he was president of Brown University pointed with pride to the fact that colleges offer their clientele relatively reasonable accommodations, abundant food, trained security, endless entertainment and special events, with even some educational opportunities thrown in—all for about $125 per day, or less, cheap at the price. Less even than the antiunion Marriott Corporation can provide. Gregorian's account is true, of course. I will acknowledge, too, the self-seeking and pettiness, the excesses of specialization, the nesting of privilege that characterize academic life. And, as I will say later, academic institutions are, in many respects, training students to be comfortable and compliant inhabitants of a selfish order. But it is still a terrain worth struggling over. The U.S. academy remains among the rather few institutions still receptive to efforts to resist the gospel of the bottom line now virtually uncontested as the proof of value in American democracy. It is *not* that academies are in some meanings of the term essentially subversive; but I do think they provide spaces within which ways of thinking about societies and cultures alternative to accepted or imposed wisdoms can grow, and perhaps even flourish. Know-nothings the world over have devoted considerable attention to preventing people from being educated. That seems to me one meaning of the savage attacks on educators from Cambodia to Algeria to eastern Germany, and many places between. And of certain events like the recent "culture wars" closer to home.

But even if one does not share my attachment to the academic enterprise, I think one might well be alarmed by present trends, or, rather, the conjunction of the policies and events on which I shall touch. In response to these, I wish to ask what the role of those of us in American studies might be in contesting the ongoing transformations of higher education and in offering alternative visions, policies, and forms of work, particularly by bringing class more fully into the discussion.

To begin, then, with two of the basic versions, not altogether distinct, of current policy initiatives; I'd call them, to reflect the nature of contemporary political discourse in the United States, the Most Right versus the Less Right. The Most Right has made the withdrawal of public support from higher education, the privatization of its costs, and the consequent shrinking of the educational sector—especially in terms of its access to "disadvantaged" students—central to its program. The logic of this strategy is not hard to follow: by making higher education an increasingly dear commodity, one restricts access to it to those able to pay the freight; or, more accurately, in the old Selective Service metaphor, one "channels" potential students into different categories of higher education, supposedly more "suitable" for them. Those who can pay, to Dartmouth and Yale; those who can pay less, to Michigan and Texas; less still, to Kent State and Potsdam; and least, to Borough of Manhattan and Isothermal Community Colleges. And then there are other institutions to gather in the altogether unwashed—or unwashable. This is, of course, a formula for institutionalizing one of the key processes by which privilege reproduces its structures. One does not often see thoroughgoing proposals for reforming educational institutions from the Most Right for two reasons: first, the desired model already exists, at least in imagination, in the elite institutions of the 1950s. More important, however, is that Most Right ideas are grounded on the view of the world articulated by Elliott Abrams; "Where liberals see 'problems,'" he wrote, "neo-conservatives see 'conditions.'"[1] That is to say, certain conditions of poverty, intelligence, inequity are not amenable to amelioration, certainly not by mere educational programs; it doesn't pay to try educating some people, for, as *The Bell Curve* seems to argue, discrepancies in IQ and other measures of intellect seem genetic. Designing inclusive educational programs would therefore be a labor lost.

Lest one think that this strategy is merely a rhetorical exercise among conservatives, one might consider recent developments in Texas and California and at City University of New York. The clear design of Governor Pataki, of Mayor Giuliani, and of their appointees and trolls, has been to cut back on the number of students, particu-

larly those from minority, recent-immigrant, and working-class populations, attending CUNY, especially the four-year institutions. By ending remedial course work at such colleges, the CUNY trustees do *not*
bar anyone from attending—that would be undemocratic! No, they
only make it less likely that poor and minority students will surmount
the new hurdles to admission; thus the policy has the practical effect of
reversing the purpose of "open admissions," that is, to open wider the
gates to educational opportunity for poor, working-class, and minority
aspirants. Further, by massively cutting back on CUNY funding, the
state and city have further restricted both access to courses and to
faculty as well as curricular options for students.[2]

Likewise, in California and Texas, the ending of affirmative action
programs does *not* reinstate the de facto segregation of those states'
flagship institutions that largely obtained thirty and more years ago.
That would be politically inexpedient. But the objective impact is once
more to place barriers in the way of less well-prepared and in practice
often minority and working-class students. In both cases the method
is that made familiar by the Selective Service's infamous "channeling"
memorandum of the 1960s, which extolled the "American or indirect
way of achieving what is done by direction in foreign countries where
choice is not permitted. Here, choice is limited but not denied."[3] In
this case, the workforce is "indirectly" being channeled or, more simply, divided by seeming to push decisions onto individuals about how
much of one's young life to invest in an educational enterprise.

Underlying these tactics is, I think, the assumption that too many
students who cannot "profit" from it are now enrolled in higher education, straining institutional resources, pushing down "standards," and
contributing to the creation of an "overeducated" and thus restive
workforce.[4] Instituting direct bars to the admission of such students
is, even in the current reactionary political dispensation, politically
impossible; thus such indirect approaches, and significant cutbacks of
educational funding on grounds of fiscal prudence, must be made to
serve the purposes of the Most Right agenda.

Not incidentally, the reduction in minority student participation in
higher education also serves the cultural interests of the Right. In the
late 1960s, the increasing presence of unprecedented numbers of
black, Latino, and other minority students, as well as a new generation
of activist women, provided the impetus, the urgency, and the political

muscle crucial to the development of black studies, women's studies, multiculturalism, and similar academic innovations. Removing significant numbers of such students may have the effect of undercutting the base of student support for such programs and thus their rationale for existence—a long-term goal of right-wingers. The logic of that strategy is revealed in the new attacks by Ward Connerly, leader of the anti–affirmative action initiative, on ethnic and minority studies programs in the University of California. Removing such programs, or even occupying them with self-defense, would further strip away institutions supportive of what we once called "historically bypassed" students on campuses they already experience as chilly, if not downright hostile.

The Less Right strategy can be exemplified by the reports of the Council for Aid to Education, called *Breaking the Social Contract: The Fiscal Crisis in Higher Education* (1997) and of the National Commission on the Cost of Higher Education, titled *Straight Talk about College Costs and Prices* (1998).[5] The council's report begins from two premises: first, that postsecondary education is increasingly necessary both to individual advancement and for maintaining the American economy in a competitive world. And second, that rising demand will, in perhaps two decades, swamp colleges as declining resources force them to limit access. "Access" is the central term in the council's idea of an American "social contract," the "guarantee that all citizens who can profit from higher education will have access to it." It is this "social contract," the council offers, that will provide the magic elixir to overcome the growing divide in America—and the world—between rich and poor.[6] The council's proposals boil down to two related propositions: colleges and universities must undergo "reorganization," like businesses, both in order to save money—something like $15–18 billion by 2015, according to the council—and in order to persuade federal and state authorities to increase funding by a like amount to close the gap between what is presumably necessary and what current trends would provide. Here's how the report puts it in its own graceful language:

> Unless the higher education sector changes the way it operates by undergoing the kind of restructuring and streamlining that successful businesses have implemented, it will be difficult to garner

the increases in public funding needed to meet future demand. . . .
Institutions of higher education should make major structural
changes in their governance system so that decision makers can
assess the relative value of departments, programs, and systems in
order to reallocate scarce resources. This will entail performance-
based assessment, defining and measuring faculty productivity,
and integrating accounting systems. (P. 3)

The council offers no solid evidence to indicate that legislatures will be
persuaded by reorganizations of any kind to begin increasing funding,
nor that savings produced by such reorganizations would come anywhere close to what they calculate—accurately or not—will be necessary. And anyone who reads *Business Week* will remain suspicious of
the claims for organizational genius attributed to the business leaders
who, the report maintains, ought more closely to be involved in collegiate decision making. Indeed, there are those who would argue,
given the startling upward flow of wealth in the United States, the
stagnation of ordinary people's wages, the degeneration of most working conditions, and the disintegration of once prosperous cities like
Flint, Youngstown, and Hartford, that business is part of the problem,
as it used to be said, rather than part of the solution. The council's
prescriptions are not precisely new ideas; in fact, similar notions about
placing colleges under business leadership seem to emerge regularly
whenever American commercial culture is at its most prosperous—
and arrogant—as it seems again to be in this fin de siècle moment. I
recall Beardsley Ruml's pamphlet "Memo to a College Trustee," which
in the fifties was the occasion of much misdirected energy at Dartmouth, among other places. Its shtick was replacing the term with the
quarter system.

Indeed, it would be hard to take seriously the disingenuous proposals of *Breaking the Social Contract* for placing in the hands of busi-
nesslike "decision makers" power to reevaluate programs like cognitive science, reallocate resources now applied to physical chemistry,
and reshape departments like history, but for two reasons: first, some
of the names attached to them, like Gregorian, Barry Munitz, and
Thomas Kean, all of whom carry some weight in educational circles;
and second, the fact that the council's work helped in part to establish
the agenda for a National Commission on the Cost of Higher Educa-

tion, established by Congress, June 12, 1997. The commission's charter and its work focused on issues driving increases in the "price" of higher education. It studied the impact of administrative costs, faculty remuneration, facilities construction, student financial aid, and federal policies, among other things, on the rates at which tuition and other college expenses have risen over the last two decades. The commission's report focuses in something of a restricted way on why colleges seem to cost a lot and what can be done about that. It begins its "straight talk," for example, by characterizing education as but one among many important commodities: "The phenomenon of rising college tuition evokes a public reaction that is sometimes compared to the 'sticker shock' of buying a new car. Although this reference to automobile prices may irritate some within the higher education community, it serves to remind all of us that higher education is a product, a service and a life-long investment bought and paid for, like others" (p. 2). The virtues of the strategy of focusing narrowly on questions of costs and how to reduce them are twofold: it fits with a consumerist model familiar and deeply subscribed to by most Americans. And it allowed the commission to avoid many of the more contentious matters lurking just under the surface of any effort to alter, much less rationalize, the American system of higher education. In fact, given the heavily conservative constitution of the commission,[7] I felt a certain sense of relief that it did not directly address certain of the issues outlined in its mandate. For example, one of the subjects in its charge was to examine "trends in faculty workload and remuneration (including the use of adjunct faculty), faculty-to-student ratios, number of hours spent in the classroom by faculty, tenure practices, and the impact of such trends on tuition." The sequence of items here is telling: it certainly seemed more likely that such a commission would ignore the exploitation of adjuncts and focus on the "problem" of tenure. The abortive attack on tenure in 1996 at the University of Minnesota, the abrogation of tenure at Bennington, and the establishment of tenureless institutions like the Arizona International Campus (tenureless except for its administrator) were only some of the straws that seemed to make a weatherman superfluous. In fact, however, little in the report actually engaged these more conflicted issues. The commission's studies revealed "little evidence to suggest . . . that changes in faculty hiring practices or workload have driven up college costs in the past decade. In fact, there has been movement in the opposite direction" generated, no surprise, because "institutions have hired more part-time and non-tenured faculty and increased the number of hours faculty spend in the classroom."[8]

Its recommendations include an effort "to study and consider alternative approaches to collegiate instruction which might improve productivity and efficiency" without really specifying what alternatives might be feasible. And its few comments on tenure, while including a potentially dangerous "posttenure review," are relatively benign. To be sure, in characteristically corporate liberal fashion, the commission places its major emphasis on "productivity" and "efficiency," in order to rationalize the disorderly and opaque higher education industry. And the commission's approach to the financing of higher education differs from those of the Most Right at least in one key respect: these proposals represent an effort to maintain broad access by sustaining—indeed widening—state funding for, rather than principally increasing privatization of, educational opportunity. At the same time, Less Right proposals reflect an enormous step away from the ideas which, in the United States, once underwrote public education, including public higher education. The Commission insists that

> all the recommendations in this document were developed with one goal in mind: to keep open the door of higher education by maintaining access at prices students and families can afford.
>
> But institutions, governments, and the philanthropic and higher education communities can only do so much. Students and families have a responsibility to do their part as well. Because a major beneficiary of a college education is the individual involved, those with a genuine commitment to their future rightfully shoulder part of the load.
>
> The weight of that load can be substantially lessened with careful financial planning. Families obviously need better information in order to plan well. (Pp. 28–29)

The rhetoric here is familiar to us from the world of urban transportation, health care, and similar areas of what was once known as the "public sector": the roles of government and other institutions are assumed to be sharply limited, an assumption that rationalizes the shifting of financial burdens to private individuals and families, who are, as we all know, equally entitled to ride efficient and convenient mass transit in Los Angeles, to find an HMO that places quality of care over profits, or to sleep under the bridge. Or, as Allen Ginsberg once put it, apropos *Time* magazine: "It's always telling me about responsibility. Businessmen are serious. Movie producers are serious. Everybody's serious but me. / It occurs to me that I am America" ("America"). Fundamental differences about the allocation of the social costs of education, health, and transportation—class conflicts, in short—are thus hidden under the thesis that better information will enable all of us to get the best available services in this best of all consumer paradises.

In fact, both Most Right and Less Right approaches to colleges and universities have much in common, like the Republicans and Democrats. What is at stake here? It seems to me that two parallel processes are at work, one primarily affecting the "clients" of higher education, the other its workforce. Education has always been touted in this country as the path to social mobility. In certain historical circumstances, for certain specific groups of people, it has been. I am myself a product of the post–World War II policy of better assimilating second- and third-generation white ethnics into the American middle classes, a process in which college and university education played an important role. At that time, high schools primarily tracked young people into class categories: to be admitted to college was itself to step across a great divide, which, for many of us *arrivistes,* separated us from our family and class cultures. To be sure, graduating from Harvard meant something different from graduating from Hobart, but as traditionalists never tire of pointing out, a degree from City College of New York could be as potent a wand for opening doors as one from any Ivy League institution. Moreover, in many critical ways, the primary role of college education, whatever its vocational implications, was inducting students into some form of national culture: that was the meaning of the coveted "liberal arts" degree, the general education requirements, the fundamental processes of acculturation to which all students who survived were subjected. We paid certain dues, of course, to be admitted, if not to Skull and Bones, then perhaps to Dunster House or at least the Hall of Graduate Studies. The benefits of upward movement in the obscure system of class stratification in America certainly seemed worth whatever prices we were paying.

But the very meaning of the term "college" began to change, particularly in the 1960s. A far greater proportion of the population clamored for opportunities to enroll in one or another form of postsecondary education as community colleges and new state institutions proliferated. The forms of study most closely related to the acculturation of upwardly mobile students were those most directly affected by the changing roles of college education. I well remember the debates in the early 1970s at the SUNY College at Old Westbury over whether we should mount a traditional liberal arts core precisely because our students were largely *not* traditional undergraduates or whether these "historically bypassed" students required an altogether distinctive curriculum, more appropriate to their experiences and needs. We opted, of course, for the latter, a strategy largely followed over the next two decades, as previously nontraditional students became the norm, especially at many of the newer public institutions. These curricular debates, aka the culture wars, are by now a twice-told tale I do not wish to rehearse here, except to point to certain contradictions in both the major sides of this debate. Traditionalists wished to sustain older versions of the liberal arts curriculum, ignoring the shift Bill Readings pointed to from the university as an instrument of nationalist acculturation toward one more systematically directed to fulfilling capitalist priorities, in particular, training and habituating students, in quite different ways, to their distinctive "places" within advanced market capitalism.[9] Ironically, the determination to use higher education to carry out such functions, to divide and stratify the workforce, was given strong impetus by the right-wing fiscal policies initiated in 1972 and 1973, which have led to the sharply increasing divisions of wealth in the United States. In other words, cultural conservatives have continued to want colleges to initiate students into an intellectual order made increasingly irrelevant by the policies of economic conservatives. The fall-back position of all conservatives, as I have suggested, is to separate out those students who, by virtue of class position and training, can "profit" from such an education from "others" who cannot, will not, or should not.[10]

In this important respect, the goals of Most Right advocates become practically identical to those of Less Right policy makers. For the latter wish to rationalize the process of reproducing the class structure of American society by emphasizing "role differentiation" among distinct tiers of higher education institutions and channeling students into those colleges most "appropriate" to their origins and career "possibilities." With institutional "role differentiation" comes solidification of student tracking. So as not to "duplicate" curricula, undesirable on fiscal grounds, anthropology and film study, say, might disappear from Keene State's menu, since these might not fit the role laid out for such a "state undergraduate institution," as *Breaking the Social Contract* puts it: that is, taking "the lead in teacher training and areas related to regional economic development." For after all, "the liberal arts undergraduate mission" in such a structure would be the role of "the independent college sector"—that is to say, Dartmouth. In that direction lies a system even more stratified along class lines than the systems of our European colleagues. The plan here seems to me an elaboration on the older three-tiered California design: community colleges, state universities, the University of California. That model for stratifying the oncoming generation was, to some extent, compromised by the impact of politically inspired programs like affirmative action and open admissions. One should not, therefore, expect advocates of the Less Right designs I have been sketching to hold out for very long against the desire of Most Right ideologues to scrap such policies.

A different kind of contradiction has always troubled those advocating curricular innovations based primarily upon identity. The problem can be seen by recognizing how frequently in practice class falls out of the picture presented by categories of experience and study such as "race," "class," "gender," "sexuality." To be sure, progressive practitioners of women's studies, gay and lesbian studies, or ethnic studies have since the beginnings of these forms of academic discourse tried to raise the question of class. But the American academy has remained largely impervious to investigating class issues. It has generally offered an attenuated approach to the study of class, mostly restricting it to economics departments primarily devoted to making businesses tick. Political economy, wherein one looks at the class-inflected intersections of political structures and economic power, remains rather an orphan in our universities. In fact, at my own college, not a single course description in economics so much as mentions the word "class," not "Poverty in America," "Labor Economics," "Industrial Organization and Public Policy," or "Urban Economics," though women and even race are occasionally referred to. While virtually every university will offer a variety of courses devoted to race and racism, to gender and sexuality, as well as to the social movements that have worked for change in such areas of life, in few indeed would one find a course called, for example, "Class in America." To be sure, social scientists and historians, mainly those influenced by Marxism, have often provided opportunities to study class issues by tucking the subject into courses on inequality, immigration, ethnicity, and the like. But where one studies the ideas of writers like Raymond Williams or Carolyn Steedman has always been a problem in the United States. And it is only within the last few years that a Center for Working-Class Studies has emerged, appropriately at Youngstown State University.

My point here is certainly not to set those concerned with the study of race, gender, ethnicity, sexuality, and so on against those who see class as a central category of analysis. There has, in fact, been a certain tendency, especially among some white men of the Left, to appropriate class as "their" cultural home, and thus to place themselves in tension with, if not altogether in opposition to, those espousing other forms of identity politics. No—if the development of new forms of class analysis comes to be the identity politics of white men, it will be a barren and divisive study. Rather, a new emphasis upon class must be designed to help students—whatever other categories of identity they share— understand how the institutions molding their lives, most particularly the institutions of higher education, are being reshaped to rationalize and to secure the operative class system of the United States.

That study might best begin by examining the implications of both Most Right and Less Right policies for the higher education workforce itself. For this is the second major area to which current policy initiatives are addressed. Built into these proposals for financing colleges and universities are ideas for reorganizing the work of teaching that would not only significantly speed up and disempower educational workers in the name of productivity, but which would even more deeply institutionalize the present three-tiered system of the academic workforce. That consists of a relatively privileged but smaller and smaller professoriat at one end, which increasingly identifies socially and culturally with its managerial peers; a larger and larger army of the underemployed—graduate students, adjuncts, and temporaries—at the other end, rightfully enraged at the disparity between their hopes and desires and the debased professional world they inhabit; and between them an anxious set of younger faculty aspiring to permanence but terrified lest a step to the wrong drummer cast them forever into the bottom ranks. That is a formula, as Yale has demonstrated, for keeping workers divided, always an important consideration for managers and those to whom they report. In such a context, for example, an attack from the Right on tenure, which primarily protects established professors, could win, if not support, at least strategic silence or casual assent from those on the bottom, against whose job prospects the existing tenure system seems to incline.[11] Similarly, efforts by full-time faculty to roll back the exploitative use of adjuncts can be experienced by part-timers as an attempt to eliminate the fragile livelihood of those trying to maintain their tenuous hold at the fringes of the profession. Furthermore, as the 1998 debate within the National Education Association (NEA) over joining ranks with the American Federation of Teachers (AFT) indicates, the ideology of professionalism still prevents many teachers from discovering themselves as workers, having more interests in common with other workers, including those who clean and serve and type, than with managerial bureaucrats who never enter a classroom, whether to teach in it, clean it, or learn in it.

The managerial strategy should be clear from other industries, like the airlines, in which long-employed workers, especially privileged ones like pilots, possess benefits and salary schedules not available to new hires, especially those in less skilled categories. The point is fundamentally to keep the workers divided, by crafts when available, by seniority where feasible, by culture if possible. The relatively successful United Parcel Service strike of 1997, in which full-time workers supported the demands of part-timers, and in which very different categories of employees stood together, demonstrates why maintaining divisions among workers continues to be such a central managerial objective.

Furthermore, at the institutional level, different ranks of colleges have already found themselves with distinct, and sometimes contradictory, objectives: for example, increases in funding to community colleges, as in New York, have entailed cutbacks at other kinds of institutions. The mandate to eliminate skills courses at CUNY's four-year colleges will inevitably shift a large student population to the community colleges; the likely impact is, on one hand, to overburden the two-year institutions and, on the other, to undermine the current budgets of the soon-to-be-smaller senior colleges. Thus maintaining any kind of unified front in relationship, for example, to state or city authorities becomes more and more difficult. Indeed, the very concept of a higher education "community" seems to me altogether anachronistic as different interest groups within the "industry" vie with one another for lebensraum. In fact, a better metaphor than "community" might be a disfunctional family, wherein competing interests sometimes set members against one another.

Thus what is at contest is not, to my mind, some minor set of reforms of the higher education system designed to increase its efficiency at a time when state funds have increasingly flowed into prisons and profits. The assaults of the culture wars, the emblematic anti-union policies of New Haven's biggest employer, the systematic attacks on tenure, affirmative action, and remedial courses, and the new policy initiatives—all seem to me parts of a characteristically decentered but broad-scale effort to reshape the institutions of higher education to fit the agenda of triumphant global capitalism.

The problem for an opposition, it seems to me, is to reinvigorate class struggle on the campus. Saying it that way sounds, I know, like an opera libretto by Leonid Brezhnev. In fact, what I am talking about is not nearly as remote or as monumental as the archaic phrasing: it involves bringing into the campus mix a greater presence of working-class institutions and of class-focused curricula, and real efforts to carry the resources of the campus and faculty to public teaching opportunities. These are dialectically related. To the extent that working people have a stake—rather than an enemy—in the academy, they support and in fact invigorate a class-conscious curriculum. Likewise, efforts to connect campus and communities force upon academics a discourse to which a wider constituency has access, as well as greater clarity about conceptualizing class. What this amounts to is a kind of challenge to respond to changes in the political economy, among them the greater presence of working-class students on many campuses, the increasingly uneven distribution of income and wealth in the United

States, and the ever new institutional forms and ideologies that mask class conflict in this country.

But what of American studies? We have, alas, significantly contributed to the processes of obscuring certain class realities at the center of American experience. I want to illustrate that by propounding, in the spirit of this book's epigraph, Lauter's "Frontier Thesis." Frederick Jackson Turner's "Frontier Thesis" has, of course, been destroyed as a credible intellectual construct by scholars,[12] but it continues to live a kind of unnatural afterlife in the social and political culture of the United States. His idea that the presence of the "frontier," whatever precisely that was taken to mean, fundamentally marked American experience remains alive in slogan, in image, and in popular fancy. Indeed, his notion that the "closing" of the frontier distinguished the earlier period of eighteenth- and nineteenth-century America from the modern world stimulated historians of his school, and politicians of many persuasions, to search out or to reenact conjectural versions of the frontier and the pioneer to affirm the equally suppositious values of that earlier time. Criticisms of Turner's ideas and those of later historians like Ray Billington have focused on the ambiguities of the term "frontier," a concept so fluid and ill-defined as to be practically meaningless; on the lack of empirical evidence to support Turner's underlying historical accounts of American development; on the implicit ethnocentrism of the notion that at a "frontier" something called "civilization" confronted something other; and on the "American exceptionalism" functionally underwritten by the Frontier Thesis. But few mainstream or even revisionist historians have asked why the concept continues to hold place in the popular imagination, or what role it has played in helping sustain fundamental American ideological structures.

Turner was, in part, trying to account for a phenomenon widely observable on this continent, certainly since the advent of Europeans: the willingness of many Europeans to pull up stakes when things got bad, and to move on. Turner conceptualized that process within a geographical framework: while there was a frontier, people were able to take the role of pioneer and move into the supposedly lightly inhabited territory ahead. Geography was, in this sense, destiny. But the phenomenon of moving on continues to this day, without anything faintly resembling the frontier of Turner's or anyone else's thesis. What the geographical framework obscures is the cultural work of individualism as an ideology; or, rather, it insists upon glorifying a largely individualistic response to broader social and economic changes. Turner's argument structures a drama in which the individual hardy pioneer takes upon himself responsibility for moving on when things aren't working right in the current settlement. Implicitly, those who try to stick it out at home aren't pioneers, don't share the great adventure of the Newest Frontier, are themselves responsible for being stuck in the traps of "sivilization." So if Youngstown Sheet and Tube leaves their city in the lurch, or if General Motors wrecks Flint, it's up to individual workers and their families to pull up stakes, pack the wagon, hit the road, and seek out their fortunes on the frontiers of the Sun Belt.

I would not make too much of Lauter's "Frontier Thesis" except as a way of suggesting how an excessive focus on the idea of the frontier in American studies—as compared, say, with a more class-inflected concept of urbanization—has been a factor in how our discipline has over the years helped rationalize American individualism. So the question for me comes back to our role in bringing such self-serving ideologies under scrutiny and in illuminating alternatives. Historically, American studies practitioners had a long tradition, particularly before the field took on academic garb in the post–World War II period, of efforts to participate in working-class institutions. To cite one of the more obvious examples: at Yale in the 1920s, F. O. Matthiessen had taught English to a group of men at the New Haven Hungarian Club and had discovered "a kind of comradeship" with them he "never wanted to lose."[13] Later, he became an activist in the Harvard Teachers' Union— its founding vice president, later president, as well as delegate to the American Federation of Teachers and to the Boston Central Labor Council.[14] In 1944, he helped to found the Sam Adams Labor School in Boston, served as one of its trustees, and taught a course there on the subjects with which he had dealt in *American Renaissance*.[15] Matthiessen had also written about the persecution of miners in Gallup, New Mexico,[16] actively supported the left-wing Harvard Student Union, fought against the deportation of West Coast longshoremen's leader Harry Bridges, and canvassed working-class districts for the Progressive Party in 1948, among other activities. To be sure, Matthiessen's is an ambiguous and therefore instructive case: he never seemed able to reconcile his socialist convictions with his patrician aesthetic preferences (for Henry James, for example) nor the concern of the Left in which he participated about issues of race and gender with the white and male American literary canon he helped so forcefully to establish (as in the *Oxford Book of American Verse*). What was taken to be his sentimental and Stalinist fellow traveling was excoriated by critics like Irving Howe and Lionel Trilling even as he was being condemned as politically mushy by the left-wing *New Masses*.[17] His ironic self-description, "an outdated middle-class intellectual," no doubt haunts the political dreams of many an academic. There is a good deal to be learned, I think, precisely from the unresolved contradictions of Matthiessen's career, probably unresolvable given the social position of those embedded in the academy, even today.

What might be useful contemporary equivalents of such out-of-classroom and -library (I do not want to say "off-campus") practice? Here I want to emphasize one central to Matthiessen, unions. I would not pretend that unions offer a one-size-fits-all solution to the kinds of problems now faced by an opposition to the corporatization of colleges and universities. In fact, as is well known, unions have also often been part of the problem rather than part of the solution. In the United States particularly, they have acted as mechanisms to discipline and control the workforce, to deflect working-class militance, and to shift attention from fundamental issues like who bakes the economic pie and what's in it to the question of how large a slice the boss will cut you. Teachers' unions have, unfortunately, too often shrunk themselves to fit this narrow view of working people's organizations. Yet unions are among the most basic of the forms of working-class institutions, even in America.

In the beginning—the 1950s and before—the American Federation of Teachers (AFT) represented in many respects a progressive force. It insisted, on one hand, that public employees had the right to organize, an idea not widely accepted (then or now) in the U.S. of A. Moreover, it opposed the collaborationist strategy of the National Education Association (NEA), which included in its membership not only rank-and-file teachers but the very managers who controlled their work lives. To be sure, some AFT locals suffered from endemic and organizationally crippling anticommunism, not to speak of the kind of racism that set them against many of the communities teachers were supposed to be serving. But on the whole, one had good reason to be proud of one's union card—I've kept my first one, in fact, ever since 1959.

Over time, however, two problems developed. In the first place, teachers' unions—like some others—came in practice increasingly to represent only a narrow, and usually privileged, fraction of the workforce: the tenured faculty. My own union in SUNY, for example, once in a burst of democratic enthusiasm negotiated a salary increase in the form of a flat sum rather than a percentage. The full professors—especially the doctors—were outraged, and that was the last time such an arrangement was even seriously considered. Percentage increases obviously benefit most those at the top of the scale and, more to my point, increasingly divide those at the top from those at the bottom. But that was no new thing, for few teachers' unions really tried to organize, or do much to serve, those on the bottom—not just the untenured faculty but the adjuncts, the other part-timers, the TAs, the lab assistants, in short, the increasing army of those mostly being exploited by colleges and universities, including, sadly, by their unionized bosses. In virtually every case in which part-timers were seriously organized, the efforts were made not by existing unions of full-timers but by newly developed organizations. And even when that was not the case, the unions were dominated by full-timers whose interests—in terms of compensation, loads, and even course content—differed substantially from those of part-timers or the untenured, much less TAs or other employees.

The second problem, widespread in the labor movement generally, had to do with the basically defensive outlook of American labor. A kind of social settlement, advantageous to some groups—particularly white, ethnic, northern, and originally urban—had been consolidated during the cold war. Union members could then count on decent pension plans, reasonable security, meaningful health plans, secure and economical suburban housing, educational opportunities for their children, and the like. The price, of course, apart from the infectious spread of cold war ideology, was the increasing impoverishment of the cities and most of those, largely unorganized, stuck in them.[18] But that was not of major concern to most unions, which saw their job as servicing the members, not organizing the unorganized, forget caring for the clients. There were, to be sure, honorable exceptions to such generalizations, like the Farm Workers, the Meat Cutters, the Furriers, and Local 1199, Drug and Hospital Workers. But teachers' unions were, for all their social democratic rhetoric, not generally to be counted among the militants, much less the progressives.

In saying that, I do not mean to denigrate the real efforts of unions to hold the line against attacks on tenure, retrenchment provisions, and arbitrary layoffs. Nor do I want to forget the significant efforts of the NEA and some AFT locals to implement affirmative action plans, often against administrative intransigence and manipulation. But unions proved to be weak reeds when push came to shove, and shove to assault, as was often the case in recent decades. Most particularly, unions were seldom able to act forcefully in the interests of the least privileged members of the academic enterprise, the teaching assistants, groundskeepers, secretaries, and dining hall employees, for example.

But that has, I think, been changing, and unions now—or so the vignette opening this chapter is intended to suggest—are going to be increasingly important not just in the struggle against academic downsizing but in the wider contests over power and direction in the academy. Why? First of all, the logic of downsizing has led many institutions to offer desirable retirement incentives—bronze parachutes—to large numbers of senior faculty. Meantime, the bull market has increased pension benefits to unprecedented heights: the value of CREF stocks, for example, shot up over 19 percent during 1997. Thus a significant number of senior faculty, even in the humanities, find themselves with retirement packages close to and sometimes exceeding a cool million. Retirement beckons. In many places, therefore, the ranks of the privileged have been significantly thinned. Meanwhile, the ranks of the unprivileged swell daily. The balance of power within unions has been shifting in significant ways, and it is no longer visionary to imagine many of them being taken over by younger, more militant, and also more socially progressive groups and caucuses. Furthermore, in situations where that seems unlikely, those struggling to organize have—like the Wisconsin TAs of the 1960s—turned away from existing teachers' associations to other workers' organizations which, in some cases, can bring greater pressure to bear on recalcitrant institutions. Such is the case, for example, of the Union of Student Employees, which is affiliated with the United Auto Workers, or the Iowa Committee to Organize Graduate Students, affiliated with the United Electrical Workers, just as in the 1960s, the Wisconsin TAS had been affiliated with the Teamsters. There is, too, a fresh sense of urgency about organizing beginning to be displayed by the labor movement more broadly, as well as an increased readiness to seek common ground with academics, long viewed with suspicion by older trade unionists. Some of these elements underlay the Yale commencement demonstration as well as the formation of an organization like SAWSJ (Scholars, Artists, and Writers for Social Justice), which has developed a series of teach-ins and a variety of other projects—like the anti–sweat-shop campaign—linking the academy to progressive forces within the labor movement.

Finally, however, I do have to say that unions continue to be the most likely forms through which struggles against the corporate transformations of higher education I have been discussing can be contested. This has little to do with ideology, but with the internal logic of capitalism. The sanctity of contractual relationships is central to that logic. And while individual capitalists, like individual managers, are forever violating contractual relationships, every one of them would insist on the truism that national polity is based upon "the rule of law, not of men." Contracts are rules of law; collegiality is the rule of men—and generally, still, "men" in the generic sense, too. Whatever else they are, unions are mechanisms for enforcing, or at least pursuing, rules of law.

To me, then, one major tool in the struggle with downsizing, educational corporatization, and managerial control has to do with finding ways to build in to enforceable contracts enforceable goals. So far, most academic organizations have been too bound in by the economist precepts of business unionism. We do not, in fact, begin to know what it would be possible to negotiate, even within the accepted rubrics of wages, working conditions, and job security. For example, can a contract provide for "goals and timetables"—terrible words!—for instituting equitable pay, benefits, and other rights for part-timers? Can the struggle to institute such contractual provisions, as in the 1997 UPS strike, be used to organize workers and communities behind them? Can such struggles become the means for teaching students and colleagues about class?

Finally, there are the implications of the NLRB's decision to charge, and then try, Yale for unfair labor practices because of its refusal to bargain with its TAS. Faced with the likelihood that they would lose, Yale came to admit that its TAS are, in fact, workers, thus undermining its ludicrous earlier arguments that they were primarily serving as apprentices to caring mentors. Still, the unfair labor charge, if it is upheld, may well have the kind of impact the *Yeshiva* decision did two decades ago: *Yeshiva* proved a main roadblock, emotionally as well as legally, to organizing in the academy for in it the Supreme Court ruled that faculty in private colleges were managers and thus not eligible for collective bargaining rights. The Yale case could generate considerable energy in the opposite direction. It is not that Yale's TAS have necessarily constituted a vanguard, though they were—pardon the expression—pioneers. Still, there are well-established TA organizations at sixty-three institutions across the United States for example, and in a number of cases they have won meaningful gains. But Yale's reputation as a presumably leading private institution make developments there nationally visible, part of the news that's "fit to print."

It is striking to me that at Yale and elsewhere a significant number of graduate students from American studies were among the leaders of TA unions and other forms of organizing. So far as faculty at Yale were concerned, almost all the militant support for the students came from those in the American studies program. I don't see that as accidental. Kathy Newman's essay in *Will Teach for Food* suggests some reasons why. She points out that "graduate students are increasingly unhappy about material issues, such as TA compensation, teacher training, professional development, health benefits, and the collapsed job market. But the greatest controversies are over issues of representation and power."[19] What two terms could better characterize the preoccupations of American studies folk? Further, as Newman illustrates, the tools developed in this discipline for analyzing patterns of representation are wonderfully adaptable to political struggles, like those over the unionization of graduate students. Newman examines, on the one hand, the largely negative representations of graduate students not only in the popular media but in Yale's own press in an effort to understand the cultural dynamics central to winning people to your side. At the same time, she demonstrates how such an understanding can usefully enable participants in the struggle to generate images and arguments with the power to persuade. As she puts it: "When we explain our role in the university as teachers, rather than as subsidized consumers, we generate more sympathy and understanding. Moreover, by framing our union drives in the larger context of academic downsizing, we link our issues to the issues of the average working American—in almost any profession. These days, everyone is getting downsized. But not everyone is organizing to fight it" (p. 121). In these and other respects American studies can provide what Corey Robin and Michelle Stephens, in their essay, from *Will Teach for Food,* "Against the Grain: Organizing TAs at Yale," present as a necessary ingredient to a successful organizing campaign. "Organizers assume," they write, "that while people do not need to subscribe to a radical ideology in order to join a union, they do need an analysis of their experience as individual graduate students that enables them to see what they share with their fellow students" (p. 59). In other words, the practical experiences of real class struggle generate understanding of how the world and its institutions, including the academy, actually operate in class terms. No surprise. Or as H. H. Lewis put it, in a poem resurrected by Cary Nelson:

Here I am
Hunkered over the cow-donick,
Earning my one dollar per
And *realizing,*
With the goo upon overalls,
How environment works up a feller's pants-legs
   to govern his thought.[20]

Obviously, such understandings do not emerge only from organizing or from participating in unions. In fact, American studies practitioners have only begun to test out ways in which our work as intellectuals can usefully be integrated with the variety of working-class organizations, on campus and off. The American Studies Association has long had a minority scholars committee, a women's committee, a students' committee, and has even changed the structure of its International Committee so that the group will henceforth represent the international members. But it has until recently had no committee to address issues of work, workers, or even—whisper the word—class. Such a committee, which may emerge, could be of value in helping teachers alter what, how, and where we teach, especially about class.

Here's a simple idea: drawing a lesson from the early days of women's studies, such a committee could collect and issue a volume of syllabi and essays that address class questions, and the difficult problems of teaching about class in American educational institutions. Why class remains the unaddressed item in the familiar trio "race, gender, and class" is at one level quite obvious, but in other ways very complex.[21] Clearly, class analysis flies in the face of America's predominant ideology of individualism and has long been associated with communism and other presumably "foreign" ways of thinking. But many other issues sharply inhibit discussion of class in (and out) of the classroom: the embarrassed reluctance of most students to acknowledge, much less discuss, class identity; the tendency to "study down," and thus to assume that class is a phenomenon associated with workers rather than a set of relationships helping define all of us; the often confusing intersections of class with other markers of identity, such as gender and race; perhaps above all, the ways in which patterns of consumption both manifest and obscure class relationships. In any event, a critical part of initiating a curriculum focused on class is understanding more fully what has stood in the way of such study. Equally important is examining the variety of definitions of class with at least as much intellectual energy as has been devoted to analyzing other conceptual frameworks such as race, gender, and sexuality. Left intellectuals have obviously been pursuing this inquiry for decades, but their analyses have made surprisingly little impact on curricula in the United States. In what ways is that related to the tiny proportion of the American labor force that is unionized? Or to the tinier proportion of organized academics? Or to the systemic and long-standing alienation of the academy from the labor movement?

The development of a class-conscious, much less a working-class conscious, curriculum will not, I suspect, take the forms that feminist and minority scholarship and teaching have produced, in part because the connections between campus and a class-conscious community are so attenuated. We do not have very good contemporary models of the practice of linking American studies intellectual work and working-class organizing and social projects. But more such models exist than most academics realize. It may well be the case that new institutional structures, hybrids of campus and community or workplace educational programs, will have to be devised. Curricular forms will, I suspect, emerge as connections begin to be developed between academic intellectuals and working-class organizations. We may even in the process learn to speak together.

Of course, communication is not the primary issue; it is power. Moreover, the lessons taught by educational institutions are not always, or even primarily, those communicated by the talk of teachers, even the most inspired. Lessons, powerful lessons, are taught by how things are managed, and thus by the managers, however unfamiliar they may be with the inside of a classroom. Indeed, the lessons of power are often those modeled by how classrooms are organized, employees managed, decisions executed—and how a college interfaces with the community it often dominates and always shapes. In a sense, the demonstration with which I began this chapter can be seen as dramatizing a great and increasing divide between undergraduate Yale students, who learn every day that they are powerful behind their walls of privilege, and most of those who tend to them in the dining halls, classrooms, buildings, and libraries. To be sure, some students and a few faculty at the time of the demonstration wore buttons and armbands stating their affiliation with those outside the walls. And it was no doubt true that more sympathized with the demonstrators than news reports, which concentrated on parental anger at "interference" with the commencement ceremony, would have led one to believe. Still, the issue is not generalized sympathy with the cause of two or three small unions. It is, rather, what an institution teaches day by day and year by year about class norms and expectations; those things it teaches not by its generally liberal rhetoric but by the force of example, by what it countenances and what it does not. One remembers Karl Shapiro's poem "University":

> To hurt the Negro and avoid the Jew
> Is the curriculum.[22]

What, then, is taught by what we might, after Jules Henry, call the "noise,"[23] the "hidden curriculum," of university education?

I want to emphasize three areas: relations between gown and town, relations between people who study in academe and people who serve them, and the question of truth, that ambiguous tabernacle theoretically at the center of the university. I should preface these remarks by emphasizing that they are speculative and impressionistic rather than based in ethnography or survey research of students at Yale or else-where. I offer them as a kind of challenge to those better situated and able than I to apply such social science tools to the issue of what students actually learn in the school.

The first lesson, I think, is that large corporate entities have no meaningful responsibility to the communities in which they exist. To be sure, there have always been primarily student organizations like public interest research groups (PIRGS) as well as numbers of individ-ual students involved in community-focused tutorial projects. I do not wish in any sense to demean these. But part of the problem is precisely what is taught by the contrast between what are constituted as individ-ual actions—joining a PIRG or doing tutoring—which of course are based upon ethical values—and corporate actions—far more formida-ble and overwhelmingly rooted in bottom-line factors. The university argument that policy must be based on what managers interpret as the institution's "responsibility" to students is the equivalent to the corpo-rate canard that it necessarily answers (more accurately, "they neces-sarily answer") only to shareholders. That is a disingenuous argu-ment, first, because it leaves out the self-interested role of managers and, second, because it places communities, and ultimately employees as well, outside the processes by which decisions affecting such peo-ples' lives are made. Thus Yale was able to rationalize its efforts not only to outsource food services and cut down the number of jobs available in New Haven, but also to deny its dining-hall workers the year-round employment of which they had previously been assured. Outsourcing, cutbacks, speed-up, and the like are familiar, of course; the claim I am raising, however, is that the naturalization of a division between ethical individual behavior and venal corporate actions is an essential part of higher education's hidden curriculum today. Lesson one.

The second, linked lesson has to do with the divide between those who are served at the university and those who serve. Of course, there has always been a certain potential for class tension between them, rooted, in the case of faculty-student interactions, in their differing relations to that form of cultural capital called "grades." But today more and more of the students at state and larger private universities are taught by part-timers, temporaries, teaching associates, and the like, whose job status, pay, and working conditions are rather more like those of the groundskeepers than those to which students, particularly at fancy private and "flagship" state institutions, look forward. A subtle shift in the balance of authority has taken place, abetted by what was, in the 1960s, a progressive innovation, student evaluations of faculty performance.[24] Abetted too by the consumerist philosophy fostered by managers claiming the necessity to make their institutions "competitive." In such an environment, undergraduate students expect to be waited upon, amused, stimulated, but not too challenged— they are, after all, paying clients, and faculty among the service personnel, easily intimidated by the threat of complaint or withdrawal to a more accommodating venue.[25] What is being naturalized here is the lesson of class separation, increasingly important to learn as divisions of income and wealth widen in the United States, and as more and more people are forced to accommodate themselves to pervasively antidemocratic economic and social arrangements.

The third issue concerns truth. Here it is useful to recollect the ardent columns and letters produced by Yale faculty in support of the proposition that teaching assistants were not employees but apprentices benignly supervised by their senior mentors.[26] Did anyone believe this stuff? Certainly not the Yale administration and legal staff, who jettisoned the argument and acknowledged that TAS were, indeed, workers when it became legally convenient to do so. But no one should be surprised: as Micaela di Leonardo has pointed out, books and articles which utterly falsify the political and social history of New Haven have continued to be taught at Yale to generations of students.[27] Does anyone think undergraduates are stupid and don't perceive reality? Perhaps. But what is at stake here is not truth but ideology, what is being defended is not the idea of a university but the basis of privilege, and what is being taught is a lesson popular in nineties America: spin it hard enough and people will believe a lemon is a coconut.

It is against such lessons—and one could describe others—that, it seems to me, the best of American studies scholarship needs to be deployed. For that, we have some excellent models, among them the work of Sandra Patton, of Richard Flacks and Scott Thomas, and of Micaela di Leonardo cited earlier. What characterizes such work? First of all, it is based on empirical study: Flacks and Thomas use surveys of students at the University of California–Santa Barbara, and elsewhere; di Leonardo employs ethnographic tools to examine in detail the New

Haven neighborhood in which she lived. Patton uses the work of Michael Agar to argue "that the boundaries of ethnographic study can be usefully reconceptualized to include a focus on the relationships between individuals, social institutions, and the State, rather than solely considering relationships between members of a particular cultural group."[28] By pointing to such fundamentally social science approaches, am I promoting a direction away from the cultural turn of American studies, projecting an announcement akin to Stanley Fish's that the moment of theory in literary study had passed? Of course, I am not Stanley Fish, nor was meant to be, and I am not predicting the demise of cultural study as central to the enterprise to which this book is devoted, American studies. I would argue, however, that such empirical research will, and should, play a substantially larger role in American studies than it has the last decade or more.

The reasons have to do with a second quality in the work I have cited: it is directed to questions that inform fundamental policy decisions in the United States. Di Leonardo attacks the " 'underclass' concept," exemplified in books like William Julius Wilson's *When Work Disappears,* which bases its analysis of American urban problems "on passive-verb, ahistorical political economy and 'blame the victim' sociology."[29] Her object is to replace the hegemony of ideas about defective "others" with "carefully historicized empirical work" that can locate the sources of American poverty in specific government policies—like those that shifted resources out of cities and into suburbs—and in uncontrolled forms of capital movement—of the sort contested in 1998 between General Motors and the United Auto Workers. Her point is not that knowledge of the truth about capital will make any of us free, but that such knowledge will arm those challenging policies and legislation based on false models of urban poverty.[30] Similarly, Patton analyzes the ways in which right-wing social scientists like Charles Murray and David Murray construct a *"salvation narrative,* in which White families, bearing the torch of 'family values' in popular representations, are the only families—or even mothers—who can *save* Black children."[31] Such narratives, Patton argues, locate the cause of American social problems not in poverty, deindustrialization, and the upward flow of wealth, but in the "immorality" of black mothers, which leads to illegitimacy, poor parenting, and other forms of social pathology—an analysis used to underwrite the policy initiatives that led to passage of bills fostering transracial adoption and virtually eliminating Aid to Families with Dependent Children.

The research of Flacks and Thomas emerges in the wake of increasingly successful efforts in California and elsewhere to roll back affirmative action procedures in hiring and, particularly, in college admissions. The underlying argument behind affirmative action in admissions was that earlier unfairness needed to be redressed by providing a leg up to populations—the "historically bypassed"—who had been cheated of truly equal opportunity. However historically just, that argument has proved politically vulnerable to the charges of fostering "quotas" and of cheating whites who themselves were supposedly guiltless of harming the victims of earlier forms of discrimination.[32] Flacks and Thomas begin from a different set of questions. They ask not who has been previously injured, but who is now in fact better using the social resources offered by higher educational institutions. Their evidence suggests that

> *the students most likely to be disposed to academic values and demands and to make use of the resources available on campus for their own development are today students for whom university attendance involves both sacrifice and risk—students usually regarded as "disadvantaged" because of race and class backgrounds.* Students who are supported by their parents, unburdened by debt and work demands, and raised by college educated parents are, paradoxically, more likely to be distanced from the values and opportunities provided by the institution. From a historical perspective we might say that the old "collegiate" hedonistic subcultural pattern has returned—and it is largely constituted by white students, particularly white males from relatively advantaged backgrounds.[33]

The policy implication one might draw from their research, if its conclusions are sustained, to put it in brutal instrumental terms mimicked from the studies with which this chapter began, is that in a period of economic constraint, an opportunity like obtaining a college education cannot continue to be squandered on students who systematically disregard what can be seen as a privilege and, in so doing, hog educational space better made available to those who will make the most constructive use of it. Or again, the higher education industry cannot afford to squander its resources on those who rely primarily upon social networks preestablished by class, race, and gender rather than upon mastering the intellectual content of colleges. I have used this bureaucratic phrasing to call attention to a fundamental irony of studies like *Breaking the Social Contract: The Fiscal Crisis in Higher Education* and *Straight Talk about College Costs and Prices.* Because they never ask who goes to college, who might go, who "ought" to go, or how that could be decided, they beg the fundamental economic issues they are theoretically designed to address. No surprise: those are the issues of the American class system.

Now I am neither utopian nor optimistic enough to imagine that American universities will ever be transformed into engines of working-class insurgency. But they can become instruments, as they have been in varied measure before, for helping level the playing field rather than, as too often now, tilting it further. That objective, it seems to me, is a goal both of progressive faculty and of working-class, minority, and immigrant communities, and thus an intellectual and policy basis for alliances between such groups. If the political force of open admissions, affirmative action, bilingual education, and similar initiatives is spent or fatally blocked, it seems to me that our job is to reconceive the grounds for struggling toward "a free university in a free society" (to recycle a brilliant Students for Democratic Society slogan). Besides, as I said at the outset, I do not think that a disobedient discipline like American studies has much of a future in a corporatized university. Self-interest, then, as well as idealism prompt us to apply what we know, what we learn, and what we teach to the project of sustaining in the academy the possibilities of democracy.

The building that houses one of the two big department stores in Semarang, the capital of Central Java, is laid out in a slightly flattened "V." At one end of the ground floor is a MacDonalds; at the other end something called "California Fried Chicken." Between them are smaller shops with American jeans, backpacks, and boots. Search throughout the building for a batik frock or some Javanese shorts to bring home to your grandchildren; you will be frustrated, for all the children's clothing—made in Indonesia, to be sure—loudly declares allegiance to the Los Angeles Lakers or to Planet Hollywood. And presiding over all the internal space—like audible postmodern goddesses, mostly in English but occasionally in Bahasa Indonesian—Janet Jackson, Tori Amos, Mary Chapin Carpenter.

I begin with these images of the penetration of American mass culture into an altogether remote world because they seem to bring into focus the conditions and challenges for our work today. Virtually everywhere in the world, here as well as abroad, a particular version of American ideology is in the ascendant. As people who study America, what have we to say in this distinctive moment not only to our students, their parents, the pundits, profiteers, and policy makers who inhabit our corner of the globe, but to the many Javanese kids—and their peers around the globe—who hang loose in the halfway house of those Semarang department stores?

I want to set out two propositions that may be helpful in trying to understand this moment in the study of what we call "America," and the place of intellectuals within it. The first proposition is this: while the term "American studies" is relatively new—younger, I think, than I—the things we now label "American studies" have been around far longer, indeed for many centuries. Here's my second proposition: the forms taken by American studies embody key political and social struggles of their era—or, to use Heinz Ickstadt's closely related formulation, "American studies recreates or reconstructs American history in its own discourse." In fact, to investigate the changing character of American studies is to examine the processes of change in American culture and society.

A few words about each of these propositions: American studies as it is now named is an effort to understand and, of course, *to shape* the changing dimensions particularly of society, culture, and politics in the geographical space of the United States, now generally called "America."[1] I think American studies can most usefully be understood not as a discipline that, from a remote and academic standpoint, surveys a particular historical and cultural territory, but as a framework within which people engage in those most significant of intellectual ventures, changing or policing the society in which we live. By that standard, the Zuni emergence story,[2] which narrates and thus helps legitimatize the processes by which Zuni society was supposed to have been structured, its rituals developed, and its characteristic cultural forms determined, is as much an exercise in "American studies" as is Henry Nash Smith's *Virgin Land*. And Bradford's *Of Plimouth Plantation* is as characteristic an example of American studies for its cultural communities as—and neither more nor less tendentious than—say, Morrison's *Playing in the Dark* is for some of ours.

Now, one might feel that such an argument dissolves useful intellectual boundaries and obliterates what little there might be to mark out American studies from any other kind of intellectual enterprise. But I want to suggest that that response—indeed, the very idea that

American studies is an academic enterprise, or even predominantly an enterprise of academicians—signals a particular historical era. The mark of that era is also inscribed in the name we have given our work, American *studies*. The domination of academic narratives in American studies embodies the period of the ascendancy of the university in the United States during, roughly, the middle fifty years of the twentieth century. To give the project another name—for example, "Magnalia Christi Americana," *A New Home—Who'll Follow?*, or *Darkwater*—is immediately to illustrate how the academy is but one locus for, and the academic mode but one form of, the study of America. To be sure, in the lives of most of us who teach and study, that locus and that mode have been enormously powerful. But that is because for most of us, and certainly for those of us to the academic manner raised, the academy has itself been so powerful. American studies as a name emerged just as the academy was reaching the peak of its cultural authority in the post–World War II years. The name represented at once a statement about the institutional power of the academy—*we* do the vital task of studying America—and an effort to stake out turf *within* that increasingly significant institution against the Eurocentric forms of study that dominated American universities and colleges.

I raise these considerations because it seems to me that the era of academic ascendancy is over. American colleges and universities are undergoing a transformation as profound—and far more painful than—that which converted them from citadels of a small, monied, and largely white and male elite, into vast enterprises serving businesses, the state, enormously increased numbers of students, and—not incidentally—us. We are all familiar with the signs that, read aright, proclaimed in the early 1990s the academy's transformation: large-scale budget slashes accompanied by course reductions, program reorganizations, and even salary cuts in real dollars; the shifting of costs from public sources to individual students and their parents; speed-up, mainly in the form of larger classes. More and more, the academy has come to resemble other institutions within American society, with the creation of a small army of the un- or underemployed, the proliferation of part-time and temporary workers, the downgrading of the future expectations of most young teachers—not to speak of the gross corruption that has increasingly marked the behavior of many senior administrators, whose salaries are regularly ten to twenty times and more those of library clerks and groundskeepers, or even of the grunts in the freshman composition trenches. Such changes represent fundamental shifts now underway in the social and economic missions of higher education,[3] shifts I would characterize as the shrinking of the objective of producing student self-actualization and independent learning and the intensification of the role of colleges and universities in stratifying the workforce, training it in habits of consumption, and preparing it for more narrowly defined jobs—if any—in an increasingly constricted economy.

What is often not so clearly seen, I want to argue, is a comparable shift in cultural authority; it is this shift which leads me to questioning ideas about what constitutes the work we call "American studies." And this set of questions leads, in turn, into a few paradigms we can associate with the site of the 1994 American Studies Association meeting, where I first presented these ideas: Nashville. The "versions of Nashville" I have in mind are but three of the many one might construct. My three involve, first, the Nashville Agrarians, who were and are so enormously influential in the practice of literary study in America; second, the Nashville movement of the late 1950s and early 1960s, to me *the* defining force for nonviolent struggle among students and other young activists, black and white, during that hopeful time; and, finally, Robert Altman's film *Nashville,* in retrospect an oddly prescient, perhaps postmodern exercise in satire and . . . American studies.

I don't propose that I can add anything very significant to the many studies of the Agrarians by scholars such as Richard Gray, Alexander Karanikas, Louis Rubin, Lewis Simpson, and Thomas Young.[4] In light—or, perhaps it is more accurate to say, in sound—of today's politics, *I'll Take My Stand,* the primary text that emerged from the Agrarians' work, seems less quaint as doctrine than it did to most of those who picked it up at its first publication in 1930. Indeed, there are many passages in it which one can easily imagine being spoken by William Bennett or Roger Kimball: "But why, it may be asked, have the best and most scholarly colleges of our country recently demanded from their freshmen one year's obligatory work in English composition if the present-day high-school product has really learned to read and write?"[5] Other passages, and particularly the volume's central attack on the impact of industrial capitalism, might well have been grumbled by Thoreau or contemporary radicals—such as me, for instance—or, more to

"Nashville." Photograph from Photofest

the point, by conservatives of the previous century, such as Ruskin and Carlyle. For the fundamental measures of *I'll Take My Stand* are traditional, arguably medieval values; in the words of the song from which it derives its title: "Old times there are ne'er forgotten." The particular form of tradition that the book poses as the only true bulwark against the anomie and materialism of modern industrial life is, of course, Agrarianism. The term "Agrarian" is much used and, as John Crowe Ransom acknowledges in his introduction, little defined. Lyle H. Lanier, a psychologist at Vanderbilt, was only more overt than others in propounding this agrarian theory. Community, he believed, true "association among individuals,"

> exists, for the generality of people, only in the agrarian community and in the villages and towns which are its adjuncts. It depends upon a stable population, upon long acquaintances, since human beings do not bear spigots by which "fraternity" can be drawn off for the asking. The city necessarily means a diminution of these associations. . . . Another phase of the same problem is the decline of the family. This is perhaps much more important than any other phase of contemporary disintegration, since the family is the natural biological group, the normal milieu of shared experiences, community of interests, integration of personality. The segmentation of

helped in some sense to produce the New Negro Renaissance of the 1920s; or about the role of the Nixon administration's persecution of the sixties' social movements in helping to produce the seventies' turn toward theory. So I would not argue that the failure of the Agrarian program led in any direct or simple way to the critical work taken up by Ransom and his colleagues. Still, their condemnation of industrial society and of socialist solutions to its problems remained strong. And, unlike in France, there was no significant fascist movement within which to pursue political alternatives. Moreover, for Ransom in particular, perhaps the fundamental weakness of industrial society was its failure to take the aesthetic—that is to say, civilization and the conditions for its cultivation—seriously.[10] In poetry, moreover, one might find, or at least seek, precisely those values of balance, harmony, affection, tradition, and—most of all—maturity that *I'll Take My Stand* hypostatized in agrarian life. The agrarianism of the Nashville group dwindled away, but its ideology, as Karanikas argued thirty years ago, reemerged in the New Criticism, and with the vast postwar expansion of educational institutions came to play an absolutely central role in American culture.

In nothing is this so fully dramatized than in connection with race. The Agrarian project altogether marginalized black people; indeed, as Gray argues, African Americans served as the unspoken other whose "structural absence" was "constitutive of the text":

> We could surely argue that the absence of any significant reference to slavery in *I'll Take My Stand* is not only remarkable; it helps us to locate the vision of the world—or, to use Raymond Williams's phrase, the structure of feeling and experience—that underpins all the essays in the symposium. It helps us to establish the models of belief and behaviour, the habits of language, that enabled the Agrarians to pattern the real and perform various crucial acts of exclusion. Like any code, the one the Agrarians employed is as notable for what it does not say as for what it does, for the absences by which it is haunted; and *their* code seems intent on not bringing into speech, and therefore into the orbit of its attention, one figure in particular—the black.[11]

This process of exclusion, of "not bringing into speech," seems to me to describe with equal power the "habits of language," the structures of "feeling and experience" that characterized the dominant forms of academic criticism until well into the sixties. To say this another way, the canon debate begun midway into the sixties, which has often been taken to be an academic dispute about what goes into a syllabus, has fundamentally to do with what will be heard and thus taken seriously within the precincts of what had, by then, become one of America's key institutions, the university.

The founders of this nation were well aware of the importance of being heard. The first amendment to the Constitution, as we all know, upholds "freedom of speech . . . of the press" and "the right of people peaceably to assemble, and to petition the government for a redress of grievances." And courts have been careful, especially in the last half century, to identify as forms of free speech a variety of physical acts: picket lines, leafleting, sit-ins, for example. For courts have recognized the political meaning of an old romantic saying, "Out of sight, out of mind." The second of my versions of Nashville, the movement of the late 1950s and early 1960s, had as its central goal placing clearly before the eyes of America the injustices constituting the central experiences of black people in the South. Like the Agrarians, the movement offered a way of thinking about a pervasive and central social disease in America; like them, too, the movement proposed alternatives to existing arrangements. That much seems obvious; less apparent are the precise qualities implied in that analysis and in those alternatives.

One reason for something of this obscurity may be the surprising dearth of writing about the Nashville movement. I have gathered around me some ten books and dozens of articles which, in part or in whole, deal with the Nashville Agrarians; I have found only two books which discuss the Nashville movement—in relatively a few pages.[12] Yet out of that movement came a surprising number of individuals well-known for their leadership, like Representative John Lewis, Marion Barry, Diane Nash, James Bevel, the Reverend C. T. Vivian, not to speak of the movement's generative force, the Reverend James Lawson, and the hundreds of other activists who marched, sang, endured violence, took jail rather than bail, and wrote history with their bodies. The Nashville movement provided a primary impetus for and ideological development of nonviolence as a central feature of the civil rights movement among younger people during the first half of the 1960s— and from that base outward into the wider movements for change of

James Lawson being escorted by police. © Bettmann/CORBIS

that period.[13] And the Nashville movement represented the flowering of a social endeavor radically distinct from that of the Agrarians, but whose roots reach back to the very time in which they flourished. So I find it more than passing strange that not a single book, and precious few articles, have been written about this movement, its history, ideas, and personnel. I ask my historian friends in particular why that should be.

Part of the answer, perhaps, has to do with the form of discourse the Nashville movement adopted and the venues in which that discourse was deployed. I want to use as my literal text here the "Negro Students' Code," developed by James Lawson and a group of college students from Fisk, Tennessee A&I, and the American Baptist Theological Seminary, who constituted the shock troops of the Nashville movement.[14] Students carried this code with them to the lunch counters of Woolworth's, McLellan's, and Kress's when they began sit-ins on February 13, 1960. From one point of view, this code amounts to little more than a statement of the discipline demonstrators had agreed upon for carrying out their actions. From another point of view, however, the code embodies the movement's ideological roots, an implicit conception of the sources of America's disorder, and a clear design for change. I want to read the code, partly because its cadences register so sharp a contrast with the learned rhetoric of *I'll Take My Stand*, but partly to invoke for our own work something of the spirit which moved in the light here in Nashville.

> Don't strike back or curse back if abused.
> Don't laugh out.
> Don't hold conversations with floor workers.
> Don't leave your seats until your leader has given you instructions to do so.
> Don't block entrances to the stores and aisles.
> Show yourself friendly and courteous at all times.
> Sit straight and always face the counter.
> Report all serious incidents to your leader.
> Refer all information to your leader in a polite manner.
> Remember the teachings of Jesus Christ, Mohandas K. Gandhi and Martin Luther King.
> Remember love and non-violence.
> May God bless each of you.

I resurrected this code, which had held a dim place in my memory these thirty-some years, from the files of the religious pacifist Fellowship of Reconciliation (FOR), now at Swarthmore College's Peace Collection. Reading those files back into the early thirties, I was stunned by the dissonance between the world in and around Nashville seen by the Agrarians and that pictured, for example, by the FOR's interracial secretary in the South, Howard Kester. Kester had written in a 1933 report, for example, "The terrific power of the anti-social forces in the South has steadily driven the Fellowship into the position of a revolutionary movement. In doing this we have merely accepted the historic position of Jesus who definitely recognized the class struggle and set his face steadfastly against the oppressors of the poor, the weak and the disinherited."[15] To be sure, Kester's language, no less than that of the Agrarians, is much of his time. In another way, however, it reflects the community out of which he spoke.

The FOR's southern race relations work was for more than thirty years largely centered in Nashville; in the year in which *I'll Take My Stand* was published, the fellowship's Southern Advisory Committee contained far more people from Tennessee than from any other state, and the executive committee, drawn from the Nashville community, included the president, dean of women, and minister at Fisk, as well as professors at Vanderbilt and at Scarritt College.[16] After a certain hiatus during the postwar years, when an FOR spin-off, the Congress on Racial Equality (CORE), carried the burden of interracial activity, James Lawson, then one of three black students at Vanderbilt's Divinity School, was hired part-time by the FOR to develop nonviolent solutions to race relations problems.[17] In 1959, Lawson conducted a series of workshops on nonviolence that helped prepare a large group of students in and around Nashville for direct action. In fact, late that year—about two months before the first widely publicized sit-ins in Greensboro, North Carolina—two such test actions were held at Harvey's department store and at Cain-Sloane's in Nashville.[18]

I mention these details not to establish a meaningless priority for Nashville but to underline the long-term continuities of a movement often portrayed as essentially a departure from the culture of the black South. The Negro Students' Code emphasizes in particular the connections of the movement with the forms of religious radicalism represented by the names of Jesus, Gandhi, and King. Lawson himself, apart from being a minister, had served a prison term for being a conscientious objector to the Korean War and had also worked in India with the Methodist Board of Missions for three years before returning to divinity school.[19] In commenting on an FOR Institute on Nonviolence in July, 1959, he had complimented the organizers for providing "excellent psychological background on nonviolence." But, he continued, "the theological and biblical were sadly neglected." Such matters were particularly important, he believed, since—like many of the students with whom he was working in Nashville—"most of the people who attend these Institutes come from churches and think in these terms."[20] Similarly, the first statement of purpose, heavily influenced by Nashville delegates, proposed for the newly organized Student Nonviolent Coordinating Committee (SNCC) began by affirming "the philosophical or religious ideal of nonviolence as the foundation of our purpose, the presupposition of our belief and the manner of our action."[21] Implicitly, the ground of conflict is here posed not in economic, legal, or structural but in "philosophical or religious," that is, moral terms— terms, I want to stress, available to the power of individual action.[22]

The code and the forms of action preferred by the Nashville move-ment—sit-ins, freedom rides, direct actions—carried this ethical im-perative into particular forms both of individual and group conduct: controlled, open, polite. For some movement activists, of course, these were no more than the tactics of a physically weak minority, designed to clog "by its whole weight," and even to mask a deep-running sense of anger. In the long run, as is well known, the view of nonviolence as a useful maneuver prevailed in the movement. Most of the Nashville group, however, emphasized less the tactical virtues of nonviolence than its transformative potential; again in the words of the SNCC state-ment: "Nonviolence as it grows from Judaic-Christian tradition, seeks a social order of justice permeated by love. Integration of human en-deavor represents the crucial, first step toward such a society." The issue, that is, is segregation, "the problem of the color line," as Du Bois had said in chapter two of *The Souls of Black Folk*.[23]

The foe, then, is not a system of ownership or a structure of laws but—to borrow once again a phrase from Thoreau—"the all but uni-versal woodenness of both head and heart, the want of vitality in man, which is the effect of our vice."[24] The students' nonviolent conduct, their discipline, their very mannerliness, were designed to transform such fearful, wooden responses. For, to cite one last time the SNCC statement, "Through nonviolence courage displaces fear. Love trans-forms hate. Acceptance dissipates prejudice; hope ends despair. Faith reconciles doubt. Peace dominates war. Mutual regard cancels enmity. Justice for all overthrows injustice. The redemptive community super-cedes immoral social systems."

As we all know, the movement was gradually to step away from this emphasis on the ethical high ground, to the issue of the ballot, to the courts, and later, tentatively, toward the economic questions that every day grow more intense. My point, however, is again not so much to question what might well be seen as the utopianism of the advocates for religious nonviolence. I want, rather, to emphasize the forms of learning and the venues therefor that this movement provided. These students and their supporters were engaged, I believe, in a kind of study of America widespread in the 1960s. It is encapsulated in sen-tences I found myself often citing then: "If you want knowledge, you must take part in the practice of changing reality. If you want to know the taste of a pear, you must change the pear by eating it yourself."

Many of the students engaged in these practical studies also devised means for carrying on alternative kinds of learning, freedom schools in unlikely locations. Pauline Knight, who had been arrested as a freedom rider in 1961, described some of her time in Mississippi's Parchman prison:

> . . . we organized to pass the time. In the morning we first had a quiet hour and then meditation. Then we all took exercises. Next came devotions. There were Protestants, Catholics and Jews among us, so we read from the Old Testament, the New Testament, and the Catholic prayerbook.
>
> After that, we conducted workshops in the Gandhian philosophy of nonviolence, and shared our experiences in nonviolent action. Then we would have discussions on many different topics. Different ones of us would give lectures on our major fields of study at school; we had a wide variety—biology, education, economics, all the liberal arts, Greek and Roman history. It was very educational.[25]

Ironically, many of you may remember, James Lawson's career at his educational institution, Vanderbilt, was terminated when he—alone of all the Nashville protesters—was expelled for engaging in civil disobedience.

That action came early in the process which would lead many students during the sixties to discover with revulsion the complicity of their educational institutions in the social policies, including segregation and war, they sought to change. Indeed, in certain important ways, the transformation of colleges and universities from the institutions they were in the 1950s to what they are today can be traced back to the civil rights movement and to the demands it articulated for equal access. On the other hand, a central part of that process has to do with the rise in importance of the media, and that brings me to my third version of Nashville, Robert Altman's film.

My first two versions were driven by their ideologies; therein lay both their power to compel and, from a postmodern perspective, some profound weaknesses. Altman's film self-consciously offers no ideological center; indeed, the center of the film is a void inhabited by Hal Philip Walker, the presidential candidate of the prescient Replacement Party, who in fact never appears. Around this abyss dance an enormous number of characters marked primarily, like the film itself, by contradiction and, like the images of a metaphysical poem, "yoked by violence together." While Altman has not in this film altogether abandoned plot, it is surely not the soul of his tragedy—if tragedy it is. The film is remarkably episodic and improvisatory, held together to the extent that it is by its general focus on the Nashville country music scene, by a very large number of self-conscious visual parallels, and by the general drift of events toward an outdoor rally for Hal Philip Walker. In fact, Altman's directions to his screenplay writer appear to have been limited only to the concentration on Nashville's music setting and the seemingly arbitrary stipulation that someone die at the end.[26] Even the dialogue was subject to the actors' emendations; many of the songs were created by the people who sang them. Not surprisingly, then, interpretations of the film have been wildly divergent and evaluations contradictory. Like a poststructuralist theoretical text, it invites, indeed valorizes, contradiction and seems designed to resist closure.

For example, one of the more powerfully affecting songs in the film is "I'm Easy," created and sung by Keith Carradine. In effect, however, the song comes down to yet another of the many ambiguous gestures the Carradine character uses to captivate one more woman into his bed. Again, in the end, after Country-queen Barbara Jean has been shot, Albuquerque, who has been hanging around the edges of the music scene hoping for a break, calms the crowd and wins a place by leading them in singing. But the song itself, "It Don't Worry Me," turns out to be a paean to political apathy and emotional disconnection—a far cry from "We Shall Overcome," whose communal singing, Ann Fitzgerald has suggested, it ironically evokes. I think it's fair to say that no one of the film's characters escapes its corrosive cynicism, and the entertainment industry is subject to hilarious satire, yet the film feels, at least to me, not precisely cheerful but by no means an exercise in gloom or even skepticism.

I think Altman is able to sustain these contradictions by a gambit which, I fear, has not been unfamiliar to us in academic American studies. It is a move to replace the force of ideology with the play of culture, to substitute *jouaissance* for *credo,* and to marginalize civic debate as nothing more than the suspect gestures of what passes for politics in the United States. In this vision, Nashville is not the staging area for a backward-yearning attack on modern industrial life, not the ground upon which citizens are immersed in a moral drama, but the platform upon which people play out in larger-than-life images the contrary dimensions of their fragile humanity. I confess I find that unsatisfying. Not because I yearn for the relative certainties of sixties politics—though I do. Nor, I think, because I'm largely bored with forms of celebrity gossip—though I am. But because, for me at least, politics does not consist in the sleazy sound bites which now fill the air around us—and that Altman so aptly expresses through Hal Philip Walker's sound truck. Politics is, rather, that form of moral philosophy concerned with the social organism as a whole, the *polis*—concerned, that is, with how we work things out together—or don't.

Altman's film brilliantly captures—and is also, I suspect, captivated by—some of the major social processes of the last quarter century and more: the shift in cultural authority toward the media, including his own; the erection of the market as today's golden calf; the reduction of politics to Tweedledum choices or, at best, to what Sid Lens used to call "lesser weevilism"; and the substitution of Wonderbread, Ringling Brothers, and heavy breathing for bread, land and peace. All of these tendencies have likewise opened dangers in what we do as American studies practitioners.

It seems to me that there is a certain lesson that one can draw from my versions of Nashville; it is a lesson having to do with American educational and political history. (And I have to say parenthetically that, being an old fogey, I'm much less nervous than some of you might be about drawing lessons and constructing master narratives.) In the period subsequent to the First World War, colleges and universities rapidly increased dominion over culture relative to other institutions, so that by the fifties it was virtually impossible to imagine success in America without first acquiring the habits of mind as well as the decorum and largely the cold war values of the academy. Universities were, of course, material supporters of such democratic institutions as Ngo Dinh Diem's police, the Institute for Defense Analysis, segregated professional schools, and ritualized patriarchy. But I want to stress that higher education was more critical to the processes of shaping our minds and spirits to a kind of Mandarin culture than even those of us who came to be "radicals" understood. A major component of the imperial culture that much of the academy, until after the sixties, seemed committed to sustaining was, of course, the form of literary study given shape and impetus by people like T. S. Eliot and his Nash-ville champions.[27] Our ability to thrive within the precincts of this cultural stockade calibrated our reliability as well as our maturity, our capacity to maintain "balance" and "perspective," even as our hopes for transforming America slid away in the jungles of Vietnam.

Still, while many of us in Students for a Democratic Society (SDS) during the sixties focused on the grotesque perversions of higher education represented by Columbia's gym and Michigan State's police program, we generally also acknowledged the academy's capacity, however limited, of fostering human rationality, and its potential, however attenuated, to play a significant role in human liberation. When the civil rights movement turned its attention to colleges—whether in demanding admissions, black studies, or jobs—it largely did so with what I found to be a genuinely touching affirmation of the fundamental values of educational institutions. We believed—as an SDS slogan of the time had it—in "a free university in a free society." Both were, we thought, imaginable; and American schools and colleges could be leaders in that ethical quest.

That hope was short-lived, I'm afraid, not because of the academy's lack of virtues, but because its authority has so thoroughly eroded. Today's students hardly look to the academy for their social values, much less for their ideas of cultural significance. These, I think, they derive much more from the media, and its attendant complex of entertainment, advertising and promotional activities. The underlying message of the media in late-twentieth-century American practice seems to me to come down to the one inescapable motive of marketplace ideology: everything can be made into a commodity and sold for profit. Everything: stories, obviously; intellect, of course, AZT, babies. And kidneys, hearts, livers, teeth, eyes, genitalia, identities, hopes, prayers, desire, the air itself, and the grass we tread to the graves we must buy. Perhaps I am merely rationalizing my work and constructing one of those simplistic Enlightenment binaries, but I think that at this moment the values toward which the academy at its best struggles *do* stand over against the corroding hegemony of marketplace doctrines and their underlying assumption that competition, profit, and self-aggrandizement are the only reliable sources of human motivation.

It was such a conjecture that led me to interrogate our visions of American studies, which in this talk I have tied to "versions of Nashville." We cannot retreat into self-enclosed forms of cultural study: emptied of politics, cultural study, indeed culture itself, becomes an exercise in self-acclaim or even managerial control.[28] Nor do I believe that American studies can be backward yearning, however apt its critique of contemporary society. Yet I think it's time we insisted upon exploring and teaching the powerful expressions of democratic values many of us have experienced right here in the United States, like the civil rights movement of the fifties and sixties—especially now, when outrageously racist ideas about human beings are rationalized as science and validated in the front pages of influential newspapers and journals.[29] For it seems to me the duty of those of us who study the past to help sustain those rare moments in which humane values emerged into human practice.

In declaring ourselves students of America we undertook a certain responsibility—not only to those we encounter in the corridors and classrooms of the institutions we inhabit, but to those in less congenial institutions, to those Javanese kids hanging out in Semarang's Americanized department stores, to the folks we meet at Nashville's malls and lunch counters. It is a responsibility we cannot execute walled in by obscure language and academic assumptions. To contest the prevailing veneration of peddle, purchase, and profit with which America has become identified, to challenge the runaway individualism that has always threatened to bury ideas of community in this country, requires that we speak and act in all of those worlds my versions of Nashville invoke. I want to offer as a concluding symbol for the directions in which I think we are traveling the move, in 1994, of the national American Studies Association office from the Francis Scott Key Building at the University of Maryland, to 1120 19th Street NW, a block and a half from DuPont Circle in the District of Columbia and perhaps half a mile from the White House. The move expresses a stride from the consolations of the campus and into the circle of politics, wherein we are finding a voice. There will be times when, like Jonah, we will curse the cold and blackness there near the belly of the whale. And while I do not see us as instruments for the repentance of Ninevah, I want to, indeed I can, imagine us as, in Father Mapple's words, "speaker[s] of true things" to the "proud gods and commodores of this earth."

27 October, 1994

CHAPTER FOUR
**CULTURE AND
CONFORMITY IN
WARTIME AMERICA:
MY JUNIOR HIGH
SCHOOL SONGBOOK**

This essay addresses some of the ways in which wartime culture was constructed and sustained in the United States in the mid-1940s. The complex way of perceiving, experiencing, and understanding the world, and acting in it, which we call "culture," has many sources. These include formal education, popular songs as well as more literary texts, movies and other media, reference and peer group as well as parental pressures, and the formative power of such factors as race, gender, class, and sexuality. Studying culture therefore requires an eclectic methodology, which borrows from literary criticism, art history, psychology, anthropology, among other disciplines, and even from autobiography—since cultural meanings emerge in the particular yet diverse ways individuals perceive and act. Consequently, in what follows I have used a variety of analytic strategies, some of which may at first seem unusual in a scholarly paper. But they are calculated to bring to the reader as "thick"[1] an account of wartime American culture and its construction—at least in one significant place—as I can provide.

I have chosen this varied approach also because American studies as it is now being practiced in the United States is itself an eclectic discipline. American studies was always in some significant degree concerned with culture,[2] and it has also prided itself on its interdisciplinary strategy. But it has in recent years increasingly been attentive to popular culture[3] and visual imagery as shaping forces in society and politics. In looking at a particular cultural artifact of the World War II period, my own junior high school songbook, I am less interested in its autobiographical implications than in how it can be used to learn how varied cultural forces come together in a particular place and a particular moment to shape the feelings and thoughts that underwrite that most total of human behaviors, warfare.

Fifty years ago, when World War II was approaching its bloody conclusion, I was a twelve-year-old student at Joseph H. Wade Junior High School in the Bronx. Wade, Junior High School 117, a relatively new school with excellent facilities, was part of a plan to divide New York City schools into three tiers instead of two. At an earlier time, students went to elementary or grammar school for eight years and then—if they continued—to high school for four. Now, students would attend elementary school for six years, go to junior high school for three, and then go on to high school for three more. The point of this arrangement, so far as I have been able to tell, was to separate out kids in their most unmanageable, hormone-driven adolescent years—eleven through fourteen—from the younger children in grammar school, on the one hand, and from the presumably more mature older adolescents in high school, on the other. In junior high, that is, the physical and sexual development of kids would be channeled into socially acceptable forms of behavior and thought. We were, in short, to be socialized into young adults. The idea of young teenagers becoming mature adults did not then seem so far-fetched as it might today. After all, Jews, who constituted the vast majority of students at Wade, celebrate the coming-of-age ritual called a bar mitzvah at age thirteen. And in the 1940s and 1950s a popular line from that ritual, to be spoken by the bar mitzvah boy, was "Today I am a man."

Located in the midst of a largely working and middle-class and primarily Jewish enclave, Wade like similar schools served another critical function in that time. It played a role in the process of drawing white ethnics—Jews, Italians, Poles, and others—from marginal positions in American society to the American mainstream. During the Great Depression many people from these groups had turned to the Left or at least to left-leaning unions and other organizations; many had been bitterly disillusioned by the manifest failures of American capitalism. In the postwar order, being planned as early as 1943, it was important for social harmony to hold out opportunities for upward mobility to such groups, and especially to the children of first and second-generation immigrants. To accomplish this process of assimilation—for that is what I am describing—the federal government would devise a whole range of incentives in the postwar period: inexpensive higher education, cheap mortgages for new homes, a suburban infrastructure of highways, support for good and often union-backed pension plans, among other things.[4] Those were the postwar carrots; the postwar sticks may be represented by loyalty oaths, purges of government workers and teachers, the pre-McCarthy McCarthyism of the Truman administration, and the execution of the Rosenbergs.[5]

But that is a somewhat later story, the story of the construction of cold war culture. We kids in junior high school in 1944 knew none of this. What we knew was that we had to settle down, do our homework, follow instructions. Discipline was tight in junior high school. For the first time in our school careers, we moved from classroom to classroom for different subjects, and the two big, ex–football player assistant principals patrolled the halls and stairwells to maintain silence during these periods between classes. That much was obvious to us. What was much less obvious were the lessons we were learning, often not from the explicit subject matter of our English, social studies or math classes, but from the assumptions and attitudes that underlay these courses. Of course, America in 1944 was a society at war, and virtually all institutions in the United States, the schools included, were turned toward achieving victory in that war. But patriotism was not the only value being inculcated in our curriculum. As I shall suggest, what we were learning, in fact what it was essential for us to absorb if we were to take our new places in the postwar order, was the culture of mainstream America.

The artifact of that time, fifty years ago, that I am using to examine these processes of acculturation is, as I have said, my junior high

Cover

school songbook, which I have preserved over these many years. In some ways, the music class, where there seemed to be much less of a set curriculum than in English or history, offers an excellent index to the teachers' ideas[6] about what it was important for us to learn. But because of the ways in which the book was compiled, it also provides some real insights into how I, a reasonably typical product of those times and circumstances, understood the culture I was being taught.

As I recall it, many classes from one grade level, as many as six or seven, gathered together in the auditorium for music. We would sing one or more of the songs we had learned. And then one teacher would dictate a new song, and we would write down the words in our books. At home, we were expected to make a fair copy of the text—preferably by typing, though many families did not have typewriters—and paste the fair copy over our scrawled transcription of the text. Then we were to find an appropriate picture to illustrate the song and to paste the picture into our books on the page opposite the text. Ann Fitzgerald has pointed out to me how enterprising this pedagogical tactic was, for it encouraged our creativity and imagination, as well as, in good American studies fashion, breaking down disciplinary barriers between language, music, and the visual arts. I did pretty well, I guess, for I got a grade of 100 percent every time, perhaps because both my parents could type and thus help me prepare a decent copy, but also, I think, because the pictures I used found approval from whoever my teacher was at the time. I should say that I remember her not at all. Undoubtedly, she was ingenious and energetic; she had to be to hold together a class of maybe two hundred young adolescent girls and boys. Of one thing I am virtually certain: she, like almost all our teachers then, was white and Christian and from a community distinct from the one to which I returned every afternoon.

That central Bronx community was, of course, a very different world from the one portrayed today in American movies and television. Its main artery, the Grand Concourse and Boulevard, was modeled on great Parisian avenues, running in broad, tree-lined splendor along a low ridge from the area around Yankee Stadium, the Concourse Plaza Hotel, and the Bronx County Courthouse in the south to Mosholu Parkway, near the northern border of New York City. It was lined with fine, middle-class apartments, and cut at regular intervals by wide shopping streets, the traffic from which was guided through tunnels under the Concourse. A number of small parks dotted its sides, one of which held a tiny low-ceilinged cottage in which Edgar Allan Poe had lived with his child bride and cousin, Virginia Clemm, and her mother. The Grand Concourse was also the scene, probably in 1940, of a grand cavalcade of automobiles, in the grandest of which sat the president, Franklin D. Roosevelt.

Later, in the 1950s, much of that area was devastated by the process of constructing the Cross Bronx Expressway.[7] Most of the Jewish families moved to Long Island, New Jersey, or Florida, and they were replaced by poorer Puerto Rican and other Latino populations, whose bodegas now occupy the storefronts along 170th Street and Burnside Avenue that once contained kosher butchers. Many areas, in fact, fell into serious disrepair as the city increasingly withdrew services from this once middle-class district, and it has been a common sight these last twenty years or so to see from a car rushing along the Cross Bronx Expressway decaying buildings boarded up or reduced to piles of rubble. But in the time I lived on Sheridan Avenue, one block east of the Grand Concourse, the area was comfortable, stable, homogeneous. But, I believe, it was at some level jittery—if that is exactly the word. For we were Jews, and it was not altogether clear, even in this war against Nazi fascism, what would be "good for the Jews," as a common phrase

(*Top left*) "Marine Corps Hymn" (*Right*) Field Artillery (*Bottom left*) Coast Guard

of the time put it. What was clear was that our job in junior high was to do well, to ask fewer questions, and to get ahead.

The primary theme of my junior high music class was the armed forces, the subject of at least thirteen of the forty-three songs we learned that year. We memorized every supposed song of every branch of the military: the "Army Air Corps Song," the "Song of the Seabees," "Anchors Aweigh," subtitled the "Song of the Navy," "The United States Marines Hymn" (it's always fascinated me that the Marines alone had a *hymn*), "The Field Artillery Song," "The Coast Guard Forever," not to speak of other ancillary ditties like "Comin' In on a Wing and a Prayer" and "The Song of the Bombardiers" (not to be confused with the "Bombardiers' Song," which we also learned). Navy fliers seemed to be a particular favorite; we learned "Hail to the Wings of the Navy," as well as "Navy Wings," and "Sky Anchors." Those naval aviation songs were among the most forgettable; indeed, unlike most of the rest, they are utterly gone from my memory. But I suspect that fliers, the subjects of seven of the forty-three songs, were the most glamorous and modern of the various kinds of warriors we were learning to celebrate.

There's a certain quality of the collegiate fight song to these very widely known military chants, explicit in "Anchors Aweigh":

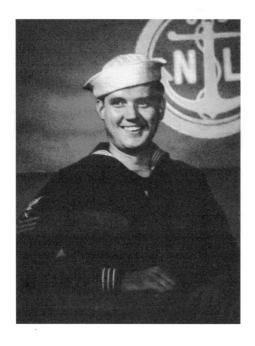

"Anchors Aweigh"

Anchors aweigh, my boys, anchors aweigh,
Farewell to college joys,
We sail at break of day, day, day, day.
Through our last night on shore,
Drink to the foam,
Until we meet once more,
Here's wishing you a happy voyage home.

Indeed, "Anchors Aweigh" has served in peacetime to rally midshipmen at the Naval Academy to "beat the Army, beat the Army, ray!" A quality of undergraduate pep rallies, young, hopeful, poignant, pervades even those songs which faintly address the possibilities of death:

Off we go into the wild blue yonder,
Climbing high into the sun,
Here they come zooming to meet our thunder,
At 'em boys give 'er the gun.
Down we dive spouting our flame from under,
Off with one terrible roar,
We live in fame or go down in flame,
Nothing'll stop the Army Air Corps.

(*Top*) "Song of the Bombardiers" (*Middle*) "Wing and a Prayer" (*Bottom*) Army Air Corps

Our Country

In these songs, the battlefield is assimilated to the playing field, and these lively marches become testimonials to the competitive spirit of the various teams in our own collegiate league, like "Bulldog, bulldog, rah, rah, rah, Eli Yale," or "On Wisconsin, On Wisconsin, forward to the fray." "If the army and the navy," crows the Marine Corps Hymn, "ever look on heaven's scenes / They will find the streets are guarded by / The United States Marines." It is boy culture projected on to the large canvas of wartime patriotism. Big boy culture, in fact, full of brews, and bonding, guns, kicking butt, and contempt for age: "If you'd live to be a gray-haired wonder, / Keep the nose out of the blue." In a way, what the songs do is legitimate the aggressive, indeed belli-cose spirit of American boy culture by providing it with a patriotic rationale and a nationalistic framework. At the same time, by incor-porating the martial, pugnacious spirit of these songs into what could otherwise be regarded as an effete music class, the teachers strove to solve a basic problem of American education: how to sustain in boys the aggressive individualism that is the ground note of American middle-class ideology without allowing such fundamentally antisocial behaviors to disrupt school itself. The fact that eight of the first ten songs we were taught were military, and mostly lively, marches, may as much be attributed to the restlessness of adolescent boys as to the war itself. It's a version of that wise advice given to the new teacher by the veteran: select readings the boys will like; girls will read anything at all. Whether there is anything uniquely American about these processes, I must leave to others to contemplate.

Just as many of these songs emphasize forms of male-to-male bonding familiar to masculine institutions from the football field to the barracks, others focus on that other central element of American ideology: a pugnacious and often self-righteous individualism. Two of the more "serious" songs—ones not to be played by your high school oompah marching band—illustrate this characteristic. One, a setting of W. H. Henley's poem "Invictus," proclaims:

> It matters not how straight the gate,
> How charged with punishment the scroll,
> I am the master of my fate,
> I am the captain of my soul.

How little at one level I understood the song is suggested by my typing error in the next to last line: "faith" rather than "fate." But the illustration I chose is powerfully suggestive: the American farmer in work boots and jeans, outside his home, under a robust, upthrust oak, relaxed yet fixed into a four-square wooden chair, which, like the tree and one of his feet, seems almost planted in the earth. The last rays of the sun illuminate his face, the chair, the tree, and the distant hills. Inside the house, an orange light seems to extend no further than the windows. The iconography of the picture, identifying the simple, separate man with natural images of strength and durability, and placing him outside the almost unnatural brightness of the home, may not actually be appropriate to Henley's text. But it does suggest how fully a certain image of the "Unconquerable" had been instilled in my mind.

The other song along these lines was "Stout-Hearted Men," as I recollect, from some Victor Herbert operetta or the like.

> You who have dreams,
> If you act,
> They will come true,
> To turn your dreams,
> To a fact,
> It's up to you.

"Invictus"

I illustrated this summa bonum of American individualism with a picture hardly needing comment of a state trooper standing next to his motorcycle.

While warriors, domestic and international, constituted the dominant characters of my junior high school songbook, god was not far behind. Indeed, the first eight military tunes were sandwiched between "Thanks Be to God," the very first song we learned, and "Forget Me Not," about which I had reverently typed "by John Sebastian Bach." Apart from these hymns, we were taught the Lord's Prayer, something called "Graces of Humility," and two Protestant anthems, "Come Thou Almighty King" and what was called the "Netherland Hymn"— "We gather together to ask the Lord's blessing." Learning the last has served me well, since it is sung regularly at the matriculation ceremony by which Trinity College inducts each new class of students— though I notice that the line I learned, "We all do extol Thee, Thou leader in battle," has been altered in these more peaceful times to "Thou leader triumphant." We were also given "Say a Prayer for the

(*Top left*) "Stout-Hearted Men" (*Top right*) "Thanks Be to God" (*Bottom*) "Forget Me Not"

Boys over There" and "God Bless Our Land," which blended prayer and patriotism into a peculiarly insipid brew.

It might have struck you as odd that my illustrations reflect a largely Christian image of religion: a priest, the Virgin, a church funeral ceremony, a colonial cleric. I believe that—all unthinking—I captured in

(*Left*) "Say a Prayer" (*Right*) Graces of Humility

these choices my teachers' norms, indeed the norms of the society in which I was learning to live. In its public manifestations, religion meant Christianity for me and for most of my friends, all of whom were Jews, no less than for our Christian peers. It was not that we rejected Judaism, though for our generation the question of what it meant to be a Jew was perplexing. It was, rather, that the default of American religion was Christian, and therefore the ways in which one illustrated songs involving god and prayer and the like was obviously with Christian imagery.

That perception is, I think, underlined by the single concession in music class to my school's predominantly Jewish clientele, an odd and interesting psalm called "Consider and Hear Me." In the Lord's Prayer, "Come Thou Almighty King," and "We Gather Together" the operative words are "we" and "us." "*We* gather together," "Help *us* thy name to sing," "Lead *us* not into temptation." And while "Graces of Humility" is focused on a "me," it has none of the anguish and personal intensity of "Consider and Hear Me":

> How long wilt thou forget me?
> Oh, Lord, forever?
> How long wilt thou hide Thy face from me?
> How long will I seek counsel in my soul
> And be vexed in my heart?
> How long will my enemies triumph over me?

This prayer, taken from Psalm 13, is the one rather gloomy text in an otherwise relentlessly cheerful year-long paean to American pop culture: "Morning Song," "Spring Morning," "Home on the Range," "Easter Parade," "Sailing Song" from *The Merry Widow*, "Skip to My Lou," even "Walking at Night":

Walking at night along the meadow way,
Home from the dance with my maiden gay.

Just as we were learning to admire and identify with warriors, and to understand religion as a basically Christian public display, so were we studying cheerfulness as the appropriate demeanor of a true American. In fact, the only songs apart from "Consider and Hear Me" that, in retrospect, now strike me as ambiguous in tone were the two derived from African American sources. One was the familiar spiritual, or sorrow song, "Go Down Moses," which I illustrated with—as I look back at it—an even more equivocal picture. Viewed one way, we are presented with the very cliche of a "Negro" choir—as it would then have been called—hands upraised, mouths wide in ecstatic song. But the mouths and hands, with the orange and black background, also form into a tableau of anguish. Interestingly, the version of the spir-

"Morning Song"

(*Top left*) "Go Down, Moses" (*Right*) "Shortnin' Bread" (*Bottom left*) Lord's Prayer

itual we learned stops when god commands the waters to divide; what happened afterward, whether the people were finally let go, remains unresolved.

The other "Negro" song was the familiar folk tune "Shortnin' Bread":

> Three lil' babies lyin' in bed,
> Two was sick and the odder most dead.

My picture is strikingly discrepant with these lines, or with the end of the song: "Spent six months in jail makin' shortnin' bread." On the other hand, it aptly portrays the place of black women in the political economy of my Bronx, that is, as housemaids. As, in fact, very cheerful, upward-smiling housemaids. Jews and blacks, then, while acknowledged in my junior high school songbook, inhabit anomalous crannies, into which the cheerful morning sun, so prevalent in many other places, does not fully shine.

If, as I am arguing, some groups were so marginal to the defining qualities of junior high school music, why include them at all, whatever the strictly musical values of their songs? I think that what we see reflected here is the still strong ecumenical folk tradition of the thirties, which persisted for those of us brought up on popular front culture even through the worst of the cold war in the melodies of Paul Robeson, Pete Seeger, and the Weavers. It is probable that a New York City teacher, especially one working with music, would have been exposed to such a tradition, indeed have been a participant in its development. A high priority of the popular front ideology informing this 1930s music was to expose people to a variety of cultures—especially those of the "United Nations" opposed to the "Axis Powers"—and, wherever possible, to other languages as well. And so we learned "The Pedlar," a wonderful Russian traditional:

> "Lovely lady tell me which
> Of these things do seem to you most fair."
> "Pedlar will these pennies few,
> Buy this pretty bit of lace so rare."

And we learned "Hans Skal Leve Hojt," the meaning of which is as mysterious to me today as the untranslated Hebrew I studied in schul for my own bar mitzvah.

I have already alluded to the basic dominance of boy culture in my book, but women and girls are by no means absent, as you will have noticed. It is important to observe, however, that apart from smiling, and dancing, the dominant posture of females is worshipful—of god or of the men in their lives, more or less equally. "Rosie, the Riveter" is not a song we studied; "Keep the Home Fires Burning" might well have been. There is nothing unusual, of course, in this division of spheres, nor was it distinctively American. Yet at a time in our lives when hormones were stirring intensely and sexual identity often seemed perplexing, this sharp division helped reenforce the conventional definitions of gender even as, under the stress of wartime needs, they were being stretched.[8] Moreover, the gender definitions registered so plainly in the songs and in my pictures by no means conformed to the realities that obtained in the largely ethnic households from which the students at Wade came. As with the military songs, we were being offered a particular version of American ideals—in this instance female—toward which we, or at least the girls, would be expected to migrate. In that process, the boundaries separating boys and girls, men and women, would be sustained, indeed elaborated—even in a nation at war.

In an important sense, the cultural work these songs performed was to confirm the students' places in a society then—and still—deeply stratified by race, religion, gender, and social class; and yet, to teach us something of the cultural learnings we needed to know should we aspire to move up—as which of us did not? These were, I think, relatively benign objectives, not terribly different either from the other forms of acculturation embedded in the curricula of urban ethnic enclaves of the time. More innocuous, for example, than the chauvinistic, cold war social science and history I was soon to encounter in high school.

In fact, one central element of the songs surprised me when I restudied them a few years ago. I hardly ever discovered in them an "enemy," the demonized other so characteristic of the movies and comics of the period—the Nazi storm trooper or the buck-toothed Japanese infantryman. Indeed, only in "Anchors Aweigh" do we encounter any reference to Japanese or Germans at all. What the songs did *not* teach us, that is, was to hate. I am not quite sure how to explain that: perhaps it was peculiar to Junior High School 117, and the sensibilities of its largely Jewish student body. Perhaps it was the character of the music teacher, she who had devised or creatively applied the pedagogically remarkable way of putting our books together. Perhaps it was the age of the students—though we were exposed in many other venues to plenty of hate and, when one considers the Holocaust, many reasons to fear it. Perhaps it had to do with the nature of music, which does not easily lend itself to one-dimensional definitions—though one thinks of Scarpia in Puccini's *Tosca*. I have, in short, no very satisfying explanation, except to say that, as my cover picture suggests, the groundtone of music class was the drive toward the dawn of victory in the war and in what might transpire afterward. And for some in charge of these twelve- and thirteen-year-olds that involved less the sense that we had enemies than that we had hopes and desires.

CHAPTER FIVE
DINOSAUR CULTURE:
FROM *MANSFIELD PARK*
TO *JURASSIC PARK*

It is June 10, 1953. The *New York Times* is continuing to run a battle-field report from the Korean War daily on page 2. Five university faculty from Chicago and Kansas City have refused to testify before a Senate committee investigating subversion in education. The Supreme Court has just ruled that a Washington, D.C., café must admit black people—so long as they are well behaved. Selinko's *Desiree* and Costain's *The Silver Chalice* lead the *Times* bestseller list, along with Norma Vincent Peale's *The Power of Positive Thinking*. Herman Wouk's *The Caine Mutiny* has been on the list for 112 weeks. It is a sopping 90 degrees as I march with about seven thousand others to Ohio Field on the old Bronx campus of New York University for our commencement. A few adventurous souls slip off items of clothing from beneath their clinging black gowns.

That same month, Dwight Macdonald, the independent socialist critic (as he liked to be described), published an essay called "A Theory of Mass Culture" in a long-lived magazine supported by the Ford Foundation and called *Diogenes*.[1] I am certain that I did not read Macdonald's essay that June. I was busy. Commencement aside, I was preparing to get married less than two weeks after and begin graduate study the day following out in the wilds of Indiana. Really, though, I didn't need to read Macdonald's piece for I already knew, comfortably inside, what he had to say. I had absorbed from my NYU education, or from my parents, or from the zeitgeist an understanding of the great divide Macdonald outlines between the high culture, the art, we studied in our classrooms and whatever else we might get involved with out in the great city itself.

The lines between kitsch and culture were clearly drawn. There was, on the one side, movies—even of the arty kind I went to at Cinema 16 of a Sunday morning. On the other side was literature, including drama, of course: Shakespeare, Marlowe, Sophocles, Goethe, and such. Or, as Macdonald put it in one of his memorable binaries, the difference between Columbia Pictures and Columbia University. On the one side was the bebop I caught up on 52nd Street or down a few blocks at the Village Vanguard—Bird and Prez and Dizzy. On the other side, the Schubert and Mendelssohn lieder I struggled to reproduce in "Sight Singing," a class required for my music minor. On the one side was the recently developed major in radio—a strictly vocational choice I'd toyed with before the invitation to enroll in the English honors program came along; on the other side, that English honors seminar, fitting me for I knew not what, but certainly something genteel and sophisticated. Back in 1951, when I had been interviewed for the honors seminar by Charles Davis, its director, I had felt uncertain about how I ought to lay out my cultural credentials to him. I so feared appearing uncultivated—even vulgar—that I asked for a second interview, at which I reassured him not only that I was reading Jane Austen novels—on my own!—but that I had been listening to and enjoying the music of Pergolesi. What Davis, as a black man a *rara avis* in English studies, made of my performance I cannot tell; at any rate, he admitted me to the honors program.

And so by 1953, I had climbed at least a few small rungs in the cultural ladder. Not only had I read most of Austen, but I had made my way up to Columbia (University), as I recall it, to hear Lionel Trilling lecture on *Mansfield Park*. I remember nothing of the lecture itself except for a remark Trilling made, which I do not find in the printed essay,[2] which irritated and frightened me quite beyond comprehension, to the effect that it took a certain maturity to be able to read well certain mature writers, like Austen and James. It was not very clear to me what he meant by "maturity," nor precisely how one managed to contract it. But I caught hints of that some years later when I actually read the essay in *The Opposing Self.*

Like many of Trilling's essays its inner subject is less Jane Austen than irony, less *Mansfield Park* as such than one more elaboration on Trilling's characteristic theme: how the "moral life," as Austen was the "first" to show, is "so complex and difficult and exhausting" (p. 200). At twenty-one, I did not find it particularly so. Nor could I see why one would, as he wrote, feel a "necessity . . . to demonstrate the purity of our secular spirituality," whatever exactly that meant. And thus I could not comprehend why he represented *Mansfield Park* as "the Great Good Place," wherein the self might be free from the "terror of secularized spirituality." Above all, I had no idea of what the self Trilling was so assiduously constructing might, in the key term of his book, be "opposing." What were the "politics"—I would not then have used the term—that aligned the cultivation of spirit that Trilling recommended, by exemplifying, with the values of *Mansfield Park,* as I understood them. What *was* clear to me was that if I was to rub myself free of residual vulgarity and gain a place of safety within that "Great Good Place," the academy, I had best accede in the judgments men of sensitivity and power, like Macdonald and Trilling, had set out for me and other new critical apprentices. If *Mansfield Park* was the "Great Good Place"—a utopia, however "fallibly governed" and however snobbishly defined—and if the precincts of high culture, of Eliot and James and Proust—however exclusive and remote from my home in New York's Washington Heights—defined whatever was not vulgar and one-dimensional, well then, so be it. I would lock myself up with them, dropping movies from my agenda, shoving my 78 rpm jazz collection into an attic, and turning my English honors degree into a passport to Yale.

It is July of 1995. I have been asked to give a seminar at Diponegoro University in Semarang, Central Java, on the subject of soap operas. This is a bad joke, I think, for I haven't "listened" to a soap since *Portia Faces Life.* I realize that I have brought this assignment on myself, for the previous time I had been there in Semarang I had gotten in the middle of a minor dispute between some students and their teacher. For their advanced English class, the students had to write a term paper analyzing a whole book; one wanted to write on *I, Robot,* the other on *Jurassic Park.* Their teacher's view was that such books weren't real literature. "Well," I argued, "it may not be fine literature, but after all, Poe had written the equivalent of today's sci-fi; one couldn't always know what might withstand the test of time; in any case, they would learn from whatever texts they examined." I don't think I was very persuasive, but here I was back again, and—if I was serious—should I not talk with faculty about the popular culture on which the students seemed so keen? Fortunately, I had seen *Jurassic Park,* the movie, on the flight across the Pacific, and so I had an alternative to offer—a good alternative, since virtually all the students had seen it, and the faculty, if they had not themselves gone, knew what it was about.

Now I am well aware that no such conflict between the study of canonical literary texts—as interpreted by English faculty—and popular culture—consumed and enjoyed by students—could still exist at any of the progressive universities where I have delivered versions of this essay. And there may be something ludicrous in invoking *Mansfield Park,* wherein the New World is mostly a source of trouble, to make points about American studies. All the same, it may be useful for me to track out how I, together with many American studies practitioners, have in the last quarter century deviated from the well-trimmed paths of Austen and James and found ourselves hacking through the underbrush of "Jurassic Park."

My narrative will not be very startling to those who have followed the increasingly serious affair being conducted in the United States between the charming overseas claimant, cultural studies, and the sometimes reluctant widower, American studies. The American Studies Association convention has, in fact, become the venue of choice for the consummation of this courtship. I do not wish to declare it a marriage, not quite yet. Rather, I want to describe four stages in this continuing romance. And I want to propose some reasons why this may be a more fruitful relationship than the earlier liaisons of American studies with that upright citizen, history, or even with that somewhat doubtful fellow, English.

What I write about here, to shelve my metaphors, is how various ways of reading the movie *Jurassic Park* embody significant shifts in how one does American studies.[3] Ultimately, I will return to the question of the social functions performed by established academic institutions, like English departments, and their definitions of knowledge. But first, I want to emphasize four steps in a process of change: the first, what might loosely be termed the Stuart Hall step (and I have to emphasize that my names are a bit arbitrary and certainly personally inflected), has to do with the alteration in definitions of a "text" to include works not encompassed by traditional categories of literary, art, and music courses and discourses. And, along with that, the application to this broadened set of "texts" of analytic tactics gathered, somewhat eclectically, from literary formalism, film and music criticism, anthropology, psychology, and the like.

Second, what might be termed the Michel Foucault step, paying attention to what is *not* given narrative (or significant visual) life through the text, but which is nevertheless present, often powerfully, *in* it.

Third, perhaps the Stephen Greenblatt step, placing the art work back into the world in which it is actually produced, circulated, and consumed—moving, that is, from more strictly formal concerns to those emerging from a historicizing lens.

Finally, the Jane Tompkins step, to speculate about the cultural work the text is performing in the particular moment of its production and consumption and, if it remains alive, in our own.

Obviously, the questions raised in this process are quite different from those formulated by Dwight Macdonald and his peers. They were interested in trying, like a cultural border police, to reestablish proper divides between cultural and, in significant degree, class realms. High culture versus low or pop culture. We, I think, are concerned with why people *create* and *consume* various forms of culture—call it high, low or Mr. In-Between—in some particular moment. They, *la Migra culta,* were invested in separating the sheep from the goats from the asses. We're not sure we can always tell them apart—and anyway, we find it more interesting to figure out why people choose one over the other and to what ends. Why *Nozze di Figaro* in Vienna 1780, *Le Bâteau Ivre* in Paris 1870s, *Portia Faces Life* in America 1940, and—to approach the object of our study at last—*Jurassic Park* round the world in 1993?

Our first step, then, focusing on such a film rather than on, say, *Mansfield Park* or "The Beast in the Jungle," as I might well have done forty-some years ago. *Jurassic Park* can effectively be read using many of the standard tools of literary analysis. I want to illustrate that point by looking at its themes, not a surprising choice given its thinness of plot and characterization—except, of course, of the dinosaurs. Most obvious of the film's themes is its critique of science, or at least technology, gotten out of control. The dangers of technology arise here, as they often do in comparable works from the Western tradition, from a lack of modesty in the scientist, a lack of respect for old Mother Nature. This is a familiar notion, and if one of my students were to do it, he or she would likely point to analogies to and differences from such well-established texts as Mary Shelley's *Frankenstein* and Karel Capek's *RUR*, not to speak of a variety of works by Hawthorne. This was, of course, the theme that attracted the most serious journalistic attention when the movie was released, stimulating the *Los Angeles Times* to hope, editorially, that it would not have the effect of turning kids against science.[4]

Second theme: the monsters get loose—in this particular case, since they are all female, it is the bad mothers, indeed the "teeth mothers," broken out into the world. Buried within us and projected into the world outside, are threatening demons, which, set loose, will consume us and those we love. We keep them in check—to pursue the obvious Freudian structure—by consciously establishing rational boundaries, like electrified fences. But then comes a great natural storm and, before we can properly react, the monsters are unleashed into the world, threatening every moment to ingest us—like the T-Rex does with Jurassic Park's lawyer. I don't need here to elaborate upon how the film thematizes the irruption of monstrosity into the world except to point to the impact of Spielberg's desire that his dinosaurs appear precisely *not* as monsters but as animals—not, that is, as "others" but as creatures peculiarly like ourselves. (The implications of this perspective become clearer, incidentally, in the sequel, *The Lost World.*)

Third theme, one central to most of Spielberg's films, the separation and reuniting of the family. One remembers, for example, "E.T. phone home." The people responsible for these separations are, of course, adult men; their efforts—contrived or accidental—are generally opposed and usually thwarted by the women and children. Here, there are two males in need of rehabilitation: Grant, the paleontologist, who is pretty down on kids, even the flirtatious Lex, and John Hammond, the billionaire entrepreneur, who places his grandchildren in jeopardy (they are with him, by the way, because their parents are

Lex, the girl, reprograms the computers. Photograph from Photofest

sorting out a divorce). This theme comes into focus most fully when it is the prepubescent girl, Lex, who, at the moment of truth, is able to reprogram the computers, thus enabling the reassembled family to make its escape from the island. I think it is hard to exaggerate the underlying power of this theme in the film. A friend of mine had been trying to get me to see it when it opened, but I was resistant: monster movies scare me—I get nightmares and spilling anxieties. Perhaps my own monsters are too close to my electric fences. In any case, I said I wasn't into death and danger. "But," he said, "no one is killed in the movie." When I finally did see it, I had to try figuring out those words. What he meant, I guess, is that no one *in the family* dies; which in the movie's emotional space, translates—like Huck Finn reporting on the steamboat explosion—into "no one."

Fourth theme: commodification. Anything, the film offers, can be turned into a commodity and that is B A D. How do we know it's bad? The people most immediately responsible for commodifying the dinos and their embryos are the corporate lawyer, who represents the shareholders, and the techie, who is engaged, like the druggie he is, in dealing. The lawyer it is who meets the most ignominious end, plucked from a port-a-pot by the Tyrannosaurus Rex—or would it be more correct to say Tyrannosaura Regina? And the techie, who is portrayed as a food junkie, gets spritzed by a dilophosaur and is himself consumed.

Finally, there is the theme which I can characterize only by the words of the dullard chaos theorist, Ian Malcolm, "Life will find a way." Against the tyranny of the mind, especially the mastermind, we have here a kind of primitive hopefulness, an inert optimism that, in our age, sometimes passes for progressive politics. It offers an unearned sense of virtue to those who hold to such positions, unearned because one needn't work at it, agitate or legislate to clean up environmental pollution, for instance, since "life will find a way." Or invest in curative sciences rather than circuses, for "life will find a way." Indeed, work—planning, organizing, testing things out—becomes suspicious since, nature, being governed by chaos, will find a way to thwart the planners.

I could go on in this vein, but I think it's obvious that such traditional analytic tactics work as well on *Jurassic Park* as they would on *Mansfield Park*. I want, therefore, to turn to my second step and ask about the themes that are present in the film but functionally *unstated*, *not* given narrative form. We are here looking for the ghost in the machine, the repressed, the other, on the premise that what is repressed, socially or personally, reveals most fully what drives people and societies. As Toni Morrison points out in *Playing in the Dark*, excavating the Africanist presence in American literature enables us to understand the distorted structures, contradictory plots, and incomplete people that characterize so many of this nation's significant books.

The film, in this light, offers a paradigm of colonialism. The land on which the park sits is, to all intents and purposes, appropriated from its "native" inhabitants, one of whom is the first victim of the scheme, pulled through a fence into the jaws of the velociraptors. The deployment of that familiar tool of third world repression, the helicopter, is striking here: the whites are taken in, and at the end, out by choppers. It's almost as if Spielberg is rehabilitating the chopper after its sinister deployment in films like *Boyz in the Hood,* not to speak of Vietnam and Afghanistan. What one doesn't see, of course, are the folks left behind, who, when Hammond and his entourage leave, can expect to be little except prey to the dinos.

Their fate is peculiarly cruel. King Kong was discovered on an island somewhere the "far side" of Sumatra. Other such beasts swim up from twelve thousand fathoms, stomp down from remote Japanese mountains, or appear from outer space. Here, the beasts are not discovered but created. They are, in this sense, the visible products of technocolonization, elaborate monsters formed out of banal stuff, which end by threatening their creators and consuming, offstage, to be sure, the ordinary folk who helped to make them. Once again, this kind of repressed theme flowers in the sequel.

I want now to take my third step by setting the film in its real historical—that is to say, economic and social—milieu, what is perhaps too seldom done in American cultural studies. Here we quickly discover a revealing set of contradictions. The film offers, as I have said, a strong indictment of science and technology gotten out of hand. But no movie before or since has been so utterly dependent upon advanced technologies as *Jurassic Park*. The film's creators used robotics, "computer-generated imagery," "advanced morphing techniques," the range of technologies developed for everything from pilot training to theme parks to create its effects.[5] For example, one of the central problems was activating the T-Rex puppet, sixteen weeks in sculpting, twenty-five feet high, forty feet long, and weighing in at about nine tons. To create the realism central to Spielberg's conception, the T-Rex was placed on a flight-simulator platform to facilitate movement; its horrifying eyes were radio-activated; and most of all its movements were controlled through the use of a telemetry suit. This is a device so rigged electronically to the hydraulic systems of the puppet that a movement of the person wearing the suit is immediately translated into that movement in the puppet. Likewise the raptors were played by men in raptor suits, using radio and cable controls for the eyes, arms, and tail, regulated by an elaborate mass of cables under the set of the visitor center kitchen. It was, as someone commented, like a ballet played out above a tangle of wires and chips. The striking scene, so often used for TV ads, of the stampeding dinos was entirely created by computer techniques developed from those used in *Terminator 2*.

If one thinks about what is memorable in the movie it is, I suspect, the dinosaurs, and they were, of course, entirely creatures of the very technology the film seems to bring into question. I want to emphasize how seriously that critique was taken. A *New York Times* story raised the question of whether or not we *should* revive dinosaurs,[6] ignoring the scientific reality that the methodology proposed—extracting dino

Hatching a baby dinosaur. Photograph from Photofest

DNA from a mosquito trapped in amber—was altogether impossible, as Steven J. Gould pointed out, given the instability and fragmented nature of the available DNA.[7] The movie's exposition of the underlying science appears to have been sufficiently realistic not only to help audiences suspend disbelief but also to get reputable newspapers to suspend reason. Moreover, the dinosaur models have themselves become exhibits at museums, like the American Museum of Natural History and the Boston Museum of Science,[8] and the film itself has been used to teach aspects of science to kids. The film, then, uses advanced technology *both* to mount a critique of science and to produce a resonating example of its outcomes.

I'll return to this contradiction in a few moments, but I want first to explore a couple of others. One of the movie's major points has to do with the immorality of turning science, and the dinosaurs it creates, into commodities. And yet, of course, *Jurassic Park* was—and is—one of the most successfully marketed commodities in the history of the world. It was sent into that world via a $65 million marketing campaign.[9] Over one hundred merchandise licenses were issued, for over a thousand products—toys, video games, clothing, food items, and the like.[10] MacDonalds, one of the major investors in these ancillaries, was for a time worried about the potential of the film's violence to turn parents away from its product line.[11] We will probably never know to what extent, if any, such considerations modified the final product. At any rate, the initial projection of about $1 billion in sales seems to have long been met.[12]

The film itself made $100 million in the first nine days (*Batman* had taken ten days to reach that plateau).[13] By mid-September, about three months after opening, it had grossed $600 million.[14] In domestic sales alone, the film has grossed $356.8 million;[15] overall, it has grossed $951 million.[16] Of that, Spielberg himself has made well over $200 million.[17]

And the revenues have continued to pour in. For example, in April 1994, the film was released in India and Pakistan. In the first week it made $710,000 in India and $110,000 in Pakistan—small potatoes, relatively.[18] But by August, it had made $5.8 million in India alone,[19] and that success story was repeated across the globe. How valuable was this commodity? That might be estimated by noting that in 1995, when it was released for TV, a thirty-second commercial was selling for, dig it, $650,000.[20] The latest spin-off is located back at Universal Studios, "Jurassic Park—The Ride," where for about $40 a pop you can (in the words of the brochure) "ride a runaway raft deep into the Jurassic Jungle and go face-to-face with Raptors, Spitters, and a towering T-Rex."[21]

The huge profits *Jurassic Park* accrued had the effect of bailing out of an immense hole the parent company, Matsushita Electric Industrial Corporation, which had virtually run aground in the early nineties recession.[22] No surprise, for the film was above all other things a triumph of commodification. For not only was it tremendously effective in selling products associated with it—as is the case with soap operas and magazine stories. But it was also, unlike soaps, itself the T-Rex of that commodity jungle.

One last poke into the real world inhabited by *Jurassic Park* and one more striking set of contradictions: The film offers, as I have suggested, a persistent critique of the mastermind, the controlling male who through arrogance, monomania, intellectual complacency, or whatever places everyone's life in danger. But the film itself is a triumph precisely of that kind of auteur-director. One never forgets that it is Steven Spielberg's film. How could one forget? He arranged the deal for the book with its author, Michael Crichton. He marked up the book for the screenwriters, meeting with them weekly to review scripts. He did the drawings for most of the storyboards. He provided the idea and name for Mr. DNA, who offers a canned explanation of the science.[23] Here is Spielberg in his own voice: "I never thought I wanted to do a dinosaur movie better than anyone else's, but I did want my dinosaur movie to be the most realistic of them all. I wanted the audience to say 'I really believe this could happen today.'. . . And there was a credibility in [*Close Encounters*] that I drew upon in attacking *Jurassic Park*. I wanted my dinosaurs to be animals."[24]

In this connection it seems to me interesting to note that the largest changes Spielberg seems to have made in translating the novel into a movie concern John Hammond, the controlling entrepreneur. In Crichton's novel he is a far more sinister character, who meets a decidedly nasty end. Here, there is something appealing in Hammond. His persistence, imagination and energy seem worthy of a better fate; and if he is initially overbearing, he is finally sympathetic. I want to suggest why in a moment, and in order to do so, I now want to take my fourth step by prying open these seeming contradictions and speculating about the cultural work in which the film is engaged.

 In doing this kind of work, I find it useful to think about how comparable patterns in a set of historically coincident texts may be seen in relation to specific historical events. *Jurassic Park* was not, of course, the only film of its time to focus on issues of, even as it deployed, advanced technology. *Terminator 2*, for example, emerged at about the same time, in the post–Gulf War moment. One wonders whether such movies are capturing something of the ambivalence Americans felt about advanced technology in that moment. On the "positive" side, so to speak, technology provided a most engaging kind of explosive spectacle, available in one's living room thanks to nose-cone TVs and satellite, and without the inconvenient layers of blood and muck that accompanied Vietnam footage. Furthermore, technology provided, or seemed to provide, the power needed for control in an increasingly shifty world—especially the power to control those "others" who needed to be taught better than to upset the post–cold war settlement of international issues. On the "down" side, however, there were many questions: did the technology really work or were its successes, like those of the Patriot missile, finally a sham and even dangerous to its wielders? Were we, once again, to become victims of oversell, doomed to disappointment with our latest expensive gadgetry? Was the promise of the future itself, then, compromised, even negated, by the ascendancy of yet one more Dr. Strangelove?[25]

It seems to me that such anxieties are converted into pleasure in the dark of the movie theater—a fundamental dynamic in connecting movies to the human imaginary. Indeed, more broadly, science and technology themselves become sources of pleasure. They turn out *not* to be either so mysterious or so threatening, for they can functionally be controlled by a girl child. And, as the screenwriter, Koepp, put it, she shows the paleontologist, Grant, "the real value of children and the optimism they bring for the future"[26]—the future into which we all depart via helicopter, leaving behind the nightmare world inhabited by raptors, Republican Guards, and voodoo priests.

I am, as Robert Gross pointed out to me, playing somewhat fast and loose with my "we" here: is the experience of the film I am supposing in some sense "universal," or am I assimilating a wide set of rather different experiences, worldwide, to those of a particular set of Americans? That is a reasonable question. A less speculative answer to it than I will provide would no doubt depend either upon ethnographic or historical evidence, and these elements are often absent from forms of "reading" characteristic of American studies. Understandably, too, since the kind of project I am modeling, an effort to get at the underlying imaginary to which a text like *Jurassic Park* speaks, does not easily lend itself to the accumulation of ethnographic or historical data. The real measure may remain whether a given speculation "rings true"; but that may depend, to circle back to the question of "we," upon the reader. Still, the danger of altogether substituting text-based speculation for empirical data remains a significant problem in the practice of American studies.

For all that, to return to *Jurassic Park*, it seems to me that the impact of the film is to neutralize the very critique of commodity production that it mounts. Commenting on his own ambivalence, screenwriter Koepp said: "Here I was writing about these greedy people who are creating a fabulous theme park just so they can exploit all these dinosaurs and make silly little films and sell stupid plastic plates and things. And I'm writing it for a company that's eventually going to put this in their theme parks and make these silly little films and sell stupid plastic plates. I was really chasing my tail there for a while trying to figure out who was virtuous in this whole scenario—and eventually gave up."[27] It's a conclusion, I want to suggest, that the film encourages.

Critchton, a knowledgeable commentator, himself raised a fundamental question about the economics of advanced capitalism directly related to such issues: who will pay for scientific work? "I think if dinosaurs ever *are* cloned," he wrote, "it will be done by somebody for entertainment." That is, he suggests, the lesson one might read from the commercialization of genetic engineering.[28] For Critchton, the assimilation of science to technology may be as problematic as the absorption of high cultural prerogatives by mass culture was to Macdonald or Trilling.[29] To be sure, that is not a theme given real narrative development within the film, certainly as compared with the issues of overreaching what science might properly accomplish or how the economic imperatives of industrialized entertainment establish the parameters for scientific work. But in fact, as I have been suggesting, technology had already in the Gulf War *become* entertainment. In the context of TV news, science, technology, and entertainment had become inseparable.

Jurassic Park is thus one more factor in the cultural tide that has been moving through the last half century to naturalize commodity production. The film helps, indeed, to neutralize the very critique it proposes. For as we emerge into a lobby outfitted with "Jurassic Park" sweatshirts and mugs, we recognize that *rightly used*, commercial science can and does create pleasure. That that, indeed, may become its main excuse for being.

Finally, I want to look at another contradictory source of pleasure, the critique-which-is-not-quite a critique of the auteur director, the controlling intelligence of *Jurassic Park*. Here it seems to me useful to think about the film in the context provided by those venues for the ultimate commodification, Geraldo, Sally Jessie Rafael, Ricky Lake. On such shows people are provided with the opportunity to turn themselves into commodities for the sake of entertaining an audience. They offer the chance for us to mark an indifferent world, like a male cat, with our particular scent. And they justify a process by which we can reveal our otherwise hidden desires and anxieties for a potential profit. TV isn't the only nineties venue for self-revelation, of course; the summer 1996 issue of the *Women's Review of Books,* for example, focused on memoirs.

So here, I want to suggest, Steven Spielberg is revealing many of his own innermost qualities . . . for some $200 or $300 million, to be sure. It makes Woody Allen look rather a piker. One finds in *Jurassic Park* a decidedly boy's view of monsters getting loose; a family romance which is all but a trademark of Spielberg; a mix of anxiety over power and control with the continuing desire for them. The film thus feeds and satisfies, like the TV shows, that great yearning in today's American audience for large life experienced at second hand. In turning self into art, I'm suggesting, Spielberg is also turning self into product, which helps to explain his wish to have another auteur-director, Richard Attenborough, play Hammond, and also the altogether ambiguous treatment of Hammond as a character.

I have been constructing a narrative in which *Jurassic Park* plays the central role. The subject of this narrative has been the development of American studies—at least in North America—during the last couple of decades. I have tried to suggest a number of ways in which, to my mind, what we call American studies functions as a tool for comprehending cultural production, distribution, and consumption. But in a sense, I have elided the more fundamental reason I have focused on this movie. That reason is, I think, suggested by and dependent upon my last step, some speculations about the cultural work accomplished by productions like *Jurassic Park.*

Culture and entertainment have, of course, come to be among the major industries of international capitalism—they are certainly among its primary sources of income. But more than that, as I have tried to suggest, a movie like *Jurassic Park* operates not only as, first, a successful product, a commodity produced in America and marketed throughout the world; not only, second, as a catalyst for many other sales; but also, third, it functions as a major way in which capitalism in the late twentieth century is rationalized and thus sustained. Its primary cultural work, that is, involves making visible contradictions within commodity capitalism, and then emotionally grounding them in a microcosm of spectacle and pleasure.

I always wonder about the extent to which Spielberg perceives this process as a source of ambivalence. And then I recollect that the movie he was beginning to work on as *Jurassic Park* was being completed was, of course, *Schindler's List,* just as the movie that followed *Jurassic Park's* successor, *The Lost World,* was the one on the Amistad slave revolt.[30]

I do not want to conclude—though I did begin—on a biographical and what may even appear as a derogatory note. In certain ways Spielberg's career marks *not* the outer limits, surely, but the normal range of political dialogue in the United States today, *Jurassic Park* to *Schindler's List,* so to speak. To say that, however, is to underline precisely why it is vital to study him—and also, perhaps, why right-wing governments and conservative commentators have so energetically tried to marginalize or trivialize such study. As Andrew Ross has been at pains to show, naturalizing the supposed triviality, the necessary baseness, of what Macdonald called "mass culture" remains one means of obscuring the significant work it actually performs.[31] In the United States today, a debate has developed about whether to refocus English studies back on to the close reading of grand literary texts and their great interpreters. Or, as most writers to a forum in the spring 1997 issue of *PMLA* argue, to extend the reach of English departments more systematically in the direction of cultural studies. The problem, as I experienced it forty-some years ago, is that a primary cultural role of English departments in Western universities has been, in the words of Paul DiMaggio, to transform "social distinctions" symbolically "from social accomplishments to natural facts."[32] That has been one primary function of the divisions of knowledge that have underwritten, until quite recently (or still?), the academic departments, like English, in their work of helping legitimate high culture and its values in the structure of American society and thus to obscure the critical social and political work being done by the other cultures we were taught to despise. The difficulty of resurrecting such traditional cultural roles in today's very different dispensation becomes all too apparent when one reads the 1950s cultural commentators like Dwight Macdonald and Lionel Trilling. It is a step backward in time far greater than a journey to Jurassic Park itself could prove to be or even, perhaps, an expedition to the "Lost World."

Of course, one might propose that how a culture designs its utopias, and the ways in which they *fail* or, perhaps worse, succeed, tells us as much as anything what is at issue in a society. Maybe someone should try persuading Spielberg to undertake *Mansfield Park,* a painfully successful paradise, to balance *Jurassic Park,* that quite failed utopia. Jane Austen is, after all, a hot Hollywood property, and the book has many of Spielberg's themes already nicely deployed. But that is another essay, no doubt, as well as another script.

PART TWO ★ AMERICAN STUDIES IN A RACIALIZED WORLD

INTRODUCTION TO PART TWO The phrase "American studies" is sometimes deployed to emphasize the field's differences from what is done in other venues, academic or geographical. In some institutions, American studies is configured separately from—occasionally in tension with—ethnic studies, African American, or other "minority" studies programs. Similarly, American studies in the United States is sometimes constructed as altogether distinctive from overseas programs. Boundary maintenance, as I argue in the following essay, has in the past been something of a preoccupation among some American studies practitioners. And it would be misleading to deny certain of the field's peculiar qualities, just as it would be foolish utterly to dismiss distinctive elements of United States culture in the name of combating that supposed scourge of our scholarship, "American exceptionalism."

It would be even more foolish, however, not to explore and try to understand the multitude of ways in which what is done within "American studies" is deeply implicated with, indeed constituted by, other worlds of scholarship and politics. The essays in this section are devoted to that task by looking at "borderlands" ("American Studies and Ethnic Studies at the Borderlands Crossroads"—originally a paper for the 1997 Eichstätt conference), at Americanists abroad ("Of *Chadors* and Capital"—for a 1996 conference at Dartmouth), and at the cultural politics of Charles Chesnutt during the turn of the twentieth century ("Fiction as Politics"—a version dates back to Moscow, 1992). They have in common an effort to complicate whatever the boundaries of American studies have come to mean.

CHAPTER SIX

**AMERICAN STUDIES
& ETHNIC STUDIES AT
THE BORDERLANDS
CROSSROADS**

In 1989 United States military forces invaded Panama, their ostensible objective to arrest the country's leader, Manuel Noriega, and bring him to Miami for trial as a key player in the Colombian drug trade. He now resides in a federal lock-up, a convicted felon, guilty of having violated U.S. federal law. The case raises a number of peculiar issues, not so much because anyone apart from his lawyers seems intent on defending Noriega, but because the case so obviously stretches the borders within which U.S. law is taken, at least by federal authorities, to operate—and the fatal consequences to so many Panamanians of that extension. What constitutes such borders? Simple military might, an imperializing definition of "American," some mutant version of extraterritoriality? As these questions suggest, national boundaries have seldom been written in steel, though generally with guns.

What of the boundaries taken to distinguish national identity, or those that define disciplines focused on national cultures, like American studies? How are these borders settled; indeed, are they? And how do definitions of national identity, professional discipline, and law interact, particularly in a historical moment at which many kinds of borders are being newly contested and in which we are constantly being prepared for the supposedly inevitable brave new world of triumphant globalized capital? In this chapter, I wish to speculate about such questions, an issue generally known as "borderlands." I wish to examine in particular border regions where American studies intersects with other disciplines, like the various ethnic studies programs that have developed over the last quarter century.

My approach to questions of national and disciplinary boundaries begins from the observation that in key respects American studies at any given time reflects, indeed incorporates, tensions and changes in the wider society. Conflicts that emerge in the United States, new departures in cultural production like the Internet, or political campaigns that evoke or play changes upon traditional imagery—all quickly become the subjects of inquiry for Americanists. But not only that: the strains *within* American studies hold close affinities to those which mark the society as a whole. As Heinz Ickstadt put it, "American studies recreates or reconstructs American history in its own discourse." Thus, as I have said in an earlier chapter, "to investigate the changing character of American studies is to examine the processes of change in American culture and society."[1] In particular, the tensions between American Studies and ethnic studies helps illuminate the conflicts in the United States over the politics of nationalism, immigration, the local and the global.

Whatever their precise forms or specific contents, most instances of American studies from the past can be thought of as working spatially from a center outward. This structure can be represented by Richard Caton Woodville's well-known painting *War News from Mexico* (1848).[2] An excited white man, perhaps the postal agent, reads from a newsprint broadside to seven other white men framed by the pillars of the small portico of the "American Hotel." An older white woman listens worriedly from a nearby window, and at the base of the two steps leading up to the entrance, a black man and a black girl in a tattered dress look on with ambiguous expressions. Mexicans are nowhere to be seen, although they are, of course, central to the whole drama. The painting presents two frames for the viewer, one constituted by the literal frame itself, the other by the pillars. It thus offers, in effect, three levels of signification: that central to our visual attention, filled by white excited men presenting and learning about the state of the nation; a margin that contains those peripheral to but visible within the painting's narrative, female, black, reserved, restrained; and *los desaparecidos.*

I would raise two issues here, one having to do with the frames or borders of what is pictured as American, the other concerning the contents of that picture itself. Revisionary criticism, as we know, has moved the peripherally situated characters (here blacks and a white woman) within the frame of attention, but, as I shall argue, the "American" frame persists, however eroded. Not incidentally, Mexicans and Indians largely fall outside it. Whatever the content of the picture offered as "American," and therefore presumed to be at the core of American studies (here the white men), the structures presenting such images offer striking similarities. The narrative design of the ways in which American studies scholarship has been presented has been, as in Woodville's painting, to construct well-defined boundaries (as, here, the hotel's pillars and the picture's frame). Within such boundaries Americanists have examined what they have offered as uniquely American. In a very real sense, it is the boundaries themselves rather than the contents that have most persistently defined the study of America. A good deal of what has constituted "American studies" has had to do not only with exploring the contents placed at the center, but also with contesting, defending, and policing the conceptual boundaries which, it has been supposed, are critical to the distinctiveness not only of American studies but of American identity.[3] For ideas about what, within that frame, constituted the core of "Americanness" have varied enormously, but the center stage has nevertheless always been recognizably "American," that is, not focused on "others."

What has been taken to be distinctively "American" has been a matter for debate and sometimes conflict. Henry Nash Smith, for example, provided a characteristic instance in the "Prologue" to *Virgin Land:*

> Men of Thomas Jefferson's day emphasized freedom and republicanism as the defining characteristics of American society; the definitions of later thinkers stressed the cosmopolitan blending of a hundred peoples into one, or mechanical ingenuity, or devotion to business enterprise. But one of the most persistent generalizations

concerning our society has been shaped by the pull of a vacant continent drawing population westward through the passes of the Alleghenies, across the Mississippi Valley, over the high plains and mountains of the Far West to the Pacific Coast.[4]

Critics have again and again objected to such notions of "American exceptionalism,"[5] to the assumption that quite distinctive social, political or cultural features altogether separate what is American from what is not. To be sure, there is nothing peculiarly American in this tendency of societies to mythologize themselves. And so, forms of American exceptionalism continue to reappear, like sightings of Elvis. One of the latest emerges in the pages of Toni Morrison's *Playing in the Dark,* in which Morrison speculates "whether the major and championed characteristics of our national literature . . . are not in fact responses to a dark, abiding, signing Africanist presence."[6]

It would be silly, I think, to insist that nothing substantial differentiates the life and culture of what is now the United States from that of Great Britain, Barbados, India, . . . or Mexico. To ignore difference in the name of rejecting "American exceptionalism" or because one cannot absolutely define what constitutes "American," or at any rate "North American," or at least some North Americans, seems to me throwing out the baby with the bath water. The issues are, rather, the qualities of what is distinctive, why and by whom that is deemed important, how that changes, and the politics underwritten by contesting definitions of what is supposed to be truly, essentially, distinctively, exceptionally "American."

Older narratives have usually been intended to underwrite either assimilationist politics or those of cultural pluralism.[7] But as Smith's notion of a "vacant continent" suggests, they contain the seeds of a genocidal ideology, which disappears inhabitants before the onset of the "truly" American.[8] Even a revisionary proposal like that contained in Randolph Bourne's "Trans-National America" pictured resistance to assimilation in terms that sustained boundary structures. Bourne argued that it would be better for the progress of the United States if immigrants were not simply assimilated to the dominant Anglo-Saxon, or at least Western European, culture of this nation. Rather, he urged that the dominant culture needed itself to be somewhat altered, shifted by the impact of new, immigrant forces and in that way renewed:

To face the fact that our aliens are already strong enough to take a share in the direction of their own destiny, and that the strong cultural movements represented by the foreign press, schools, and colonies are a challenge to our facile attempts, is not, however, to admit the failure of Americanization. It is not to fear the failure of democracy. It is rather to urge us to an investigation of what Americanism may rightly mean. It is to ask ourselves whether our ideal has been broad or narrow—whether perhaps the time has not come to assert a higher ideal than the "melting pot." Surely we cannot be certain of our spiritual democracy when, claiming to melt the nations within us to a comprehension of our free and democratic institutions, we fly into panic at the first sign of their own will and tendency. We act as if we wanted Americanization to take place only on our own terms, and not by the consent of the governed. All our elaborate machinery of settlement and school and union, of social and political naturalization, however, will move with friction just in so far as it neglects to take into account this strong and virile insistence that America shall be what the immigrant will have a hand in making it, and not what a ruling class, descendant of those British stocks which were the first permanent immigrants, decide that America shall be made. This is the condition which confronts us, and which demands a clear and general readjustment of our attitude and our ideal.[9]

Played out in spatial metaphor again, it is clear that even Bourne's revisionary conception maintains the centrality of defined, if perhaps shifting or somewhat reconfigured, boundaries. Perhaps there are more stars in the flag, lined up somewhat differently; or the basic blue marking the United States on the toy globe is altered by admixtures of yellow and green (or even red). But it strikes me that what Bourne is describing, with all good will, is not so fundamentally different from what T. S. Eliot describes in "Tradition and the Individual Talent" as happening to "the" tradition when something "truly new" is added and causes the whole to shift, if ever so slightly.

In recent years, however, there has been a profound change in the material and political environment within which American studies narratives are constructed. Locally, American studies has grown, even as universities, or at least their financial bases, have contracted, and as sources of support, like the United States Information Agency (USIA) and major foundations, have committed their resources elsewhere. More important, I think, globally, the circumstances and implications of studying the United States have radically altered. These changed conditions, I argue, have helped reset the conceptual frameworks—the underlying metaphors—which shape American studies narratives. The extent to which changing conceptual frameworks are, dialectically, helping alter material conditions remains a matter for debate.

This is, as Michael Geyer has pointed out, a period of "profound unsettlement."[10] The collapse of the Soviet Union and its protective empire, the rise of desperately particular nationalisms, and, above all, the integration of much of the world into a system of global capitalism have all helped to create a new set of material conditions. People, or more accurately, certain groups of people within national, language, or ethnic groupings can, do, and are sometimes forced to move far more, some out of fear of political or religious persecution, others out of economic aspiration. One can observe the multiplication in the last quarter century of international networks of people whose ethnic and language links constitute a set of bonds certainly as strong as those that tie them to the nation states in which they happen to be residing— perhaps for a long term, perhaps only temporarily. These increased movements of people across national borders have been facilitated by the extension—again, unevenly developed—of an international capitalist consumer culture. To drive in from the airport of one American city is to drive in from any of them: golden arches vie with Big Boy, and Mr. Goodwrench with "You're not gonna pay a lot at Meineke." While this pattern cannot be said to have spread worldwide—yet—television, the international distribution of products—including soaps, sit-coms, and movies—common merchandising tactics, credit and phone cards, bank machines and other forms of money transfer, and relatively cheap air transport, among other factors, have helped produce a kind of internationally common cultural coinage. That significantly reduces the barriers to movement that lie *within* people: few places, now, are altogether strange, at least to significant numbers of the bourgeoisie, and to many of the poor and exiled as well. Moreover, consumer desires and expectations—often fueled by Western TV and movies—of many such people have risen, as has their cosmopolitan outlook, their participation in international modes of exchange.

Such processes have been accelerated within the United States by the immigration reforms of 1965, which have helped internationalize the American population to a greater degree than has been the case since before World War I, especially in the cities. Large numbers of the recent wave of immigrants are "people of color," to use a vexed phrase, many from Asia, the Caribbean, and Latin America. Immigration and white flight have meant that the ten largest urban areas in the United States—places like Los Angeles and New York, where the media images of the nation are largely produced and disseminated—now contain a majority of people of color. Drawing on work by Mike Davis,[11] Troy Duster has offered statistics such as the following: in 1970, New York was 75 percent white, now it is 38 percent; Los Angeles was 78 percent Anglo, now 37 percent.[12] Similar shifts have been taking place even in relatively suburban counties like California's Orange, Monterey, and Santa Clara.[13] Overall, the proportion of whites in California has fallen from 77.3 percent in 1970 to a projected 51 percent in 1999, as the percentage of Hispanics has risen from 12.1 to 39 percent and of Asians from 6.9 to 11 percent over the same span of time; by 2025, it is projected that Hispanics in California will outnumber whites by 20.1 million to 18.2 million.[14] Census Bureau figures offer less startling changes, but they are notorious for undercounting minority populations. Even the *New York Times* reports that the proportion of whites in New York City fell from 52.0 percent in 1980 to 38.5 percent in 1996.[15] Whatever the exact figures, the changes are striking. As much as a quarter of all Americans now derive from "minority" ancestry and in some places, like California and Texas, "minorities" will outnumber Anglos within a few years, as they already do in the school-age population.

Some of the new immigrants, like some of those a hundred years ago, plan to return whence they came; some do not; some will, whatever the intent. In ways different from those of the turn of the last century, though, the cultural highways between the "old" country and the "new" are wider, smoother, more open to two-way traffic. It is not just the existence of foreign-language books, newspapers, TV and radio programs in the United States; there were probably more foreign-language newspapers circulating in Chicago in 1898 than now. But I think that among today's ethnic minorities "old country" culture now plays a greater role in defining "new country" identity, individual and group.[16] The issue is not one of descent—to use one of the terms of Werner Sollors's well-known consent/descent binary. Rather, facilitated by fax machines and the Internet, phone cards and phone parlors, videocameras and videophone centers, money transfer businesses, and the like, it has to do with continuing and much more immediate processes of interaction between the culture and dynamics of the "old world"—the Dominican Republic, Mexico, Havana, Kwangtung, Moscow, Saigon—and the politics and art of the new America.

For example, a film like Lourdes Portillo's *Después del Terremoto* (1979) is "about" Nicaraguan immigrants in San Francisco, but involves the enormously destructive earthquake in Managua, the Sandinista revolution, the ambivalence of the exile community toward the Sandinistas, and vice versa. As Rosa Linda Fregosa frames the experience in an interview with the filmmaker: "But, you could have made a documentary about the immigrants' experiences or about the struggle of Sandinistas in exile. Instead, you made more of a fictional docudrama, a scripted narrative film, where you investigate sexual freedom and the freedom to consume within the context of North and Central American politics."[17] Similarly, Cristina Garcia in *Dreaming in Cuban* and Junot Díaz in *Drown* write stories in which movement between the Caribbean and the United States, and between English and Spanish, constitute the central cultural dynamics of the newer American population. It would be hard to imagine two books less alike on their surfaces, Garcia's filled with the magic of dreams and Santaría, the shattering passions that constitute Cuban politics and class relations, and Díaz's as unsparingly naturalistic as the suburban squalor, the Dominican barrios, and the ratty jobs about which he writes. The first focused on the desires and betrayals of three generations of women, the other on the casual violence and suburban anomie of uprooted males, particularly adolescents. Yet both writers constitute narrative I's more like one another than like those of earlier generations negotiating the "ethnic passages" so cogently portrayed by Thomas Ferraro: "In writing of themselves or their people, immigrant offspring incorporate the assimilation paradigm as a framing device in order to measure it against experience. Restaging the struggle for entitlement and self-determination in America provokes them to recognize varieties of cultural persistence they previously had not suspected. Calling into doubt ancestral claims of unbroken continuity, they discover in their alien pasts varieties of cultural transformation already tending toward modernity."[18] For the central figures in *Dreaming in Cuban* and *Drown*, assimilation is not a dominant problematic. Caribbean "cultural persistence" in the United States is inescapable and fragmentary continuities—of family, language, imagery—the stuff out of which identities are being daily constituted. In these books, America is not a horizon toward which desire bends, but always an already dominating presence in the "old country."

Today's changes from the paradigm Ferraro's book so clearly anatomizes is also marked by a shift in terminology, from "immigrant" (or even "exile") community to "diasporic" and from patterns of "assimilation" to those of "travel" (as of theory or disease or capital). The terms are not equivalent, to be sure: much, at least, of the older Cuban community in Miami and around New York continues to see itself as "exiled" and to act out on that idea. It seems to me fundamentally misleading to apply the term "diaspora" to groups like the Salvadorans, for example, whose trajectory has been strictly toward the North as represented by the United States, and whose communities bear little resemblance to the widespread international networks that characterize truly diasporic peoples, like Chinese and Jews.[19] Yet both in casual conversation and in scholarly discourse, "diaspora" has become the favored term, offering a kind of cachet absent from the dreary precincts marked by "immigrant." Or, perhaps, the shift toward that term reflects a somewhat inchoate but widespread appreciation of the changed global circumstances toward which I have been pointing.

But more noteworthy and of particular importance both to American and to ethnic studies are the increasing cultural and social practices denoted by the term "borderlands." This label names a process by which cultural borders, like political borders, are eroding; or, more revealing, a process whereby the cultural territory some have called the "borderlands" has expanded, even as, on the one hand, efforts to police borders, political or cultural, have in quarters like the Congress and the offices of former California governor Pete Wilson intensified. And even as, on the other hand, processes of globalization have been loudly promoted as defining the future. Borderland art and scholarship place themselves precisely in the midst of that set of economic ironies whereby the physical borders of America grow daily higher to people even as the boundaries for (or to) American capital grow more porous.

The border is obviously a geographical metaphor, but "borderland" dynamics cannot be understood solely as geography. To be sure, the metaphor has primarily emerged from the particular experience of Mexicans and Mexican Americans, in the theoretical work of Chicana writers like Gloria Anzaldúa and Cherríe Moraga, Chicano critics and historians such as José David Saldívar, Néstor García Canclini, and George Sánchez,[20] and self-described "warriors for Gringostroika," like Guillermo Gómez-Peña and Roberto Sifuentes. But the erosion of national boundaries as a primary definition of its objects of study has also emerged in other areas of Americanist scholarship. Immigration scholars like John Bodnar had earlier turned their attention toward the economic and social forces in immigrants' native lands that shaped decisions to stay or to leave, as well as who made those decisions and when.[21] Renaissance and eighteenth-century literary study have increasingly been seen in transatlantic terms, not only metaphorically— as in the varied ways of reinscribing Caliban[22]—but in terms of publishing, reading, and viewing practices. The work of European scholars like Paul Gilroy,[23] Maria Diedrich,[24] Carl Pedersen and Fran Hopenwasser,[25] and others has helped undermine the tendency to present North American slavery isolated from its international context. And the writing of many multicultural scholars, focusing on what has differentiated the experience of people of color from ethnic whites, has brought into question the earlier paradigms or sets of assumptions that characterize the work of scholars like Sollors or Michael Walzer.[26]

Defining at once his identity and his art, Gómez-Peña interprets the personal dimensions of the borderland as follows:

> I am Mexican but I am also Chicano and Latin American. At the border they call me *chilango* or *mexiquillo*; in Mexico City it's *pocho* or *norteño*; and in Europe it's *sudaca*. . . . I look for the traces of my generation, whose distance stretches not only from Mexico City to California, but also from the past to the future, from pre-Columbian America to high technology and from Spanish to English, passing through "Spanglish." . . . My "artistic space" is the intersection where the new Mexican urban poetry and the colloquial Anglo po-

etry meet; the intermediate stage somewhere between Mexican street theater and multimedia performance.[27]

The volume *Temple of Confessions,* published in connection with the Gómez-Peña/Sifuentes performance piece/installation[28] by that name, itself stands as an illustration of borderland art.[29] An oval opening in the cover displays in vivid red and black two women, more or less dressed as nuns, in passionate embrace. The picture turns out to be a postal card—of the sort found in many trendy bars—but in this case marked in bold white "CONFESS." On the reverse we are instructed to "confess your intercultural Fears and Desires, and mail to the address at right. You may also e-mail your text, graphic or audio piece to: pochonostra@aol.com." Visitors to the performance/installation were able to "confess" into a tape or on cards supplied for the occasion. Attached to the rear of the book is a CD on which is reproduced, among other things, a selection of oral "confessions," which range from the enraged to the bizarre.[30] Also within its pages one finds a rub-on Aztec tattoo. The book itself, printed on different paper stocks, in differing fonts, is a kind of collage of "confessions," interviews, essays, poems, stories by visitors and by a number of artists, which includes photographs of the parts of the performance/installation, among them the divine black velvet parodies of well-known painters, such as "Santa Frida de Detroit" and "El Transvestite Pachuco." In his descriptive opening essay, Gómez-Peña describes the effect of the installation in these terms:

> The installation functions simultaneously as an elaborate set design for a theater of mythos and as a melancholic ceremonial space for people to reflect on their own racist attitudes toward other cultures. And depending on the cultural baggage and racial background of the visitor, and on his/her particular relationship to the symbols and to the performance characters, the space changes its meaning and even its looks. . . . The kind of recorded and written confessions we obtain through this project, I believe, couldn't possibly be obtained through field work, direct interviews, or talk radio. The extremely seductive yet threatening imagery, as well as the considerable amount of time that people stay in the space, help bring to the surface forbidden or forgotten zones of the psyche. Because of this, the confessions tend to be quite emotional, inti-

mate, and revealing. . . . Since our job as artists is not to analyze or moralize but merely to open a Pandora's box and let loose the colonial demons, we never express our approval or disapproval to the confessor.

Temple of Confessions is more about America's cultural projections, and its inability to deal with cultural otherness than about the Latino "other." (Pp. 21–22, 23)

The book has something of the same qualities, by turns seductive, threatening, hilarious, informative, provoking, even wistful. It determinedly tries to transgress borders of genre, form of publication, relationship to audience, and to express ideas about the functions of art, which Gómez-Peña and Sifuentes see not only in the psychic terms described above, but also as playing significant roles in the struggles over political maneuvers like the North American Free Trade Agreement (NAFTA), the militarization of the U.S.-Mexican border, and the recent immigration laws, which give the Immigration and Naturalization Service essentially dictatorial powers and strip travelers to the United States of virtually any right to court review of arbitrary INS actions. It isn't that Temple of Confessions engages all these issues directly, though there are many comments on the implications of NAFTA, for example. Rather, the book is, among other things, an exercise in consciousness raising about the rage, fear, and desire that provide emotional fuel to the debates over such legislation.

Nowhere, perhaps, has the borderland metaphor been deployed more richly, and engaged more intense emotion, than in connection with definitions of that element of identity categorized as gender. A "borderland" approach to gender definition begins with the common binary of masculine/feminine and the presumptively impenetrable boundary between them. It proceeds to destabilize this binary thinking by demonstrating the permeability of the border between the terms, moving to the idea that women participate in elements of "masculinity" as men do of "femininity." Or, to cite Margaret Fuller's well-known 1840s framing of this point:

In so far as soul is in her completely developed, all soul is the same; but in so far as it is modified in her as Woman, it flows, it breathes, it sings, rather than deposits soil, or finishes work; and that which is especially feminine flushes, in blossom, the face of earth, and pervades, like air and water, all this seeming solid globe, daily renewing and purifying its life. Such may be the especially feminine element spoken of as Femality. But it is no more the order of nature that it should be incarnated pure in any form, than that the masculine energy should exist unmingled with it in any form.

Male and female represent the two sides of the great radical dualism. But, in fact, they are perpetually passing into one another. Fluid hardens to solid, solid rushes to fluid. There is no wholly masculine man, no purely feminine woman. . . . Man partakes of the feminine in the Apollo, Woman of the masculine as Minerva.[31]

Contemporary theorists carry this observation further by pointing to the existence between the terms "masculine" and "feminine" of a "borderland," which participates in both and yet "belongs" to neither. And they suggest that this Borderland/La Frontera (to use Gloria Anzaldúa's term) is, in this historic moment, rapidly widening, despite all attempts to shore up a stable boundary and thus to sustain the binary idea. Moreover, those deploying this image suggest both that the flow across the borderlands has speeded up and, at the same time, that the population inhabiting the borderlands, those with diminished or virtually nonexistent loyalties to either of the traditional gender "nations"— the citizenry of a "Queer Nation"—grows apace.

The border metaphor insists upon somewhat greater historic specificity than the metaphor that presents gender as performance, since borderland conceptions acknowledge that gender boundaries, like other kinds of physical and ideological borders (national, familial, racial), rise and diminish over time and in distinctive circumstances. This is not the first time that gender or, indeed, national borders have been radically challenged, nor is the current intellectual geography a settled and permanent state of affairs. On the contrary, the ongoing "culture wars" can be seen as a struggle between those engaged in boundary-challenging practices and those often desperately involved in shoring up Berlin walls of ideology, nationality, sexuality, and the like.[32]

The border metaphor is, unlike the metaphor of gender as performance, somewhat geographically specific as well, since it is more— at least in origin—a phenomenon associated with conflicted physical borders, as in south Texas and California, where the image takes on distinctive resonance by virtue of its associations with other economic and political forms of border crossing. One might argue that "border crossing," unlike "gender bending," will necessarily entail transgressive practices, since every border expresses significant ideological, economic, or political interests. Thus, to contest borders is inevitably to challenge the interests invested in them. Further, such challenges are generally made by or in the name of the people borders are designed to corral, limit, or exclude. In this sense, I think, the border metaphor may appeal more to activists, because it links, as Anzaldúa does, the transgressions of queers and wetbacks, the politics of sexuality to the politics of immigration.[33] Indeed, Gómez-Peña distinguishes his own "borderness" from "internationalism," "a cultural identity," he suggests with some irony, "based upon the 'most advanced' of the ideas originating out of New York or Paris."[34] And here, I think, we cross from the cultural terrain inhabited by borderlands metaphors to the political terrain where such metaphors emerge transformed as resonant strategic tools for extending or contesting the domain of twenty-first-century capitalism.

The economic and cultural logic of consumer capitalism presses toward erasure of borders, at least as they remain inhibitions to the unconstrained flow of capital and goods. For consumer capitalism, difference—whether coded as "national," "ethnic," "racial," or even sexual—remains primarily a feature of commodities: Scottish wool, Japanese automobiles, Mexican chile, Indonesian carvings, butch hairstyles. Such economic processes produce identities that, as Gómez-Peña suggests, can be called "international," in something of the same sense that a primary instrument of Western (and particularly American) capitalism is called the "International Monetary Fund" (IMF). But, of course, borders mark real differences in human experience, life chances, indeed possibilities for survival. These are profoundly different as between the inhabitants of San Diego and Juarez, New York and Santo Domingo, and, indeed, between the inhabitants of New York's Upper East Side and its Lower East Side, between Sutton Place and Alphabet City, Westwood and Watts. Erasing borders, at least to the flow of dollars and of capitalist ideology has, if anything, exacerbated such differences, which helps to explain the ever increasing clamor of third- and second-world people to enter the West, and especially the United States. In such a context internationalism, as defined by the IMF, NAFTA, the General Agreement on Tariffs and Trade (GATT), or similar mechanisms of capitalist penetration and control, emerges as a threat to potential sources of resistance grounded in forms of "local" solidarity, whether in Chiapas, Java, or Michigan. One might evoke a parallel here to how ethnic identities in the United States have persisted not so much by virtue of residual and often sentimental notions of descent, but have been constructed as means to resist the power of assimilationist rhetoric, of the educational and political practices of the "melting pot," whose practical effect has been to mask the sources, even the reality, of the inequalities in opportunity, health, work, and education. "Borderland" art and scholarship does *not* attempt to deny the existence of borders nor of the profound and living differences that borders distinguish. Rather, borderland thinking challenges the processes by which such differences are naturalized, installed, and maintained, particularly as the economic and political inequalities fostered and sustained by "internationalization" are obscured by cultural imagery and ideological claims that seek to smooth out the clear differences that people prefer not to highlight.

Here lies, paradoxically, a source of tension between American studies and the various forms of ethnic studies; the tension derives from two sources. First, there is the extent to which American studies can be taken up by an unconsidered internationalizing impulse. From many points of view, internationalization represents a desirable objective, for it counterbalances exceptionalist and parochial tendencies within the U.S. academy. On the other hand, scholarship that celebrates processes of internationalization can, willy-nilly, pull intellectuals throughout the world into the ever fascinating and all-consuming study of U.S. social, political, and especially cultural forms, and can foster the establishment of American English as the sole lingua franca and American culture as the normative measure of desire. Domestically, a strong international emphasis can fixate on scenes of interaction between American and overseas cultures, no bad thing in itself, except to the extent that doing so can marginalize the intense struggles of ethnic minority and queer communities *within* the United States. By contrast, ethnic studies programs have largely been rooted in and have emerged from the struggles of ethnic minority communities in the United States for equality and freedom; "queer" or lesbian and gay studies programs have followed a similar trajectory. No surprise then that their practitioners are suspicious of an academic discipline like American studies, seemingly rootless, even apolitical, and upon occasion, like its namesake, dangerously imperial; an academic discipline, one might say, seeking rather than derived from a politics. The danger then is that internationalized American studies programs may find themselves for these reasons boosted as the glamorous, highly networked counterpart to the more restricted economic and geographic particularisms of ethnic studies.

What can borderland narratives, arising in and from ethnic minority communities and scholarship, say to American studies practice? I want to try characterizing some of the new paradigms of borderland scholarship, all the while acknowledging that the border metaphor is itself heavily inflected by Chicana/o experience and needs to be qualified carefully, the more so as one extends it into the work of other ethnic minority cultures. Nevertheless, while the border metaphor may have originated in Latina/o history, the kinds of experiences to which it refers are widely shared among immigrants and residents from many parts of the world, and resonates as well among those who identify themselves as queer.

In American ethnic scholarship such "border" study is, I think, particularistic from one point of view. It does not begin from the normative assumptions, however liberally interpreted, of earlier versions of cultural pluralism; nor is it compelled by, or often even mindful of, the agonizing about national unity heavily displayed across the political spectrum among some white and usually male commentators.[35] Rather, such narratives begin *within* identity communities. They try to distinguish cultural features not only on the basis of traditionally defined historical experiences, and certainly not on essentialist grounds, but rather in a constructivist mode, with eyes toward the future, discussing how ethnic identities are being or have been constructed. I want to say this carefully, for I do not mean to imply that prior experiences—like those of Japanese internment camps or Chinese exclusion, the Treaty of Guadalupe Hidalgo or the "Trail of Tears"—are being set at a discount. But neither can such events or earlier symbols of ethnic identity contain the present, much less the future; in a sense, the borderland intellectual exchanges certainties of a defined past for the ambiguity and contradiction inherent in any effort to reconstruct or repossess icons, as Anzaldúa does with "La Llorona" and "La Malinche," as Gómez-Peña and Sifuentes do with Catholic and Mexican symbolism in *Temple of Confessions,* or as Retamar does with Caliban.

Borderland scholarship has, on the one hand, traced how often fragmented ethnic communities have struggled to overcome division through processes of ethnicization. The first word of the title of George Sánchez's book, *Becoming Mexican American,* expresses this move. On the other hand, such scholarship has deconstructed hegemonic terms like "Asian American" or "Indian"—however necessary in their time and in certain respect in this—to bring out the historical, geographical, and cultural differences that mark group identities.[36] A different paradox: such scholarship at its best honors the fluidity of individual identity; at the same time, it acknowledges that in a racialized society like that of the United States racialized categorizations are functionally all but permanent. They have thus prevented most people of color from the real possibility of "consent," or assimilation. Borderland scholarship understands racialization more as a process than as a permanent attribute of individuals or groups.[37] And it points not only to cultural determinants of racial categories, but to the material factors like geography, jobs, and other economic influences upon the construction of ideas of race. Indeed, one fundamental quality of such borderland scholarship is how closely issues of culture and of politics are linked.

Borderland scholarship, like much of the art with which it is concerned, seems skeptical of closure, in narrative or social terms. The prospect, for example, is quite different from Whitman's triumphal vision of the poet in "Passage to India."[38] Struggle, whether definitional, political, or in terms of identity formation, is more the norm. The experience of becoming a "hyphenated" American, from this perspective, is not one susceptible to framing metaphors, of the sort I discussed earlier, but needs to be seen as a movement into and out of identity categories. To cite Guillermo Gómez-Peña once again:

> There is no such thing as a permanent, static, homogenous sense of identity for Chicanos or for Mexican immigrants. In many ways, I can say that I am a Mexican in the process of Chicanization and that I am developing a multiple identity. I am Mexican, but I am also Chicano, and I am also Latin American. When I am in Mexico, Mexicans often note the figures of speech of mine that are *pocho.*

When I am in the United States, some Chicano nationalists object to the fact that I wasn't born in a Chicano barrio, and that I don't speak Chicano slang. When I am in Spain, they call me *Sudaca*, and in Germany I'm confused for a Turk. There is a point at which you realize that to defend this monolithic concept of identity—*la Mexicanidad*—in a process of ongoing border crossing and reterritorialization and deterritorialization is absurd.[39]

Such scholarship builds outward from the particularities of its defining community to explore the extent to which its categories of analysis, like the borderlands metaphor itself, can fruitfully be taken up by other ethnic populations. And here, of course, lies an element of potential conflict. For this process necessarily engages a certain skepticism about the immediate appropriateness of others' experiences, categories, or metaphors. Thus, for some ethnic minority critics, the bipolar structure of racial categories in the United States—black/ white—can become a problem. Again, I want to be careful not to be misunderstood: "race" in the United States *is* most deeply imprinted and, historically, extended mainly along the black-white divide, and African Americans have provided predominant political and cultural leadership in the struggle for justice. Still, no single model of analysis can account for the range of differences that ethnic scholars must now examine, especially when these are so heavily inflected along class and language lines—as the divisions between blacks and Koreans in Los Angeles or Brooklyn so painfully illustrate. Alvina Quintana offers a way out of this difficulty by employing "the term Black as a political signifier that refers to disenfranchised American ethnic-minorities."[40] But as inviting as this strategy may be, it assimilates all other struggles into one, thereby effacing significant discrepancies, not only of identity but of politics. Moreover, for some Native Americans, the very concepts of ethnicity, of race, or of immigrant nationality tend to obliterate the central categories of "indigenousness" and "sovereignty" and the importance of spatial categories of lived experience.[41]

If the potential for conflict between ethnic scholars exists, as I have suggested, then so does the reality of discord between ethnic studies and American studies. Apart from the issues on which I touched earlier, one of the practical problems concerns what one is presumed to know: for those in areas of ethnic studies the expectation is a familiarity with American studies as it has emerged over the last half century. For those in American studies, however, the presumption of knowledge about ethnic studies—its contents, methods, and debates—has not generally obtained. The problem emerges if one observes what gets included in significant American studies texts, which works and authors, events, issues, understandings get valorized and which are relegated to the realm of the Mexicans in Richard Caton Woodville's picture. Consider, for example, the second edition of Hollinger and Capper's *The American Intellectual Tradition* (1993), or Fox and Lears's *The Power of Culture* (1993), or Fisher's *The New American Studies* (1991), or Cohen and Roth's *History And . . .* (1995), or even Pease's *Revisionary Interventions into the Americanist Canon* (1994).[42] All of these are extremely useful collections, but from them one would hardly know that Indians had culture, that Latinos produced intellectuals, or that Asian Americans exist in American history. One could make such generalization about virtually all the recent collections with the notable exception of *The Cultures of U.S. Imperialism*.[43] In a sense, I am being unfair here for rhetorical purposes, since a good deal of borderland writing is of recent vintage, though tied back to José Martí's "Our America" (1891) or Américo Paredes's *With His Pistol in His Hands* (1958), or Zitkala-Sa's "School Days of an Indian Girl" (1900).

Such "canon" matters raise a central intellectual issue, which I would formulate in a question, adapting Donald Pease's useful formulation: to what extent do borderland critics "offer an alternate Imaginary out of which to constitute the field of American Studies" and thus "threaten the identity of those constituted in the previous field-Imaginary"?[44] I would not in this essay pretend to answer that question; I suspect that few if any Americanists have sufficiently surveyed the field, much less probed the "field-Imaginary," to do so. In any case, my basic concern is rather more political than professional. Underneath these intellectual and learned issues lurks a more fundamental political disquietude, which inserts a certain urgency into the discussion, much as the projects of borderland artists like Gómez-Peña have done.

There have been, I am suggesting, radical discrepancies between what is manifestly visible in the frames of American studies and what emerges into prominence within those constructed by ethnic studies scholars. Are these contradictions in some measure continuous with elements that, exploited by political right-wingers, have contributed to the dynamic driving the retrogressive 1996 immigration bill passed by the U.S. Congress? Such policies as the ones embedded in California Proposition 187,[45] or even, at their worst, the aggressions directed toward foreigners, toward "others," toward the border violators, the "impure," exist not only in the United States but in Germany, France, the former Yugoslavia, and elsewhere. The cry everywhere has been for national or ethnic or racial "unity." The reality—everywhere, too— has increasingly been a growth of the borderlands phenomenon. The question for scholars, especially in a field as theoretically progressive as American studies, is whether they and we can successfully help challenge the seeming contradictions in these differing conceptions of national identity, culture, *polis*. Seen thus, what is at stake in the question of national identity is not a scholarly construction of the past, but a politically charged construction of whatever future is rising into view beyond the horizon of the new millennium.[46]

CHAPTER SEVEN

OF *CHADORS* AND CAPITAL

In the summer of 1994 I was speaking at the University of the Eleventh of March in Surakarta, Indonesia. They had just begun an undergraduate American studies program, and they were interested in curricular and organizational ideas, as well as wishing to hear about the direction of American studies in the United States—at least as I interpreted it. The university, a relatively new one, is named after the day on which, in 1966, President Sukarno had officially turned state power over to then General and until 1998 President Suharto, a fact I will return to later.

After my talk—probably one I called, echoing a tae kwon do classic, "Multiculturalism Meets Modernism"[1]—a young woman in the audience got up during the discussion period to ask a series of questions. In her early twenties, perhaps, she wore a *chador,* along with her smart white blouse and stylish blue cotton skirt. She spoke fine, idiomatic English, better than that of many of her teachers, and she stood her ground when people giggled as she unrolled a series of about six distinct questions, enough to occupy two or three such discussion periods. For me, the most interesting question went something like this: "Do you think that American studies in Indonesia serves a role something like that previously played by the missionaries?" I saved that question for last, relishing the opportunities it presented to comment on the ambiguous roles I was at that moment enacting. But as I got into my response, I realized that the question is at once quite easy to answer and very difficult.

On the one hand, there are answers with which we are all familiar: American corporations hardly need the work of American studies scholars to penetrate Indonesia's huge market for Tori Amos CD's, *General Hospital* videos, Ralph Lauren fashions (made in Indonesia, to be sure)—not to speak of airplanes and military hardware. I choose my gendered verb here—"penetrate"—with some care to represent an earlier, but still present, way of understanding this market relationship. I also spoke about the ways in which the forms of cultural exchange embedded in market associations constitute two-way streets, though frankly one would have to search deep to discover how American cultures are inflected by those of Indonesia. Indeed, until the flap over Riady family political contributions during the 1996 election campaign, it wasn't clear that most Americans knew that Indonesia was a country rather than a microbrewery. I may also have touched on how people in a nation like Indonesia, far from being passive recipients of American culture or scholarship, do actually reshape what they find into new local forms—though there again, having just come from R & R in Bali, I could not help but be aware of the many ways in which the world outside is walled off from—even as it is a presence in—whatever is distinctively Balinese. So in these by now fairly conventional responses, I felt a certain ambivalence.

As I have reflected on that question and my answers, I have increasingly stumbled against difficulties, for while my initial set of answers served the moment, they do not seem to me finally to serve the reality. My answers, after all, dealt primarily with economics, culture as a commodity, world systems theory among other intellectual niceties. Such answers seemed quite at home in the heated air of the Javanese classroom where we were meeting. People nodded, including my questioner: I was not a one-dimensional apologist, I was up at least a bit on fashionable theory, I could dance round without actually embracing cultural imperialism. But I have been more and more troubled in the intervening months.

Perhaps it was the beautifully stitched fabric she wore over her head. This is a time of declarative head coverings: yarmulkes, backward baseball caps, dreadlocks. Whatever they project toward the heavens, on earth they represent forms of separation, markers of denial perhaps, or inchoate assertions of difference and identity. In this case, I think, the *chador* offered a deeper ground tone to the question its wearer had asked. For it represented a culture—in the anthropological sense of a whole way of life—that my interrogator was at some level posing politely, hospitably, but persistently against even the most well-crafted academic responses I might make. For ultimately, what I came to see as her question, as most deeply at contest, was cultural authority and its sources. That is to say, on what bases, using what set of values, would she—and I—live our lives and teach others? To be sure, as a speaker I was not in any simple sense a missionary for Pepsico, Boeing, or Disney. But was that because much more fundamentally, being a good Emersonian, I taught what I am, not what I said, and thus became, protesting innocence all the way, a missionary of the Western individualistic, thus bourgeois, values which underwrite those particular corporate formations? To ask it differently: implicated in the word "missionary" is the idea of being sent; by whom or what, then, was I sent? Or, as Langston Hughes played it in reverse:

By what sends
the white kids
I ain't sent:
I know I can't
be President.
    ("Children's Rhymes")

Let me approach this dilemma of Americans—if not America—abroad in two ways: first, anecdotally, via another place and time, Warsaw, spring 1996, the biennial meeting of the European Association for American Studies. And, second, somewhat theoretically, to ask how culture is sustained, transmitted, altered, and to what ends. I want to argue what may seem obvious: that, from a policy standpoint, the overriding objective of American activity abroad is to foster the inculcation of bourgeois cultural norms as a fundamental condition of, a sine qua non for, the continuing spread of consumer capitalism. My assumption, implicitly, is that the cold war continues by other means. And thus, those of us who participate in work abroad and remain skeptical of or hostile to the virtues of capitalist hegemony are caught precisely in the dilemma that my questioner evoked in Surakarta. If we carry "America" abroad—as, being Americans whatever our politics, we necessarily will—can we, on the one horn, evade the missionary consequence? But if we avoid foreign entanglements, do we not deny to our colleagues and even comrades abroad whatever the values are, to them, of what we know and carry? For American studies is, or can be, not only a critique of American values and policies, but a productive account of how powerful U.S. institutions operate at home and abroad.[2] And, to sprout a third horn, do we not also deny to ourselves the understandings that looking back at home from away will provide? I want, then, to offer some concrete illustrations both of such trilemmas and also of some perhaps unexpected turns in the increasingly complicated, indeed contradictory, narrative of America abroad.

First, then, Warsaw, late March, 1996. Throughout the days of the conference, small groups of men are slowly cutting through and carting off the dirty cakes of winter ice that clog the streets and walks of Warsaw University. It seems that Queen Elizabeth of Great Britain is to arrive the Monday most of us will be leaving. The final plenary session on Sunday provided the site for a speech by an apparently well-known American diplomatic historian, a gentleman named Gaddis. I will not trouble you with many details from his speech; it can be represented by his argument that the Germans in the immediate postwar period came to prefer the Americans to the Soviets on moral grounds: Russian troops, after all, had—defying self-interest as well as cultural values by antagonizing people—raped large numbers of German women during their push west. And that, argued Professor Gaddis, was a critical moral factor in shaping postwar alliances. Never mind well-entrenched German attitudes toward Slavs, economic incentives provided by the unscathed American industrial plant and our booming postwar economy, and the like. What the speech brought home to me was how very much alive the cold war remained. To be sure, we were hearing a troglodyte who had somehow survived from the ice age, but he was different only in degree from the Kennedy School economists carrying out their free-market campaigns in Moscow,[3] or the USIA-chartered political scientists engaged in establishing empirical research methodologies in the academies of Eastern Europe. It occurred to me that these and other examples I could cite are all part of the continuing cold war. Or, more accurately, as Noam Chomsky corrected my formulation, of the longer-term conflicts between "developed" and systematically "underdeveloped" societies, of which the cold war was one manifestation. In this sense, the period in which we find ourselves is not usefully characterized as "post" coldwar, but rather as one in which the struggle has shifted from the confrontation of massive nation states and their allies (both clearly demarcated, even if their alliances shifted on occasion) to a more ambiguous terrain, on which is being fought as intensively as ever a *Kulturkampf,* or, more accurately, a series of cultural combats.

Here I need to register what is for me a problem with that many-sided, shifty term "post." However it is combined—with "modern," "colonial," "feminist"—it has always roused in me a taste of breakfast food, more promotional than nourishing. "Post" is, my dictionary tells me, "the place where a soldier is on watch, a place of duty," also "a place occupied for purposes of trade." These are, I think, especially evocative in the phrases "post–cold war" and "postcolonial." For these terms, like the piece of timber set upright in the ground, "mark a position," somehow setting the future to the right of the post apart from the past somewhat to its left. I'm deeply suspicious of such postings.[4] For, to return to my theme, the resonance of the question of missionary functions posed by the woman in Surakarta depends upon a basic continuity—rather than a break—between the earlier world of colonialism and the present still-imperialist moment. Perceiving, and acting upon, that continuity may be compromised by the very multiplication of post-designations. Indeed, while it would be foolish to ignore the differing realities produced by the collapse of the Soviet Union and the accelerated transmission of everything from cyberads to AIDS, it would be yet more dangerous to underplay the continuity of what I have been referring to as an ongoing combat for cultural authority, a struggle for hearts and minds, not to speak of economic resources and markets.

Having returned from my brief anecdotal excursion to Warsaw, I think I had best now enter into a mildly theoretical exercise. I want to explain why a form of cold war seems to me as lively today as ever, though the terrain of combat has no doubt shifted. My argument depends upon examining some of the connections I had earlier skirted between the cultural functions of Americans abroad and the aspirations of multinational corporations, between modern disciplinary protocols and the ever renewed organization of modern capitalism, or, in brief, between missionaries and Coke. It may be useful to begin from one of the more spectacular failures of supposedly "socialist" enculturation, the so-called Great Proletarian Cultural Revolution of the sixties in China. "Why a revolution, called 'cultural,' within a revolution?" our group asked when we traveled in China in 1974. We never got an altogether straight answer, but it became clear that it had to do with how culture persists beyond transfers, indeed transformations, of political or even economic authority: the behaviors, attitudes, priorities, values embedded in and fostered by culture will, like a dormant virus given scope, modify and even undo seemingly fundamental economic and social changes. The children of the former bourgeoisie, for example, would by and large qualify for a place in the university, and thus a leg up on the future, far, far more often than the children of peasants if university admissions standards remained unreconstructed. Well, that might be, we advocates of "open admissions" agreed, but still it seemed to many of us Americans absurd to imagine, as we often then heard, worrying about a return to the "capitalist road." Today, of course, that's no longer a worry, but a reality—a reality marking the failure of the cultural strategies of the Cultural Revolution.

By "failure" I mean this: the Chinese experience suggests that at least in modern mass society significant changes in the social relations of production will be sustained *only* if most people *internalize* the assumptions and values, the *culture,* such changes embody. The capitalist revolution against feudalism could be consolidated only when bourgeois cultural norms became the cultural common sense of most people in the towns and villages of Europe and the Americas. The hegemony of corporate capitalism in America and Western Europe depended upon its production not just of more, and more varied, goods and services, but of new forms of culture internalized in a burgeoning "middle class," which increasingly constructed its identity in terms of the products they acquired and the processes by which they did so.[5] The Great Proletarian Cultural Revolution attempted to instill a parallel if different set of cultural changes virtually overnight, posing as an alternative to generally long-extended processes of historical modification of values and assumptions[6] an effort to impose new cultural norms through the pressures of mass mobilizations, varieties of

144 ★ From Walden Pond to Jurassic Park

Stalinist police-state controls, and the exploitation of patriarchal traditions of authority. The venues in the Cultural Revolution for fulfilling desire were to be those created and sustained *not* by consumer production but by politics. A command economy would ensure against problems of competition, overproduction, and market uncertainty. Meanwhile, socialist selves might be created in terms not of what one came to desire and possess, but of how one fulfilled political expectations experienced, I suspect, as powerfully paternal. I think it is difficult for most Americans, including left intellectuals, fully to appreciate the turn-on, the intensity of satisfaction, bordering on and sometimes leading to sexual, to be derived from street politics. Whether it is our puritanism, our commodity fetishism, or the utter evacuation of politics from American cultural environs that so limit our perceptions, much less our experience, of the intense links between personal desire and political satisfaction—I leave to wiser heads. But I know that the Maoist project in this respect at least was not so psychically utopian (or distopian) as it has been made to seem. Still, it was a failure. In a way— to return to my Indonesian terrain—the transfer of power from Sukarno to Suharto similarly represented not a simple military coup but the failure of the leaders of the Bandung conference, of nonaligned radical decolonization, to locate the means for changing political common sense among many—probably most—of the people.

A cultural revolution of quite another sort is, as we know, now under way, especially in the nations of the former Soviet Union and elsewhere in Eastern Europe. For the so-called "market reforms" in Eastern Europe—a dainty phrase for the installation of capitalism— cannot finally be sustained unless and until bourgeois cultural norms become the common sense of people in those nations. The previously dominant political arrangements have largely been overthrown or, even in the most intransigent of states, deeply modified. Processes of capital formation, privatization of property, competition, profit and loss have been loosed upon the lands. The weight of American state power, if not always, ironically, American corporate capitalism (unsure, after all, about profits), beams down on Moscow, Bucharest, and Minsk. The claim is made that history is now over, the triumph of advanced capitalism assured, and the sole remaining task to tote up the winners and the losers in the newest and final money game. But in fact, the cultural struggle continues. The policy goals of official America abroad thus respond to the imperative of "manufacturing consent,"[7] or, in the language I have been using, asserting and reasserting the hegemony of bourgeois cultural values—individualistic, market-driven, money-defined—against the resistance of a variety of alternative cultural patterns, not all of which most of us would embrace, any more than most of my readers would don a *chador* or a penis-gourd. Do we look forward, then, to the consolidation of the new corporate revolution, the manufacturing of consent to an emergent consumer capitalism? Or will the gravitational pull of collectivist and other cultural forces begin to splinter recent capitalist institutions and forms of interest group politics? Who knows? Whether the forced march toward Disneyland and MacDonalds prescribed for the new Russia will be any more successful than the Great Proletarian Cultural Revolution remains to be seen.[8] What concerns me is better understanding our role in it.

For it is in this fractious context that the internationalization of knowledge and the cross-border mingling of scholars have been taking place in the last decade or two. I want now to turn more specifically to the forms of such interactions and the contradictions those of us participating in them continue to face, the contradictions I have coded here as, so to speak, our missionary position.

In the scholarly world, it has, of course, become a commonplace that knowledge is increasingly international, nowhere more so than in American studies. Larger numbers of overseas scholars now attend professional meetings in the United States and, instead of giving papers on "American studies in Uzbekistan," they are likely to talk about their own scholarship on Disney parks, the impact of the American military on local economies and personal safety, the continuing connections between "old country" language and culture and "new country" multiculturalism, and the variety of ways in which people outside the United States receive, transform, and recode American images and narratives.[9] In short, overseas scholars have increasingly been focusing on questions that the material conditions of their workplaces and knowledge enable them to pursue more fully than Americanists in the United States. At the same time, however, larger numbers of scholars from the United States also take part in overseas conferences; in the last few years, for example, I've participated in professional meetings from Cheju-do to Tomsk, and from Tenerife to Hanoi, and

I'm just one among many. I think, or at least I hope, we do at least as much listening in these venues as speaking. And I think we learn how differently issues which we experience as inflected primarily, for example, by race can appear when, as in a country like Denmark, they are viewed more centrally as shaped by class perspectives.[10]

We interact more immediately, too, thanks to the Internet, which is increasingly available, at least to professors and researchers, in most parts of the world except—as I've experienced it—for Africa. Of course, no invention seems to have succeeded so well as the Net in projecting English as *the* international language. And with English, American English to be sure, comes the need, indeed the inevitability, of learning American culture. When, quite innocently, I said something like that to the fortieth anniversary convention of TEFLIN (Teaching English as a Foreign Language, Indonesia) three years ago, the older, more traditional teachers of language were outraged, partly no doubt on theoretical grounds having to do with beliefs about language acquisition, and partly, perhaps, because they saw that notion as a way of opening their students to Ice-T, *Dynasty,* and Dr. Pepper. The younger teachers, of course, embraced the notion—together with the pleasures of American popular culture. Which gave me, mistrustful old man that I am, some instant missionary qualms.

However that might be, such increasing interaction, and the dissolution of national boundaries in intellectual work, has in significant ways altered the conceptions of what constitutes a field like American studies. It used to be that we looked primarily at peoples' lives only *after* they had arrived on these shores. It has now become a commonplace—perhaps most usefully illustrated in the work of John Bodnar and George Sánchez—that we need to understand the variety of processes, in Italy, Korea, and Mexico, for example, that at particular moments encouraged or enabled particular groups of people to decide to uproot and migrate, and at other moments brought people somewhat different in class, learning, or aspiration to follow the first group. Likewise, we examine more systematically the impacts of policies and economic developments in the "mother" country that have shaped, and continue to shape, ethnic identities in the United States.[11] Then, too, overseas scholars in particular have begun to study the various impacts of American personnel and policy on their own regions. For example, the work of American architects and agronomists brought in the nineteenth century to help develop the northernmost Japanese island of Hokkaido is well known in Japan. But how was their presence used in relation to establishing imperial policy toward the island's indigenous population? That's the subject currently being investigated by a young Japanese American studies scholar, Yujin Yaguchi, in Sapporo. In a certain sense, then, American studies is leaking through the boundaries that had previously delimited the field. Is that a function of the general hybridization of culture, academic scholarship included?[12] Or is it, to reinvoke political contradiction, or maybe personal ambivalence, one way in which American studies mimics—or helps underwrite—the imperial aspirations of its namesake?

At the same time, the intellectual paradigms that have structured the investigation of America abroad have themselves come into question. In the United States, disciplinary and interdisciplinary modes of studying America coexist, not always peacefully, to be sure, but civilly for the most part. Overseas, the traditional way of approaching America has been as an "area" within an established discipline, history, political science, literature. In February 1995, a new American studies association was founded in Moscow; but as it turned out, virtually all the members of the presidium, apart from being male, were also historians or economists. The association that studies American literature and culture had already met in December, and while some literary folk participated in the new organization, it remains unclear whether a unified, much less an interdisciplinary, association will emerge. Listening to some of the papers given at that Moscow meeting, I felt that some of the empiricism energetically being fostered by USIA in Eastern Europe might be healthy. On the other hand, I had also to ask the extent to which such "development"—if that is what it is—has the effect of screening out alternative, interdisciplinary paradigms of somewhat differing intellectual lineage. I mean Raymond Williams and Stuart Hall lead in somewhat different directions than Hans Morgenthau and Leo Strauss. In other parts of the world, as I shall say in a moment, that old set of academic structures, which in many ways bound the Soviet bloc intellectually to Western Europe, is being brought into question. But is filling the old departmental bottles with the still older wine of unproblematized American empiricism to be regarded as "progress" in Europe, East or West?

Such questions are open as never before. For in many Eastern

European countries, as well as in Asia, teachers are for the first time having to ask both what to teach and also how. As the question of the canon therefore appears on screens across the world, subject matter and teaching strategies emerge as problematics rather than as settled wisdom. Determining topic and pedagogy can take on considerable intensity not just in American studies programs, but in English as a second Language (ESL), in area studies, and even in mainstream courses focused on issues of national origins and history when the underlying concern is really "Why study the United States?" Or, more poignantly, "What, if anything, can we learn from American experience?" Seven years ago a group of American scholars of ethnic minority literatures was invited to a conference at the Gorki Institute of World Literature in Moscow. Part of the agenda, at least for some of the senior Soviet scholars, was what they might learn about "dealing with our national minority cultures." Since that time, of course, many then Soviet national minorities have dealt their own hands, thank you very much. Indeed, the very word "ethnic" has in the intervening time become, at least in many areas of Europe and the Middle East, a term of fear and loathing. But obviously the question of what one might learn from America remains even more insistently on the agenda, not only as a response to the forms of genocide represented by the phrase "ethnic cleansing," but also because so many societies that had previously thought themselves monocultural discover that they are not now, nor have ever been, and are less likely to be so in the scary future.

At a Salzburg seminar in the fall of 1995 on American ethnic literatures, I asked a group of scholars from Eastern Europe, North Africa, and the Middle East to write up a brief view of ethnicity in their own nations from the point of view of an intelligent observer, not a specialist (which none were). We learned about Berber nationalism and its growing opposition to other forms of North African identity, like "pan-Arabism and pan-Islamism." We learned about the illegal immigration to Romania of people from China, Pakistan, Turkey, and Afghanistan. "They want to go farther to Western, more developed countries," to quote my informant, "but they do not have the right papers and they find themselves stuck in Romania. Some of them get involved in all sorts of activities in Romania. Recently the illegal activities of a Chinese mafia have been discovered and this has created great commotion in our society. There have also been racist reactions of the well-

known type: 'They have come here and look what they are doing.'"
Our Polish participant deconstructed the official history explaining the
supposed monoethnicity of Poland; instead, he provided a brief profile
of Germans in Silesia, Kashubians in north-central Poland, Gypsies,
Lithuanians, Belorussians, the all-but-hidden Jews, and, the newest
ethnic group in a number of countries, Vietnamese. Some of these
groups are differently represented in parliament, have differing authority over local schools and television, and clearly distinct relationships with their own "overseas" communities.

The differences from American experiences of such ethnic diversity probably outweigh the similarities. But the relationships are generative. From this side of the border, the development of overseas
scholarly concern for issues like ethnicity opens more fully possibilities for new forms of comparative study. And these, I think, enable us
to return to American realities with a useful distance, a productive
defamiliarization of our own practices. For overseas scholars less pa-
ternalistic than their Soviet counterparts of seven years ago, American
experience is also instructive. It helps open study and a richer understanding of their local reality, where official dogma had foreclosed,
simplified, or pigeonholed it. Moreover, in some places, as Melani
Budianta pointed out at the 1996 American Studies Association convention, talking about American phenomena, such as elections or religious conflicts, can become a means for talking about a local situation
too fraught for direct confrontation. Indeed, there is no gainsaying the
fascination and usefulness of American experience, for all its history
of Indian genocide, African slavery, Chinese exclusion, Japanese internment—and Lord only knows what future Gingrichean horrors.

In this sense, as a colleague from Singapore, Ban Kah-Choon, then
director of the American Studies Center at the National University, put
it sitting in our living room a few years ago, "America represents
possibility, not closure." To study British literature, as he said, necessarily involves the recuperation of a fixed and largely closed set of
social and cultural relations, whereas America, in *his* world and at *this*
time, represents openness.

And have I thus come round to apologetics? Ban also underlined a
central phenomenon of America abroad: how *we* study, perceive, and
utilize the construction called "America" may be quite different from
how those outside the United States do these things. "Rome seen from

within," he said, "has many very different meanings from Rome seen from Palestine or Egypt." I want to illustrate this perception by looking at interdisciplinarity, a teaching strategy honored, I fear, more in the breach in the United States than in the practice. To do so, I want to share with you two course descriptions that Ban provided from the American Studies program at the National University of Singapore.

American Poetry: War and Science

One of the most interesting ways of looking at American poetry, and its astonishing innovations in range and technique, is as a response to the developments in science and technology which powered the growth of the country. These have contributed to war, industry, commerce, political control, and the understanding of natural processes. The module [course] seeks to show through a presentation of the tensions between poetry and science/technology some of the key elements that have gone into the "making" of the United States and the continuing presence of the factors that have contributed to its growth.

Language and Gender in American Law

The course addresses particular issues situated at the crossroads of law, language, gender, political economy, power and ethnography through an interdisciplinary approach that examines the American legal system and its linguistic context. Through one central concern that has spurred much rethinking within the American jurisprudence system—that of gender—the course looks at some of the broader issues within American society, the response to problems of gender and the revising and rethinking of American law. It seeks to provide a perspective on one of the most active aspects of recent American social thought.

Now I think these are quite fascinating course descriptions, but I introduce them not so much to praise our colleagues in Singapore but to illustrate a point. Interdisciplinarity has a set of meanings in the United States, but these by no means regulate the ways in which the practice will develop elsewhere, even if the field is called "American studies." On the contrary, just as subject matter focused on American experience plays new roles when it enters the academic stage overseas, so with method. In Singapore—and I think elsewhere in Asia—interdisciplinarity represents a way of helping students to understand actual social practice in the United States, of answering questions not about how U.S. business is organized or financed, but why people who work in it do what they do, and how; not the constitutional parameters of American political decision-making, but the connections that linked Sonny and Cher to Sonny and Newt. In Russia, on the other hand, interdisciplinarity is, in part, a lever prying at the self-interest of separate faculties trying, understandably, to sustain themselves by building up the walls of their disciplines. In Japan, interdisciplinarity may be associated with the difficult process of generational change. What is offered, in short, undergoes a sea change to "something rich and strange" when it emerges as what is accepted and used by scholars overseas.

Some of you may by now be thinking that I have worked my way into a pretty hollow: Have I surrendered ambivalence to compliment the adaptations made in authoritarian Singapore of imperial American academic methods? Do we abandon contradiction, along with chewing gum, before we exit Changi airport? Can an American abroad find comfort only on an island of 3,000,000 Chinese in a sea of 300,000,000 Muslims? These are, I think, really forms of the same question I have been worrying throughout this essay. To state it baldly: is the music accompanying America abroad, however sponsored, however self-consciously correct, always already a variation of "Onward, Christian Soldiers"? Well, sure. But then again, who decides the words? Perhaps they are those of John F. Kendrick:

> Onward, Christian soldiers! Blight all that you meet;
> Trample human freedom under pious feet.
> Praise the Lord whose dollar sign dupes his favored race!
> Make foreign trash respect your bullion brand of grace.
> Trust in mock salvation, serve as tyrants' tools:
> History will say of you: "That pack of G. . d. . fools."[13]

Deciding on the words is, I think, a matter not of historic inevitability but of human intellect and the will to shape events. Perhaps it begins, this work of American studies, of American intellectuals abroad, when we are willing to engage the heat, the doubt, the contradictions, and the possibilities evoked by a student, a *chador,* a question in a classroom in Surakarta.

CHAPTER EIGHT

FICTION AS EXPLORATION: THE NOVELS OF CHARLES CHESNUTT

One of the commonplaces of criticism about Charles Chesnutt is that he wrote in order both to make money and to advance the condition of black people in turn-of-the-century America.[1] In the years after the Civil War, a widening class of urbanized Americans with significant disposable incomes came to regard more or less exotic places—and people—as items of consumption. They bought property in quaint remote areas of Maine, North Carolina, and Florida, interested themselves in the products and habits of the natives, and were entertained by literary accounts of local characters and curious events increasingly remote from their own daily lives. As Richard Brodhead has pointed out,[2] this new market opened to many writers concerned with particular areas of the country broader opportunities for selling their stories and sketches and thus for making careers as authors. Chesnutt was one among this group—an unusual one, to be sure, since for the most part black people had been represented, at least to white audiences, almost exclusively by white authors like Joel Chandler Harris, Sherwood Bonner, and Thomas Nelson Page. Indeed, as has often been the case in American culture, blacks had become the material out of which many whites fashioned saleable products.

Chesnutt began his effort to fashion a profitable literary career within this context, initially selling stories to magazines like the *Atlantic Monthly* (first in 1887), *Family Fiction, The Independent,* and ultimately, of course, publishing as his first books in 1899, the collection of dialect tales called *The Conjure Woman* and *The Wife of His Youth and Other Stories of the Color Line.* In many of those stories, and in *The Conjure Woman* taken as a whole, Chesnutt also pursued his other, social objectives. He had posed these in a well-known early journal entry (May 29, 1880) as "the elevation of the whites," to be accomplished by overcoming the "unjust spirit of caste," and dispersing the "almost indefinable repulsion toward the Negro, which is common to most Americans," by familiarizing them with the human realities of black life and the strengths as well as weaknesses of black people.[3]

But the context within which Chesnutt wrote his journal entry was significantly different from that in which he published his stories. The handwriting spelling out the end of the reform movement entailed in Reconstruction was clearly on the walls before 1880. Reconstruction had, of course, been ended with the withdrawal of federal troops from the old Confederacy as part of the settlement leading to the election of Rutherford B. Hayes in 1876. By 1878, the use of military force to compel free and fair elections in the South was forbidden, and forms of organized terrorism directed against black voters in particular and Radical Republicans in general prevailed in many areas.[4] Still, a few blacks continued to serve in the Congress and in some state legislatures into the new century, some blacks were able to vote, despite varieties of legal and extralegal discouragement, alliances between white farmers and black agricultural laborers emerged in the 1880s, and the legalized system of Jim Crow legislation had not yet been set in place. The situation in 1880 warranted discouragement and bitterness, but not, perhaps, hopelessness; in any case, Chesnutt did not despair.

By the end of the 1890s, however, the situation for black Americans had altogether deteriorated. Alliances with white farmers and laborers had collapsed and a movement, beginning in Mississippi in 1890, to disenfranchise blacks altogether, by law and by violence, had essentially triumphed by the turn of the century.[5] At the same time, segregation was being installed as the uniform practice in Southern states: once the Supreme Court had struck down the Civil Rights Acts of 1875, blacks could be, and increasingly were, excluded from public accommodations for whites—hotels, eating places, theaters, and the like. Blacks were also segregated into miserable "Jim Crow" areas on railroads and steamboats, and, of course, into separate schools. Finally in its 1896 decision in *Plessy v. Ferguson* the High Court enunciated its "separate but equal" doctrine, which remained the racist law of the land until the *Brown v. Board of Education* decision of 1954. Meanwhile, lynchings of black people increased to a rate, by the turn of the century, of about one every three days, and large-scale assaults on black communities took place in towns like Wilmington, North Carolina— about which Chesnutt was to write in *The Marrow of Tradition*. Yet apologists for the Old South like Thomas Dixon and Thomas Nelson Page were presenting fictionalized rationalizations of slavery and the plantation system in widely circulated novels and stories. In short, by the time he had begun to publish his literary works, the conditions that might have occasioned the optimistic tone of Chesnutt's 1880 journal entry had largely disappeared. It would not, then, be surprising if he sought, perhaps with a certain desperation, to think through alternative scenarios to the prevailing horrors, or to the accommodation preached by most Negro leaders.

The form of the conjure stories, in particular, was thus shaped both by market and functional considerations. The strange, colorful, but peculiarly truthful stories of Uncle Julius are conveyed to a white and largely northern audience by one of their own, the frame narrator, John—much as Sarah Orne Jewett's stories of rural Maine are framed in the language and through the perceptions of her urban narrator. The narrative structure provides a guide, as it were, for the urban reader uncertain about how one would be expected to "read" these curious local folk. But Chesnutt also provides a second, female northerner, John's wife Annie, who models the kind of sympathetic response Julius as tale-teller and Chesnutt as author wish to evoke. As I have argued elsewhere,[6] the central theoretical story of the collection is "Sis' Becky's Pickaninny," in the course of which Aunt Peggy, the conjure woman, restores health to Sis' Becky and her child by reuniting them, and Uncle Julius begins the cure of the severely depressed Annie by engaging her feelings in that story. Uncle Julius thus presents what Chesnutt clearly intends as one model for the role of the African American creative artist: healing a sick white society by the magic of his art.

But while Uncle Julius is, from one perspective, a doctor of health, from another he is a doctor of deception, the veritable trickster puttin' on ole massa. Annie hears Julius's stories as offering, unlike the romanticized white fictions of the plantation tradition, the "stamp of truth"[7] about slavery and race relations; whereas John hears them, perhaps quite as correctly, as devices by which their teller attempts to achieve some advantage in his largely submerged struggle for dignity and survival. Indeed, some of Julius's tales liked least by his listeners—and by critics—present a less appealing, less "pathetic," less "moral" (p. 127) view both of conjurer and of tale-teller: deceptive, self-interested, alarming. These contradictory faces of Julius foreground precisely the limits Chesnutt rapidly came to perceive in the dialect story approach to resocializing white readers. For all that the conjurers in the tales can sometimes restore health or better the situations of the black people, they remain slaves, and conjure magic can only, at best, ameliorate not alter that condition; for all his narrative invention, Julius remains "in service" to John and Annie; for all the magic of his language and his ingenuity in undermining racial stereotypes, Chesnutt remains trapped within the commercial boundaries of the dialect tale. Unlike in "The Passing of Grandison," where Grandison's slavering deception covers his skillful maneuver to win freedom for his whole family, and where the failure of almost all readers to penetrate Grandison's consciousness leads them, embarrassingly, to identify with the outlook of a pompous slaveholder, the dialect tales seem to offer no exit from literary—or social—typecasting.

No wonder, then, that Chesnutt sought the wider scope offered by novels, and especially by social problem fiction—an increasingly popular form in turn-of-the-century America. But here, I think, Chesnutt confronted a difficulty somewhat different from that of many of the novelists aspiring toward social change. Faced with the racist onslaught of late-nineteenth-century Jim Crow legislation and Klan violence, even black leaders and intellectuals disagreed widely, and sometimes vehemently, about proper strategies for the advancement of African Americans. As is illustrated by the emerging conflict between Booker T. Washington and W. E. B. Du Bois, no consensus had emerged within the black community about the content the term "advancement" was meant to name. Ralph Bellamy and Upton Sinclair could press for socialism (and pure food and drug laws); Elizabeth Stuart Phelps, Charlotte Perkins Gilman, and Mary Austin could illustrate the importance of creative work to the fulfillment of women.[8] But wherein lay the road to progress for the African American—even for the apparently fortunate few who might be physically indistinguishable from the majority of whites? Never, in any case, a propagandist, Chesnutt's primary task, I want to argue, emerged as trying out, in imagined fictional worlds, what seemed to him the strategic possibilities available to black people of his period. In that way, too, he might pursue the idea that fictions could perform useful cultural work, a common enough idea of the time. I will argue, however, that as they developed, his novels came more to embody, than to offer resolutions of, the social contradictions inescapable in that historical moment.

A number of themes and images link the three novels Chesnutt published during his life—*The House behind the Cedars* (1900), *The Marrow of Tradition* (1901), and *The Colonel's Dream* (1905).[9] I want to begin with the image of the sickly child not only because this metaphor connects the novels to "Sis' Becky's Pickaninny" and, in certain ways, to some of the distraught children of stories in *The Wife of His Youth* but also because these children come in the novels to represent the question of future generations—or, more properly, of the future itself: will there be any worth considering? In *House*, John Warwick's child plays hardly more than a metaphoric role: he begins to flourish when Rena arrives at Warwick's establishment and declines in her absence. But as the book's focus shifts from Warwick to Rena, from South Carolina to the house behind the cedars, Albert disappears from view. *Marrow*, however, begins with the dangerous birth of Dodie Carteret, chronicles in detail his near strangulation on a piece of a rattle, and concludes with his near asphyxiation and bare survival. Meanwhile, the Millers' child dies of a stray bullet during the racial pogrom that forms the climax of the book. Philip, the colonel's child in *Dream*, dies together with his caretaker, Peter, under the wheels of a train. Such is the gloomy catalogue of the fate of children in Chesnutt's novels.

The elderly fare no better. Old Judge Straight of *House* assists John Walden's effort to become a lawyer and thus leave behind the identity of negro that Patesville society would impose upon him; but the judge is unable to warn Rena and her family against the catastrophe that overtakes them. In *Marrow*, old Delamere similarly represents the best of an earlier southern culture, but his heir, Tom, turns out to be a liar, cheat, and murderer, and the old man's desire to support the advancement of Patesville's blacks through a legacy is thwarted after his death by his executor. Finally, in *Dream*, the old servant, Peter, bears, however feebly, ancient traditions of kinship and loyalty into a world where neither retains real power. Peter sacrifices his own life in what turns out to be a futile effort to save the colonel's child Philip. Chesnutt's plots foreground these images of decline, frustration, and death despite the inveterate optimism that his narrators regularly assert. The novels thus seem to me caught between a wishful rhetoric and a gloomy narrative logic that belies it, contradictory impulses that at once express Chesnutt's sometimes conflicting objectives in writing and the particular historical moment within which he attempted to create an authorial career.

The question central to *The House behind the Cedars* may best be understood as one crucial to many other problem narratives of the period, and that is the issue of assimilation. That issue provides much of the dynamic in works as diverse as Abraham Cahan's *Yekl* (1896), Mary Antin's *The Promised Land* (1912), Sui-Sin Far's (Edith Eaton) "In the Land of the Free" (1909), Zitkala-Sa's (Gertrude Bonnin) *The School Days of an Indian Girl* (1900), and even the early chapters of Upton Sinclair's *The Jungle* (1906). To be sure, Chesnutt's black characters are not "immigrants" any more than the central figures of the numerous Native American autobiographies of the period. But like the period's immigrants from Europe and Asia, they are confronted with the dilemmas of assimilation: to enter the more powerful society dominated by Anglo whites (when and *if* that was truly possible) seemed to entail renouncing one's origins and vital elements of its culture. On the other hand, remaining within one's original world meant accepting the limitations implied by the words "reservation," "ghetto," "barrio" or even "the house behind the cedars." Besides, these enclaves were by no means safe spaces, within which inhabitants might feel secure against encroachment or attack. When, moreover, the defining barrier between the precincts of the "majority" and those of the "minority" was race, most members of the "minority" were in fact constrained by "descent" and seldom offered the options implied by the term "consent." Chesnutt's novel focuses on that tiny fraction of the turn-of-the-century black population that could, at least potentially, pursue the option of assimilation. By so doing, Chesnutt can explore the deeply contradictory implications of that option.

Moreover, Chesnutt, like many of the writers to whom I have alluded, locates these dilemmas within the life of a woman, Rena Walden. Men in these books often invite the challenges of assimilation, and if they are ultimately torn apart by its contrary imperatives, some at least "rise"—often at the expense of the women involved. Many of the women are more vulnerable, partly because they identify more fully with their original cultures; partly, perhaps, because the prescriptive ideals of the white, middle-class culture promotes female vulnerability; and partly, it may also be, that they are treated condescendingly by male authors. Thus in *House*, John Warwick's successful career as a South Carolina lawyer seems destined to continue, despite the fact that the secret of his and his sister's ancestry has to some extent emerged. Rena, by contrast, dies, torn apart by the conflicting demands of assimilation and family.

Or, more precisely, Rena is torn apart by the demands of the men who wish to control her life. Seen from a slightly different angle, *House* takes the form of a novel of seduction and betrayal. Warwick himself employs a seducer's stratagems to rouse Rena's desires for the larger world his life represents, and a lawyer's tactics to overcome their mother's not altogether unreasonable objections to Rena's leaving home and her. Warwick is, of course, generous to his sister and ward, sending her to a finishing school and effectively staging her debut in South Carolina society. Unquestionably, he opens life chances to her altogether unavailable in Patesville, where she is forever cast as a "cullud 'oman," however beautiful. What he cannot do, at least within the sentimental domain inhabited by the novel, is altogether obliterate her attachment to their mother and to the culture of the world in which she was raised. If Warwick is generous and if his is a richer, finer culture, his motives do not seem to me altogether altruistic. He gains through Rena a substitute mother for his lonely child and a most significant asset in the exchange processes by which social and economic alliances between men are established. But then, the "majority" society always offers tangible benefits for those willing to buy into its values. The issue is what must be sacrificed. In this case, the sacrifice involved is the permanent separation of a daughter from her mother, an event heavily freighted with implications drawn from slavery. Rena's initial distress, then, arises from the conflicting emotional priorities of Warwick's white and her mother's colored worlds. To succeed in passing, Warwick virtually bans sentiment from his personality; for better and for worse, Rena cannot.

But in the second part of the novel, when the focus shifts almost entirely away from Warwick and on to Rena, the demands of a white and a black suitor come to appear—and in practical effect to be—remarkably alike. In the second part, Rena once again leaves home, this time to take up the good work of a teacher of rural black children. That "aspiration for usefulness" turns out to be a defeating, even a dangerous calling. For in her life as schoolteacher, she is even more harshly opened to more or less predatory male designs. Her white former fiancé, Tryon, now more than ever determined to win her—though to what end remains unclear—bribes one of her students so that he can replace the student in walking Rena home. This deception has the effect of exposing her to the pursuit of the corrupt and violent mullato, Wain. Wain's evil motives are clear enough; but Tryon's are at this point obscure, to say the best of them:

> Rena's letter had re-inflamed his smouldering passion; only opposition was needed to fan it to a white heat. Wherein lay the great superiority of his position, if he was denied the right to speak to the one person in the world whom he most cared to address? He felt some dim realization of the tyranny of caste, when he found it not merely pressing upon an inferior people who had no right to expect anything better, but barring his own way to something that he desired. He meant her no harm—but he must see her. He could never marry her now—but he must see her. (P. 238)

Thus Rena becomes the "quarry," and in a scene rendered in terms drawn from the pursuit of a fugitive slave, she is driven by the two approaching males to try hiding herself in a snake-infested swamp and thus ultimately to contracting "brain-fever" and to her death.

By contrast, the one significant darker-skinned male in the novel, Rena's neighbor Frank, who "loves [her] better 'n all de worl'," remains devoted to her throughout the book and at the end rescues her and takes her home to her "mammy" (p. 260). Chesnutt puts into Frank's thoughts what is perhaps the central narrative point of the book:

> White people, with a deeper wisdom perhaps than they used in their own case, regarded Rena and himself as very much alike. They were certainly both made by the same God, in much the same physical and mental mould; they breathed the same air, ate the same food, spoke the same speech, loved and hated, laughed and cried, lived and would die, the same. If God had meant to rear any impassable barrier between people of contrasting complexions, why did He not express the prohibition as He had done between other orders of creation? (P. 255)

And Rena's last words are a benediction on Frank, "My best friend— you loved me best of them all" (p. 264). But even Frank's care cannot save the dying Rena from the impositions of lighter-skinned men. Perhaps the grimmest irony of the book is that Frank's effort to bring Rena home is twice briefly interrupted by white men who think he is abducting a white woman. Those interruptions adumbrate the larger patterns of affliction that characterize Rena's relationships with white or near-white men.

In his contemporaneous series of essays "The Future American," as Sally Ann Ferguson has pointed out, Chesnutt proposes assimilation, indeed absorption, of black or at least lighter-skinned "colored" people into the white majority. "The 'Future American' articles," in Ferguson's accurate summary, "indicate that Chesnutt's ultimate solution to the race problem is a wholesale racial assimilation achieved by the genetic dilution of the black race."[10] So committed is Chesnutt to this notion that he seems willing to sacrifice darker-skinned African Americans, for whom he sees no clear future at all. And yet, it seems to me, in *The House behind the Cedars* Chesnutt not only throws up barrier after barrier to the accomplishment of the end of assimilation, but offers a darker-skinned man as the book's moral anchor. To argue that *House* carries out the theory of racial amalgamation posed in Chesnutt's essays one must insist that Rena's demise is the result of her own failure at the demanding task of crossing the color line; indeed, that that failure is a consequence of her early socialization as a black person, which makes her superstitiously believe in dreams, feel sentimentally attached to her home, and unable to seize the main chance when it is offered to her.[11] The novel, especially seen in the light of Chesnutt's essays, is sufficiently ambiguous to support such a reading. But finally, that reading seems to me to push against much of the internal evidence of the text and also against the history of the story's development.[12]

Indeed, I would argue that the novel's very ambiguities accurately represent Chesnutt's own ambivalence. The white society into which John Walden has successfully passed presents, in the drama of the novel, few redeeming virtues to offset its consuming racism, its "obsession with 'blood and breeding.' "[13] And the black culture, out of which John would lift Rena, while often fallible and ignorant, offers values that constitute far more than nostalgic shards. On the one hand, then, in essays like "The Future American" series, Chesnutt makes an unmistakable if radically flawed argument for a future of racial amalgamation. But, on the other, as he works out the human dimensions of passing and assimilation in *The House behind the Cedars*, they turn out to be much less clearly desirable—or even possible.

That Chesnutt is attempting to work out in fictional terms the political logic of assimilation seems to me suggested by his decision to give up efforts to try to publish the earlier *Mandy Oxendine*.[14] That novel offers attractive and energetic white-appearing characters, Tom Lowrey and Mandy Oxendine, who are able to pursue the means to *personal* advancement to which Chesnutt himself gave credence: education, passing, and moving away from the environment that defined them as "black," preferably to the North.[15] But in this novel, race plays little real role in producing the actions of the plot; rather, the issues fundamentally turn on the burden of female beauty and male predatory passion. In fact, the central plot element, the killing of the most rapacious male, would change little were all the main characters considered "white" in American ideology, as they are in factual appearance. That is, the novel does not, unlike *The House behind the Cedars*, pursue in its core plot the viability of passing as a strategy for collective change in the situation of African Americans. It is not that passing is unimportant in the novel, but what happens to Mandy and to Tom does not emerge from the determination of the former to be accepted as white and the willingness of the latter to be categorized as black. Thus the novel does not centrally address a matter of politics so much as a matter of romantic pursuit and private jealousy.

The Marrow of Tradition is even more explicitly marked by contradiction and agony in its racial politics. For in that novel Chesnutt is trying out differing strategies in the face of one of the most extreme manifestations of southern racist violence: the 1898 assault on the black community of Wilmington, North Carolina. The character of these assaults—mistakenly described as "race riots"—is suggested in the novel by the preparations made for the lynching of Sandy Campbell: "[Ellis] learned that the railroads would run excursions from the neighboring towns in order to bring spectators to the scene; . . . that the burning was to take place early in the evening, so that the children might not be kept up beyond their usual bedtime. In one group that he passed he heard several young men discussing the question of which portions of the negro's body they would prefer for souvenirs" (pp. 219–220). This grisly passage, reflecting as it does the kind of ferocity identified with Captain McBane, may seem out of keeping with the ideas of more cultured and sensitive whites, like the editor, Major Cartaret. But Chesnutt is careful to point out that "McBane's sentiments, in their last analysis, were much the same" as Carteret's, though the latter "would have expressed them less brutally" (p. 87). In fact, as the conspiracy of the whites gains momentum, "Cartaret's thoughts, centering more and more upon the negro, had led him farther and farther, until now he was firmly convinced that there was no permanent place for the negro in the United States, if indeed anywhere in the world, except under the ground" (pp. 244–245). In short, the maturation of Cartaret's thinking emerges as a "final solution" to the negro problem.

In such a context, assimilation is about as relevant a strategy as it turned out to be under the Third Reich; in fact, passing is altogether absent as a viable choice in *The Marrow of Tradition*, though there are individuals who might, under other circumstances, have considered that option. It is as if the very violence of feeling, the ferocity of the whites' assault, has annealed the previously porous color line into a steely barrier. Indeed, the early scene on a train during which Dr. Miller and Dr. Burns are taught by the conductor the "beauty of the system" of segregation (p. 55) suggests an absolutism to American apartheid absent from the earlier *House.* "Consent" is no longer at issue: a person is on one side of the line or on the other, and the only question is how he or she is able to respond to that defining fact of life.

A central theme of the novel, to be sure, is the ironic absurdity of the color line. Separated from his mentor, Dr. Burns, and exiled to the Jim Crow smoking car, Dr. Miller is as uncomfortable with the vile be-havior of the white upstart, Captain McBane, as he is with the jollity of a group of black working people. Janet Miller and Olivia Cartaret re-main sisters in flesh, even if their relationship is never, until the climax of the novel, socially acknowledged—at least among the whites. And most centrally, after Dr. Miller is turned away from Major Cartaret's house on the occasion of Dr. Burns's operation to rescue the Cartarets' son, Dodie, from choking on an old-time rattle, it is only Dr. Miller who can, in the book's final scene, save Dodie from asphyxiation. Thus the plot presses toward the conclusion that only when the color line is breached can the heir of white culture and power be saved, barely, from extinction. But even in this climactic moment the issue is not passing, as such, but Jim Crow as a social and legal system—or, rather, as a force for the radical alteration of southern politics by the elimina-tion of blacks.

Against this brutal, intractable force, Chesnutt deploys a number of representative figures, representative in the sense that they embody alternative political strategies. On the white side, equally ineffectual, are the Quaker, Lee Ellis, and old Mr. Delamere. The first recognizes injustice, but cannot bring himself to side with the blacks (p. 291); the other has "outlasted [his] epoch," a fabled time of honesty and law (p. 211). The black players are more complex: they include Mr. Delamere's loyal servant, Sandy Campbell; the advocates of continued subser-vience, Aunt Jane Letlow and her grandson, Jerry; the representative militant, Josh Green; and the two figures of a presumably rising black middle class, William and Janet Miller. All by any measure lose. Sandy, like Miller, is cheated of his legacy when General Belmont hides De-lamere's new will and ends up as one of Cartaret's servants. Indeed, Sandy's inheritance is transformed from $3,000 to some of his em-ployer's old clothing—a dangerous legacy in the book's plot. Aunt Jane and Jerry, despite their desperate dependence on their white protec-tors, are both slain in the assault. So is Josh Green, as he attempts to lead a spirited if futile defense of the black community. And the Millers' child is killed by a stray bullet as his hospital is being consumed in flames.

The carnage, however widespread, is not undifferentiated. Chesnutt is clearly contemptuous of Negroes like Jerry who would try to maintain the old relationships of servility. But Josh presents a far more complex case. He evokes a mixture of admiration and doubt, apprehension and condescension in Miller: "Here was a negro who could remember an injury, who could shape his life to a definite purpose, if not a high or holy one. When his race reached the point where they would resent a wrong, there was hope that they might soon attain the stage where they would try, and, if need be, die, to defend a right. This man, too, had a purpose in life, and was willing to die that he might accomplish it. Miller was willing to give up his life to a cause. Would he be equally willing, he asked himself, to die for it?" (pp. 112–113).

Chesnutt poses in Josh's succinct dialect some of the book's most aching questions, like that invoked by the biblical injunction to "forgive our enemies": "I've heared de preachers say it time an' time ag'in. But it 'pears ter me dat dis fergitfulniss an' fergivniss is mighty one-sided. De w'ite folks don' fergive nothin' de niggers does. . . . De niggers is be'n train' ter fergiveniss; an' fer fear dey might fergit how ter fergive, de w'ite folks gives 'em somethin' new ev'y now an' den, ter practice on" (p. 113). Or whether to take up arms to defend precisely the rights to political liberty and personal freedom extolled by Miller: "Dese gentlemen [Miller and Watson] may have somethin' ter live fer; but ez fer my pa't, I'd ruther be a dead nigger any day dan a live dog!" (p. 284). Josh dies, of course, in heroic style, but, questions the narrator, "as the fool dieth?" (p. 309). This narrative ambiguity seems to me not only to define Josh's actions as marking a stage, powerful though limited, in the advancement of the black community.[16] It is also a carefully studied response to the time—neither conceding to the conventional but powerful prohibition against black violence toward whites nor altogether endorsing Josh's vengeful motivation or even his success in bringing McBane to a justice otherwise unavailable.

The ambiguities about Dr. Miller, however, strike me as less studied, arising more from a certain ambivalence in Chesnutt's views of Miller's—and his own—role in bringing health to a diseased world. The metaphor of disease and cure is central to the novel. The narrative begins as in a sickroom, with the dangerous birth of Dodie Cartaret; it ends as Dr. Miller mounts the stairs to Dodie's nursery, where the child lies near death from the croup. Dodie's repeated brushes with death are directly the result of outbreaks of that consuming disease of Chesnutt's world: racism. His difficult birth, and his mother's consequent sterility, come about because of Olivia's racist hatred for her sister, Janet; Dodie's choking midway in the book follows carefully on the first efforts of the "Big Three" to impose a racist regime on Wellington. And his nearly fatal croup arises immediately from the racial assault being engineered by his father and his father's coconspirators. In brief, every manifestation of public racism gets reflected—and humanly amplified—in Dodie's illnesses.

Who can cure such disease but a doctor . . . or, as in Chesnutt's first book, a conjurer? Dr. Miller is perfectly situated to deliver such a cure—if only those in need of it can accept its source. But Miller's antagonist here is no narrow, superstitious Scottish farmer, as in *The Conjure Woman*. Rather, it is Cartaret, a writer, an intellectual, a self-declared representative of the new (white) South. He is, in short, not just Miller's, but Chesnutt's, antagonist in the ongoing contest for the conscience of America. For, like Thomas Nelson Page and Thomas Dixon, Cartaret's work is the construction of a particular narrative, promoting white supremacy, about social and political life in the South.

In the novel, Miller "triumphs." For not only must Cartaret humble himself, but, Chesnutt suggests, he sees at least for the moment through his color line ideology to Miller's humanity as a father and his pride as a physician. Further, Dodie's mother, Olivia, must finally accept Janet as her sister, and thus the disintegration of the color barrier, as a condition for Miller's treatment of her son. Only the triumph is singularly qualified. The Millers' own child lies dead. William Miller's hospital, the legacy of his father, is in ashes. Miller's middle-class black friends, however mild, have been driven off if not killed. If Dodie is saved, as likely he will be, is Miller's role so very different from that of Uncle Julius? Is the future of blacks to rescue the future of whites?

Some of the novel's contemporary critics complained that it was an angry book. It was greeted, even by an admirer like William Dean Howells, as "bitter." And it was portrayed, even in a magazine advanced enough to have published Chesnutt's grim story "The Sheriff's Children," as "a novel written apparently by a man with a racial grievance, and for the purpose of exposing conditions rather than to gratify any literary instinct in the author."[17] The novel *is* angry, perhaps even bitter—as well it should be given the conditions that Chesnutt does, indeed, wish to expose. And yet it is also conciliatory, self-limiting, indirect—as well it had to be given the dominance of the racist ideology of plantation fiction and thus the problem of reaching an uninformed audience. Dixon's extremely popular *The Clansman* (1905) would, in little more than a decade, emerge as the even more popular movie *The Birth of a Nation*. *Marrow* is yet to find expression on celluloid. Miller's advice to the men Josh has gathered to fight in defense of their rights, is all too correct—including the final clause: "Our time will come,—the time when we can command respect for our rights; but it is not yet in sight" (p. 283).

Chesnutt had hoped that *The Marrow of Tradition* might become the *Uncle Tom's Cabin* of its era, galvanizing sentiment against the deepening oppression of black people. That it did not says something, no doubt, about the limitations of his plotting and of his typological characterizations. It says something, too, as I have suggested, about the marketplace for racially engaged fiction at the turn of the century. But the failure of Chesnutt's hopes for the book arises, too, from a functional disunity within it. The moral centers of Mrs. Stowe's novel, beginning with Tom himself and Rachel Halliday, are unambiguous. They are not in *Marrow*. To me, that is not a criticism of Chesnutt, but an acknowledgment of the contradictions into which his racial theories, on the one hand, and his narrative imagination, on the other, necessarily led him.

More than Chesnutt's other books, the ending of *The Colonel's Dream* captures—or perhaps is captured by—that dreary fin de siècle tone expressed in Matthew Arnold's lines:

> Wandering between two worlds, one dead
> The other powerless to be born,
> With nowhere yet to rest my head,
> Like these, on earth I wait forlorn.
>   ("Stanzas from the Grand Chartreuse")

The sense of defeat should not be surprising, since the novel is both a summary and chronicle of what is finally Chesnutt's increasing frustration and disillusionment. In returning to his southern boyhood home of Clarendon, the central figure of the book, Colonel French, at first believes that he has rediscovered a genteel, if somewhat indolent, community, needing only some infusion of northern energy—and capital—to transform it into a kind of Utopia. His initial nostalgia gradually erodes as he discovers that the region is, in fact, held in thrall by a New South business type—melodramatically named Fetters—a type that will become more prominent in the novels of Faulkner. French comes to recognize that the often touted combination of northern capital and philanthropy cannot break patterns of dependency and control held in place by legalized peonage, ignorance, systematic violence, and, above all, by the ideology of racism.

French finds himself becoming a social reformer, even though he maintains the fundamental outlook of a successful capitalist and a functional condescension toward black people. By the conclusion of the book, he is no longer naive, perhaps not even idealistic. But he is defeated. His son is dead; the coffin of his old retainer, Peter, has been dug up from the family plot where the colonel had buried him; his plans for a textile mill which will transform the economy and thus the society of Clarendon are abandoned. To all intents and purposes, he leaves the field to Fetters and his cronies.

This chronicle of the colonel's defeat reflects Chesnutt's, for as William Andrews has pointed out, the writer shared virtually all of his character's beliefs in liberal reform: "capital investment, industrial stimulation and expansion, educational modernization, white philanthropy and black self-help projects, quiet diplomacy and public civil rights litigation."[18] But at another level, one must wonder whether what is being called into question is less a reform agenda than the fundamental values of turn-of-the-century American society—including those of success and financial advancement Chesnutt clearly subscribed to. The writer postpones an actual meeting between the colonel and Fetters until fairly late in the novel, and when French—as well as the reader—finally does come face to face with his antagonist he turns out to look not like a fungus, a vampire, or even a redneck, as earlier images suggest, but like "any one of a hundred business men whom the colonel might have met on Broadway in any given fifteen minutes during business hours" (p. 223). Indeed, he and the colonel share certain bottom-line values having to do with running one's own business and making profits. To be sure, Fetters can conceive of no other standards to govern his conduct; whereas the colonel comes to question "the very standards of right and wrong [which] had been confused by the race issue, and must be set right by the patient appeal to reason and humanity." Indeed, contrasted with the Presbyterian minister, who is a believer in the "final solution" to the Negro problem (p. 164), Colonel French is very much a progressive: "I am rather inclined to think that these people have a future; that there is a place for them here; that they have made fair progress under discouraging circumstances; that they will not disappear from our midst for many generations, if ever; and that in the meantime, as we make or mar them, we shall make or mar our civilisation" (p. 165). So far, reasonable enough. But as the colonel's long speech goes on, one must come to wonder if this is Chesnutt's portrait of whites at their best, and if that is the case, whether it is precisely French's commitments to marketplace values as well as to racial hierarchies that defeat him: "They constitute the bulk of our laboring class. To teach them is to make their labor more effective and therefore more profitable; to increase their needs is to increase our profits in supplying them. I'll take my chances on the Golden Rule." (One cannot but stop and wonder which rule the colonel really means: that of the Bible or that which holds he with the gold rules.) "But they are here, through no fault of theirs, as we are. They were born here. We have given them our language—which they speak more or less corruptly; our religion—which they practise certainly no better than we; and our blood—which our laws make a badge of disgrace. Perhaps we could not do them strict justice, without a great sacrifice on our own part. But they are men, and they should have their chance—at least *some* chance" (p. 165). Colonel French is an energetic and attractive man; his aspirations remain admirable and his defeats, however melodramatic, are moving. Yet their inevitability cannot be attributed simply to the intransigent backwardness of southern society. What French cannot articulate, and what perhaps Chesnutt himself could then not either, is a vision of true equality before the law and of human rights independent of marketplace values. But then, it would be over a decade before W. E. B. Du Bois would write "Of Work and Wealth." And one would be hard pressed to argue that such a vision is afoot even in twenty-first-century America. In short, what keeps welling to the surface of this novel is the question of whether the problems of the South, including the problem of the color line, can at all be resolved within the framework of economic capitalism to which French, like his creator, remains committed. Chesnutt hoped that this book, too, would be successful in the marketplace and by so being would influence significant numbers of Americans to alter their attitudes toward caste and perhaps class. But in the time in which he wrote, such success would apparently be predicated on values quite the opposite of those that he aspired to promote.

One can, I think, draw certain lessons from the rise and fall of Chesnutt's aspirations both to financial success as a writer and to social transformation as a literary objective. It seems to me that, in the first place, a writer aiming at social change must speak from a unified vision. Mixed messages, perhaps even indirection, confuse the issues. It is not, I would argue, that such writing needs to be simple-minded, but it cannot be fundamentally contradictory—trying to maintain one set of abstract values while dramatizing their limits and failures in the narrative.

Second, a writer may accelerate the pace of change, or perhaps give particular direction to a movement under way. One climbs the parapet and with a series of literary gestures directs the already moving crowd toward a newly seen objective. But if the crowd is not in motion, a writer gestures in vain, appearing to those who look engaged in some self-consuming dumb show to be greeted with derision or indifference.

Chesnutt had the bad luck to be writing against racial oppression just as a tide of segregation and violence was cresting: "Post-Bellum, Pre-Harlem," as he was to entitle a late article. And he had the defects of his virtues: a powerful narrative imagination that could not be held within the bounds of a fragile progressive ideology. Out of such conflicts arise the silences to which the last quarter century of his life give such eloquent testimony.

PART THREE ★ REVISITING THE CANON:
THE QUESTION OF MODERNISM

When I initially wrote these essays, I wanted to revisit some of the issues regarding the American literary canon that constituted a central part of my last book, *Canons and Contexts*. It seemed useful to do so, first, because my own work has been devoted to the canon-challenging *Heath Anthology of American Literature,* but also, and especially, because I was rebellious at the general consensus among literary types that canon theory isn't real "theory" at all. In fact it is notable primarily by its absence from the variety of handbooks, guides, and histories that now map the territory seen as legitimate for critical exploration. For example, Charles E. Bressler's *Literary Criticism: An Introduction to Theory and Practice* (Prentice-Hall, 1994) offers snapshots of the known species of criticism at their play. The volume contains in its glossary terms like "castration complex," "efferent reading," "monomyth," and "poem"—a word undoubtedly in need of gloss—as well as sections, predictably, on New Criticism, deconstruction, New Historicism, among, to quote the cover copy, the "eight basic schools of literary criticism developed and heralded in the twentieth century." But nary a reference—at least so far as I or the indexer could tell—to the question of the canon or anything, like "contingencies of value," "cultural relativism," judgment, or even curriculum, distinctively related to canon issues. And while I enjoyed the book's explanations of marvels like "phonocentrism," "anal stage," and "latent content," I could not help but experience a certain dissociation here from what I do for a living, that is, figure out what, why, and how to teach students.

I had once devoted a whole paper at an MLA convention (from which some of the above is purloined) to tracking out the paradox that while canon questions are central to our lives as professionals, the question of the canon remains marginalized as a subject in the higher reaches of literary study. But gradually it occurred to me that the margin occupied by the question of the canon is precisely that of the borderland between literary and American studies. The issues it engages are not so much those of formal textual study as those of the impact on what we read, teach, and value of institutions like publishing and education, of professional status and power, of anthologies and the organization of the professoriat. These are not matters of indifference to literary scholars; neither are they central, the meat and potatoes of English departments. For every course on canon study, I can probably find you dozens, more likely hundreds, on deconstruction, feminist or Marxist criticism. Since this is a book on American studies, it came to seem to me best to view canon issues from that side of the border, dealing with literary figures (like Melville and Lowell—unlikely pair) and professional phenomena (like the *Heath Anthology* and *Understanding Poetry*—another unlikely pair) as evidence of processes of cultural change.

It further occurred to me that what I had to say on this subject really centered on the variety of ways in which conceptions of literary modernism had been constructed between the early decades of the twentieth century and the 1950s. No surprise, for the paradigms of modernism on which I was brought up constituted the dominant lens through which generations of teachers perceived literary study. So this has become a section whose subject focus is literary modernism, but whose concern remains how reputations and cultural values are constructed and how these are embodied in institutions like anthologies and curricula.

CHAPTER NINE
**REFLECTING
ON THE *HEATH
ANTHOLOGY
OF AMERICAN
LITERATURE***

In 1968 a group of us, radical and liberal intellectuals, mounted an effort to stir up the Modern Language Association and thus, we modestly believed, change the literary profession. We organized a series of meetings before and during the annual convention in New York, set up what we called a "tactics committee," which met three or four times a day, picketed one of the big MLA forums, and plastered some posters on the walls of the old hotel Americana. As I recall, one of them featured a picture of Eldridge Cleaver with a legend under it saying "I got my job through the *New York Times*"; another quoted Blake to the effect that "the tygers of wrath are wiser than the horses of instruction." Three of our number, including Louis Kampf, were arrested for trying to keep the hotel's security from tearing the posters off the Americana's marbelized walls, and that led to a brief sit-in in the hotel lobby, the arrival of New York's TAC Squad, and protracted negotiations with the MLA's brass.

We also introduced a series of motions into the association business meeting: one called for ending the Vietnam War, another for *not* holding the following year's meeting in Chicago. We voted all of those motions in, voted to set up a Commission on the Status of Women, and even elected Kampf to be second vice president, and thus to succeed to the MLA presidency in two years. In fact, the only vote we lost was one which called upon the MLA to stop supporting the Center for Editions of American Authors, which was engaged in publishing elaborate scholarly editions of the standard—that is, entirely white and male—American writers. The Association's members, it became clear, were quite willing to end the war—by way of passing a resolution, at least—or to forgo the pleasures of Chicago in late December, but when it came to the meat and potatoes issue of closing off a conduit to government funds and scholarly assignments . . . later, much later, for that. In vain, we argued that what we really needed were basic editions of less well-known authors. In vain, we asked "Where are the blacks?" "Where are the women?" Scholarship, we were told in those more innocent days, was scholarship, and politics was politics. Why would we insist on mixing them?

As I say, we lost that vote. But it got us to thinking: what would have to be done to change the profession sufficiently so that the idea of performing scholarship on minority and white women writers would not seem so outrageous to a majority of our colleagues? And what would have to be done so that those of us interested in learning more about and in teaching such writers might be able to do so? After all, while some of us knew a bit about writers like Frederick Douglass, Mary Wilkins Freeman, Charles Chesnutt, and Paule Marshall, and while a few of their books were actually in print, most of us had never heard of Harriet Jacobs or Lydia Maria Child or Agnes Smedley or Zora Neale Hurston, much less taught them—or, for that matter, taught Harriet Beecher Stowe, well-known, to be sure, but quite outside the pale. These writers inhabited neither our scholarly consciousness nor our college textbooks—not even our graduate school reading lists, much less that pedagogical Bible, the *Norton Anthology*. What was to be done?

I certainly had no ready answer in 1968, though it did occur to me that a collection which contained the work of such authors might be useful. But I was too ignorant, even about who they might all be, and too uninformed about how the publishing industry operated even to think seriously about such a project. What I did know, what I had learned from working earlier in the labor movement and in the peace movement, was that change did not simply happen: it had to be organized, and not just by one or two people operating alone, but by many of us, learning and working together. So, with others in 1968, I began to toil in what we eventually called the Radical Caucus in English and the Modern Languages,[1] and, soon, in The Feminist Press. We began by circulating syllabi for changed courses, and by starting to publish lost or forgotten works like "The Yellow Wallpaper" and "Life in the Iron Mills." We were part of a broader intellectual movement, which gained momentum through the 1970s. It was a movement to rewrite history, literary and otherwise, to begin including those who had been pushed to the cultural bottom, or at least out of the sight of traditional scholars. It was a movement which, in the course of a decade fundamentally transformed the intellectual work of a whole generation of academics.

But the pace of change was slow. By the end of the decade of the seventies some courses at some schools had begun to incorporate some "new"—by which was generally meant "old"—writers, but usually not that many. And the changes, like those in personnel occasioned by efforts at "affirmative action," were mostly cosmetic: the basic premises and structures of most courses and most departments remained unaltered. I felt a responsibility to work at what I knew—the part of our discipline we called, however inaccurately, "American literature." It seemed to me that the new scholarship had proceeded sufficiently far, and the changes in at least some courses were sufficiently interesting, to provide the basis for an effort that might help produce at least a small leap ahead. So in 1978, with others in The Feminist Press, I began working on a proposal to the federal Fund for the Improvement of Post-Secondary Education to finance a project which we came, modestly, to call "Reconstructing American Literature." There was a certain charming irony in obtaining a grant from FIPSE to do this work since the agency was a creation of the Nixon administration, not precisely a fountainhead for social change.

Earlier, my own scholarly and political interests in the literary canon had led me to explore the processes by which the discipline of American literature had first been established in the 1920s. I found that the men—they *were* almost all men and white—who had developed it had, more or less consciously, pursued an interesting organizing program, involving the creation of an academic network, founding a magazine, producing a statement of ideology, and publishing a set of teaching tools in the form of anthologies. It seemed to me that we might use how they had worked as a model to alter what they had set in place, for the results of their efforts were still largely with us into the 1970s. The FIPSE proposal asked for money to accomplish a set of reasonably well-defined tasks, but underlying these was, I think, a distinct political agenda. We planned to collect and publish syllabi and other course materials, to hold an institute to explore practical and theoretical issues involved in change in the canon, and finally—so our program officer, Richard Hendrix, convinced us—to begin work on what might become a new and significantly different anthology of American literature. But what we really wanted to do was develop a network of people devoted to change, to bring them into working relationships with one another, to provide them with tools they might use to pursue their work, and thus to build an active force committed to a new definition of American culture within the academy.

I have some fancy names for the processes by which, my research had suggested, those who had established "American literature" in the 1920s had worked, and which we, in our own way, wished to utilize: literary archaeology, theoretical reconstruction, professional organization, and institutional establishment. By "literary archaeology" I mean simply the rediscovery of texts that had been, for whatever reasons, lost to sight. That was an effort beginning to go on all over the country in the late 1960s and early 1970s: at the Women's Herstory Archive, at the Black Periodical and Black Fiction projects, in the process of transcribing from the walls of Angel Island the poetic inscriptions left there by Chinese workmen, in the efforts to locate and examine the content of nineteenth-century Indian and Latino newspapers and magazines. The now-defunct Reprints Committee at The Feminist Press provided one center for such activity. Toward such ends, alternative publishing enterprises were established, among many others, KNOW, Inc., Mnemosyne, and Arte Publico. More commercial ventures like Arno were also designed to provide students and other curious readers with previously "lost" or discarded texts, usually in the form of individual volumes containing single works like Rebecca Harding Davis's *Life in the Iron Mills,* William Wells Brown's *Clotelle,* or Susan Warner's *The Wide, Wide World.* That work is still going on, as is illustrated by the recent publication of works like the novels of Frances Ellen Watkins Harper,[2] *The Squatter and the Don*,[3] and poetry by long-forgotten nineteenth-century women writers.[4] Without this broad, participatory effort, nothing of what we were trying to do would have been possible for, as the old political adage has it, "You can't beat somethin' with nothin.'" The American literature scholars of the 1920s had, so to speak, beaten Longfellow with Dickinson, Holmes with Whitman, and Alice Cary with Melville. Our task was not so much to put down the white, mostly male canon as to discover whether there were, out there in literary limbo, writers of merit we might wish to know more about and share with our students. Needless to say, there were—and they have continued to emerge: Judith Sargent Murray, Cary, Harriet Wilson, Mariano Vallejo, Zitkala-Sa, Sui Sin Far, Carlos Bulosan.

That the names I have mentioned are those of women or of minority men comes, I am sure, as no surprise. For many of those out in that limbo were such people. Whether their placement at the margins could be explained simply on the basis of the fact that they were female or persons of color was more problematic. Surely, we argued, racism and patriarchy played a role in their devaluation. "Perhaps," others responded, "but can you be certain that *only* prejudice was involved? Are there not also questions of objective literary standards?" Such questions, like the rediscovered texts themselves, raised important theoretical issues. Those of us interested in change had to ask whether the standards by which works had been valued were themselves, to borrow the phrase of one early Radical Caucus member, "free, classless, and urbane," or whether such standards were expressions of particular, and limited, cultural and social interests. We were forced to articulate the bases on which we were prepared to canonize texts—or at least to include them in syllabi, reading lists, and anthologies. Writers like Kate Millett, Nina Baym, and Annette Kolodny were among the first to deconstruct the assumptions, about the fundamental importance of the search motif, for example, which helped validate the texts that students had traditionally been taught were most significant. But we also had to begin articulating and arguing for alternative standards.

I have described the principles of selection of those of us involved in the *Heath Anthology of American Literature* in some detail in the preface to the first edition of that work. Here I want to emphasize two: what one might call "difference" and "representation." They are connected. Because no syllabus, no reading list, no anthology can contain *all* the writers of interest, one is always making choices about who to include and who to drop. Long after they were out of fashion, the schoolroom poets like Longfellow and James Russell Lowell continued to be found in classes basically as representatives of a significant nineteenth-century poetic phenomenon. But that decision begged the question of what *was* and remained significant. What about the widely read domestic fictions of the mid-century or the distinctively American tradition of slave narratives? To find such texts of deep interest, as many Americanists began to do, inevitably raised questions about why. To include Charles Chesnutt, Mary Wilkins Freeman, and Sarah Orne Jewett in an American literature course, and not Henry James, as I did in my "American Voices" at Old Westbury, generated yet another set of issues.

Participants in the Reconstructing American Literature institute we held at Yale in 1982 debated these issues at some length. That meeting was obviously only one site of the ongoing effort to redefine the standards for determining curricular choices and, behind them, canons. The scholars and critics of the 1920s had emphasized American literary texts that seemed to them to embody the growing importance of the United States in an otherwise declining world and the increasing complexity of modern times. Thus their canon stressed what they took to be strong, masculine virtues in plot and theme as well as density in texture and, on the whole, a clerical pessimism in outlook. In putting together the *Heath,* we wished to represent what we perceived to be the rich diversity of American cultures, the significance of gender, race, and class to the shaping and reception of literary texts. And we wished to recontextualize culture, to reconnect literature and its study with the society of which it is fundamentally a part, to underline the often lengthy historical development of the many voices that constitute the American chorus, and to ask how texts "worked" in their world and continue to work in ours. Difference rather than nationalism came to be our touchstone, and a conception of writing as simply one among many valid forms of culture rather than as a set of more or less sacred texts.

These last few sentences amount to the briefest encapsulation of the kind of theoretical reconstruction entailed by the shift in textual focus, which was in its turn generated by the questions—such as "Where are the blacks?" "Where are the women?"—posed by the movements for social change of the sixties. But theory without practice is sterile. The question that haunted that Yale institute was how we might transform our work as teachers and writers. Because we were concerned with *difference,* we—and especially those of us who were white and male—could rely neither on our graduate school training, which had been focused on the "mainstream," nor on our professional networks, which remained largely homogeneous. Indeed, even among the women and the minority men at the institute, such problems obtained, for their closest peers tended to be people much like themselves. It rapidly became clear that precisely the professional individualism that the whole course of our education in America had taught us to treasure was, in fact, a major part of the problem. The solution, then, was to break from individualistic or mainstream paradigms of work and to seek, rather, collective and representative forms.

Since the next step in the Reconstructing American Literature project was to begin work on a new anthology of American literature, it seemed appropriate to put that idea into practice immediately. Studying the processes by which previous anthologies had been developed, I had found that in all the dozens of them, no person of color had ever served on an editorial board and but one or two women. We decided, by contrast, to make sure that the editorial board for this anthology would be as evenly balanced between men and women and between white and minority scholars as we could make it. Representation might not ensure diversity; but lack of representation, uniform experience in education taught us, ensured homogeneity. But even a representative board, we realized, would still not have the scope fully to carry out the project implicit in the words "reconstructing American literature." One of the institute participants, Margaret O'Connor of the University of North Carolina, suggested that a way out of that problem was to turn to the profession at large. Rather than have the editorial board, however diverse, perform the whole process of selection, she proposed, ask everyone interested in American literature for suggestions about which writers to include. They might also then be recruited to write headnotes and to provide the scholarly apparatus for their writers as well.

The idea, while a bureaucratic nightmare (it forced me to become computer-literate), had immediate practical as well as theoretical appeal. Such a procedure not only involved a large number of colleagues across the country in the project, but helped generate precisely the peer network necessary for its success. Together with a series of workshops, sessions at professional conferences, and similar efforts, it helped both to overcome the isolation that people interested in change often feel within their own institutions and to develop the sense of movement so critical to carrying out any new effort: at conferences, you met other people working on the project, you found colleagues whose work you valued also involved. You sensed yourself to be not an isolated scholar doing your own thing at the word processor or even in your closed classroom, but a part of an ongoing movement for change, a movement you could participate in, indeed influence. I would not argue that this Reconstructing American Literature project constituted the movement for change in the American canon; by definition, no single project *is* a movement. But the collective effort it represented helped, I think, to provide momentum and point to what had been going on more broadly in our sector of the profession.

Ironically, perhaps, this process of organizing the work turned out to have considerable commercial value as well, and it is worth briefly considering that phenomenon. I had originally seen the project not as a cultural venture with commercial potential but as a progressive tool for encouraging and supporting curricular change by my peers, for pressuring the creators of existing anthologies to alter their books, which they had been doing marginally, at best. In fact, one key part of the project—for which we were actually funded—was compiling, editing, and publishing a collection of syllabi of significantly "reconstructed" courses.[5] Such syllabi, we had found in the early days of the academic women's movement, were critical in supporting the development of a new discipline, women's studies, as well as in fostering feminist change within existing disciplines like English, history, and psychology. Still, I was apprehensive that our goals for a new anthology could be compromised by a publisher's commercial priorities. Richard Hendrix, the FIPSE program officer, was far more optimistic than I about the possibility of actually creating and successfully marketing a serious revisionist anthology. I saw the project as expressing and helping implement a cause; he perhaps recognized that, especially as we turned toward the eighties, causes needed to be sold as systematically as Ben and Jerry's ice cream. I viewed my role—at least in the beginning—as organizing other faculty members; I had been doing that for years, but this time the goals involved curricula and culture, not unions or peace or, directly, civil rights. He may have seen that there was less conflict between our organizing objectives and the commercial interests of a textbook house. At any rate, that is how it turned out.

Or, more accurately, the processes of organizing the field became virtually indistinguishable from those of creating a market for the anthology. While I had not realized that editing an author for an anthology would constitute an academically significant credential, it soon became apparent that having hundreds of our colleagues thus working *on* the anthology would go a long way to making it likely that hundreds would *use* it. At the same time, the commercial interests of the publisher became virtually indistinguishable from the promotion of our cause, which I would loosely characterize as multiculturalism. For example, the marketing division of D. C. Heath invented the idea of publishing a twice-yearly *Heath Anthology Newsletter*, which even before the anthology had been published became a significant means for promoting educationally progressive ideas as well as for transmitting concrete information about implementing a "multicultural" curriculum. In fact, the *Newsletter* became the most widely circulated "journal" in the field, thus lending further stature both to the anthology and to its cultural politics. That anything—perhaps short of overthrowing the power relationships of class in America—can profitably be sold is, of course, a cliché of contemporary capitalism. Yet one of the more interesting features of this project for me remains the rapidity with which the borders between commerce and cause became indistinct.

How to understand that? One might argue, of course, that the *Heath*'s departures from the norms of anthologies, that our "reforms," are essentially so minor that they have easily been coopted.[6] It is true that one *could* use the anthology to teach a perfectly traditional course in American literature. Very unlikely, to be sure, but possible. The anthology is also, to be sure, a commodity. Still, in the real world where it is bought, sold, and used, it has become more than that. In fact, the *Heath* has emerged not only as a practical revisionary classroom tool and a successful commercial enterprise (it seems to have become the largest-selling American literature anthology), but also as a cultural symbol. Its symbolic meanings became clearer to me when we were engaged in the first revision.

My initial concerns when we were working on that revision in 1992 were how the volumes were getting used and what, precisely, was to be in them. But as I began to think less about such pragmatic matters and to consider what the *Heath* had come to signify—both for those who approved of it and for those who did not—a new train of thinking began to open to me. I had been told—and indeed discovered for myself in interviews six or seven years ago—that some faculty were presenting use of the *Heath* in their courses as a covert symbol of being in tune with the latest professional developments. On the other hand, Fred Crews offered the *Heath* in some deluded remarks in a 1992 issue of *New York Review of Books* as the sole representative (apart from Donald Pease) he was willing to name of what he condemned about "new Americanists." In both cases the anthology was being deployed as a sign, the real content of which, I want to propose, involves a diffusion of cultural authority, a matter for applause by some, and censure by others. That is paradoxical, since whatever else it may be, an anthology is, as I have suggested, one form of codifying culture. In fact, to use the terminology I introduced above, I would describe the anthology as one of the forms of "institutional establishment" the movement for canon change has produced. At the same time, it seemed to me that the *Heath* had come to be identified with processes which have powerfully been altering the sources of cultural authority: within the academic world, the warrant of senior faculty has been eroding, as, indeed, has the influence *of* the academy in relation to other centers of cultural power. In order to carry out this argument, I want, first, to propose a modest historical framework, and then to look at the implications of the specific editorial practices that produced the anthology.

I have contended elsewhere that around the time of World War I a significant shift in cultural authority took place.[7] Certain networks, like those represented by women's literary clubs and by magazines directed to what came to be called "genteel" audiences, lost influence, whereas certain others, including decisively the academic world, gained in power. The consolidation and expansion of university cultural dominion took place, of course, after the Second World War, with the wild growth of colleges and universities, first under the GI Bill and later during the sixties. The scope of that dominion can be inferred from the extent to which, by the 1980s, the road to writing—or musical or even artistic—success ran through academic programs, and the legitimation of books of fiction or poetry depended upon the approval of academically based critics. There were countertrends, of course, like the fifties Beats in San Francisco and New York, but even many of them came, at last, to rest, or at least to reside, within the academy. And it should be obvious, as well, that such an historic design fits much less well people of color, whether musicians like Charlie Parker or John Coltrane, or poets like Etheridge Knight and Gwendolyn Brooks. Nor would I argue that the academy—whatever one means by that capacious term—succeeded in every case in imposing a hegemonic view of culture on those it paid or certificated. Nevertheless, precisely because it was able to absorb so many of those who produced or sanctified culture, even those who might violently disagree with one another, the academy became *the* institutional authority of cultural legitimacy in mid-twentieth-century America.

No wonder, then, that *what* and *how* the academy taught took on great, I would say for a time unrivaled, cultural weight. As has often been documented, the academy's "what" and "how" constituted a relatively narrow section of the cultural body. This is not a point I wish to belabor here, but consider the fact that in my own training at NYU, Indiana, and Yale, I read only three black writers, and not a great many more women of any color; that in my music minor, I studied the songs of Schubert and Mahler, but never "spirituals," much less *corridos,* that I listened to Bach on the university's recordings, but to bop only under the comforter of my bed. I carried these assumptions about legitimacy—for that is what they were—into my own teaching well into the 1960s. And I was, I dare say, somewhat advanced. To look at the American literature anthologies available even well into the 1970s is to see just how narrow that cultural slice had become. Moreover, the dominant teaching methodologies of that period—and, in some degree, of this—*explication de texte,* myth and symbol analysis, and the like, formalism, in short, helped sustain perhaps more than anything else the authoritative power of the university-trained critic. This "how" and this "what" had, I want to emphasize, largely been set in place by the 1950s, by historically documentable processes connected with the cold war. I am not arguing that American colleges and universities imposed a unified, narrow cultural "line" upon our students during the 1950s, 1960s, and 1970s. I do claim that, vested with enormous cultural authority, universities and colleges fostered a central set of understandings about what was culturally significant and how that might best be apprehended, what I will call an "imperial" version of American culture. Moreover, they promoted the conviction that institutions of higher education themselves were and ought to be society's primary arbiters of cultural legitimacy. They exercised, in short, significant cultural *hegemony*, as we have come to understand that term.

But the story does not end there. For where once from hour to hour the academy did ripe and ripe, now, as the squalor of most campuses signifies, it rots and rots. And thereby hangs my tale. For there arose in the land those who knew not Clark Kerr, nor yet Lionel Trilling. For whom universities meant little more than a stamp on one's life passport—important but not all that serious. For whom the flickering screen, the boom box, the Boss, and the Dead—not to say the Pistols, the Michaels, Madonna, Chuck-D, Ice-T, the Nike ads, and (God save the mark) Roseanne—defined the shape of culture. And the color of money. There arose, to be brief and academic, alternative sources of cultural authority from the entertainment industry and the media more generally. Their endorsement by the young found a significant echo *within* the academy particularly, as Richard Yarborough pointed out to me years ago, among those practicing what is now called "cultural studies," foremost among them African American scholars, who had always constructed a far broader conception of what constituted "culture" than the mainstream academy was willing to admit. These forces, external and within, have challenged the sway of academe and its allies precisely at a time in which the role of universities in the political economy of the United States is undergoing a redefinition as profound as that which reshaped colleges and universities seventy-five years ago. The functions of higher education are shifting, rapidly and decisively, as I argue elsewhere in this book. In that process, the cultural and ideological power of the academy has been eroding, its authority in these realms being undermined. It is in such a historical context that I wish to place the ways in which the *Heath Anthology* came in the early 1990s to signify.

What it signified was, in ways that I did not initially appreciate, deeply implicated in how we organized the Reconstructing American Literature project that led to the book's publication. In the past, anthologies in general, including those in American literature, were put together by very small groups of men with sufficient standing in the academic profession to have what they produced accepted by their peers. The preeminent examples in American literature are probably the anthologies developed by Norman Foerster, which went through something like twelve editions, and the Bradley, Beatty, and Long volumes, which—with the more recent supervention of George Perkins— have migrated over seven or eight editions from Grosset and Dunlap, to Norton, to Random House and now, I believe, to McGraw-Hill. The editorial group was seldom very large; in fact, I have sometimes suspected that publishers looked for a cadence like that set by the old Chicago White Sox double-play combination, with its resonance of "good" family names: Tinker to Evers to Chance. It was only with the advent of more recent anthologies that editorial boards swelled to six and then seven, and some less decorous names were admitted. In fact, I was told by an old publishing hand when I was organizing the *Heath* editorial group that I would add a year to the time before publication with every person I took on to the board.

Nevertheless, I put together a board that has hovered around fourteen. They were the most diverse group, in terms of race, gender, and even geography, that had been assembled for such an editorial task. I chose them because of their expertise in the multiplying fields into which what we call "American literature" has increasingly been subdivided. But I also chose them on two other grounds: first, because I had reason to think that they would speak out for the somewhat differing interests entailed in their deep commitments *to* particular areas of expertise and thus to particular populations that have actually constituted multicultural America. In addition, it seemed to me that because they were trained as academics, their—our—very identities, the subject-positions from which we spoke, were multiple and fluid, rather than narrowly particularist—if I may use that term to express an academic version of identity politics. That proved to be the case, and I have come to think that it was critical to the success of the editorial process.

No anthology, after all, just as no syllabus and no museum, can contain everything one wishes it to contain. One therefore must make choices. If the anthology were, for example, to include not only a significant selection of Stowe, but also work by Harriet Jacobs, Frances Harper, and Alice Cary—none of whom had been admitted to an American literature anthology—someone else would not be included. One makes such decisions either on the basis of established tradition— that is, one does what has more or less been done before—or on the basis of struggle—that is, by a process which brings assumptions about cultural value into conflict. Obviously, we chose the latter course— significantly but not absolutely inflected, to be sure, by our and D. C. Heath's reading of the market. Implementing that model of struggle demanded not only that many editorial board members be advocates of particular cultures but that they *not* be so particularist as to prevent our reproduction in meetings and in the anthology of the engagement and interpenetration of cultures which has so characterized what Randolph Bourne called "trans-national America." It was not only that we were always being asked, in effect, to put our professional reputations on the line, and to bring into question the prior training that, for someone like myself, made it difficult to accommodate writers like Harper, or Lydia Maria Child, or John Rollin Ridge. But also, and as critically, to accomplish our goals we needed to surrender the imperial organization of culture to which we had been trained without falling into, for the purposes of our anthology, limiting particularisms. Limiting, because, mirroring the imperial version of culture, they would defensively portray American cultures as altogether separable, distinct entities rather than as dynamically interactive, yet differing hybrids.

I want to emphasize this part of the process, for it models in its small way changes in the public sphere that have been called "multiculturalism." The assumptions that a significant number of the editorial board members had started with were, I think, those of the hegemonic academy I sketched before, what I have called an "imperial" account of American culture. That is, some of us assumed that "newer" writers (however old they were) would be assimilated to, melted into the cultural norms—perhaps slightly modified—of our earlier training. We learned, in fact, that that "melting pot" paradigm could not usefully function any more in the creation of an anthology than in the sustenance of a late twentieth-century democracy. We had no alternative metaphor—the salad bowl came up, but for good reasons did not take—but we worked toward what I have called "comparative" versions of American cultures, in which the emphasis is upon accounting for difference and understanding change. My verbs here—"learned" and "worked," for example—do not convey the difficult, often conflicted, and seldom neatly resolved transactions by which we arrived at settlements, compromises, or at least termini needed to publish an actually existing anthology.

Still, while the size, diversity, and character of the editorial board were unique, that was not the innovation which, in my thinking, has produced the *Heath's* primary character as a signifier. As I have said, at the 1982 Reconstructing American Literature institute, Margaret O'Connor had proposed that we depend not upon the expertise of even a large and varied editorial board, but that we write to everyone we could reach in the profession to ask what *they* wanted to see in the anthology. Good Sixties rhetoric: "Ask not what your anthology can do for you. . . ." That process enabled us to reach out to the mass of younger faculty and graduate students who stood on the threshold of the profession, as well as to many scholars of color and white women who had not had much recognition within it. We were therefore able to tap into their knowledge, as well as their energy and commitment. And, perhaps equally to the point, it enabled us to reach *past* those levels of the profession that have generally been determinative in structuring curricula and producing anthologies. I do not want to be read as suggesting that those upper levels of the profession were backward or necessarily hostile to the goals of the Reconstructing American Literature project. Many were not. But like *some* of us on the editorial board, most of *them* had been disciplined to an academic culture which, whatever else it taught, asserted the cultural authority of the academic enterprise.

Many younger people, on the other hand, and others the academy had marginalized approached its verities with scepticism, and a certain contentiousness. In the first place, it was not at all clear that they would ever have regular academic positions, and if they did, the jobs would not have the tweedy character an older generation had been taught to expect. Second, the younger professional generation (younger, that is, when we began) had come of age at a time in which Bob Dylan spoke as much to their condition as Dylan Thomas, the Jefferson Airplane as much as the Jefferson legacy; they were more likely to have been brought up on James Brown than on Tom Brown, and to prefer the cadences of Jimi Hendrix to those of Henry James. They doubted—correctly, I believe—the ability of academic knowledge as conventionally defined to explain, much less to rectify, the world they might, or might not, ever come to inherit. They stood, as it were, straddling what would become a widening divide between an academy that had become increasingly self-referential and self-promotional and the alternative sources of cultural authority. While these could be frankly, even grossly, commercial, they told something more about the truths of racism, environmental degeneration, privilege, and war than one might learn in the school. Sometimes, indeed, they offered up models of resistance to the commodification of knowledge, which has so deeply affected all American institutions, the academy not least among them.

For such a constituency, I suspect, both the *process* of the *Heath* and the *product* signified. The participatory process, however imperfect, deconstructed inhospitable assumptions about academic authority. It was not precisely that the *Heath* "belonged" to them—indeed, it then belonged to Raytheon, of all companies—but that seemed to matter less to a generation enlightened about the commercial exploitation of anything short of the Final Solution. The issue was what one could *do* with such a product. Here, certain quite commercial tools, like the semiannual newsletter and electronic means for exchanging syllabi and teaching ideas suggested how open to possession and repossession the anthology was. Moreover, the inclusiveness of the volumes and their insistent historicism were enabling of the desire to understand the dynamics of cultural change—and exchange—that even sophisticated formalisms had abandoned. Besides, what most offended traditionalists, such as the inclusion of "The Signifying Monkey," spoke to those wishing to poke through academic pretension and its self-defeating separation from the dynamism of popular culture.

I will not claim that I, or anyone on the editorial board or at D. C. Heath, fully understood these dynamics as we worked up the final version of the anthology or even as we came to revise it. But I do think this account goes some way toward explaining why the *Heath Anthology* came to signify—indeed, to promote—a diffusion of cultural authority, both for those who abhor the decline of academic cultural power, and for those who welcome what they see not as a decline but as a socially healthy redistribution of cultural capital.

But, one might ask, so what? Is the kind of American literature or even cultural studies course one teaches a matter of significance? Will it rebuild community in Los Angeles, much less diminish the fissures still prominent in American society? Will it even promote literacy among those who get to college, much less among those daily pushed out of schools into the streets of the 'hood or into a prison system now absorbing more of state budgets than higher education? No serious person could answer such questions with a simple "yes." And yet, as the attacks on the anthology from the Right suggest, something more is at stake here than publishing profits or minor rearrangements of the cultural landscape. The question of what we teach cannot be separated from what we value, and therefore, I would argue, from our values. To value writers who have largely been marginalized is at some level to call into question the cultural order and thus the social boundaries upon which that process of marginalization has been based.

These connections were imprinted upon my consciousness one searing afternoon in July of 1967. I was directing the first functioning community school project in the country, at the Morgan Elementary School in Washington, D.C. We were halfway through an intense and conflicted institute for the teachers and interns who would be staffing the school that fall when I was called in to explain the purposes of the troublesome institute to white and black parents active in the Adams-Morgan Community Council. Well-intentioned and seriously concerned with the education of *all* the kids in that 99 percent black and poor school, the whites in particular feared that we were embarked on what was then called a "Black Power" curriculum. The argument about our educational and political strategies heated even more rapidly than the storefront in which our folding chairs were circled. And finally one of the white mothers, her voice pitching higher and higher, said, "But if you teach the students to be proud of the fact that they're black, where does that leave my child?"

Where, indeed? The arguments that particular authors and texts propound certain values inherent in their race or gender is, of course, absurd, as the positions of Clarence Thomas and Ward Connerly are hardly needed to remind us. To give Langston Hughes equal billing with T. S. Eliot has nothing to do with some mythical essence each might be supposed to have. Rather, it calls into question established power relationships, at least as these are played out in the arena we name "culture"—one among many arenas (like the voting booth and the abortion clinic entryway) in which groups of people contest for authority.

Conservatives have, of course, claimed that the standards used to promote writers like Eliot and Stevens are "apolitical." Indeed, some reviewers of the first edition of the *Heath,* such as Mark Edmundson in the *Times Literary Supplement* and Richard Ruland in *American Literary History,*[8] constructed dichotomous models of culture wherein "political" and "aesthetic" values were held to be utterly separate and decidedly unequal. Edmundson, for example, erected a supposed "discrepancy" between what he called "traditional literary values" and " 'political' conceptions of the origins and purposes of literature." Indeed, his review of the anthology can be schematized sentence by sentence and paragraph by paragraph within that antinomy:

> "conventional aesthetic standards" / "political" standards
> "artistic achievement" / "political image"
> "writing well" / "adopting a politically progressive stance"
> "sophisticated formal concerns" / "readily accessible narrative"
> "intensity of verbal invention" / "thematic intensity"
> James Merrill, et al. / Garrett Hongo, et al.

This absolute cleavage between the realms of the "aesthetic" and the "political" seems to me theoretically naive—and sort of uninteresting. Indeed, one of the main problems that vexes the question of art is precisely its conflicted intersections with politics—as the careers of contemporaries like Clement Greenberg, Hilton Kramer, and André Malraux—not to speak of Shelley, Wordsworth, and Pound—should remind us. Art is not politics, nor politics art. Nevertheless, aesthetic standards are constructed *by* people *in* history—as the violent shifts in taste, sales, and the price of pictures amply demonstrate. Standards therefore express, in part, political values—not to speak of commercial interests. Indeed, as my two lists may suggest, Edmundson's own construction of a "discrepancy" constitutes a political argument for certain kinds of art and certain groups of artists—all white, incidentally— and against others. But that is not surprising. For we learn to value what is valued in "our civilization" (to use Eliot's telling phrase) and not those things that seem to challenge the order upon which our own status is erected.

Recognizing just how we had all been socialized to traditional academic standards of value was, indeed, one of the central problems of the *Heath* editorial board. Even with the enormous diversity of input from contributing editors, and with the significant differences of training and of priorities that characterized the editorial board, we found that our primary task involved reconstructing our own standards of value. Whatever else we were, we were academics, products of a form of specialized training that validated certain ways of thinking about, indeed of responding to, texts. We were also relatively privileged members of American society, invested in ways barely discernible to us in the system of values and power relationships which—happily (for us)—sustained the work we did and therefore the jobs we held. We *had* jobs, networks of preferment, valuable reputations, any of which might conceivably be threatened—or at least eroded—by our participation in a culturally radical project. I want to be clear here that I am not attributing bad faith or critical blindness to my fellow editors. Quite the contrary, I am trying to articulate the limits of my own practice, for I doubt that anyone on the editorial board had been so thoroughly imbued with the spirit of New Criticism and other academic norms as I, whose formative study was with Cleanth Brooks, John Crowe Ransom, and others at Indiana and Yale in the 1950s. I do believe, however, it is useful to make explicit the difficulties presented by our own positions in academe, as well as by the anthology genre and what it represents in academic practice.

For even if some diffuse pulses of self-interest were not working obscurely to brake the process of raising our cultural consciousness, we faced the even more difficult problem of not having alternative models from which to work. On what bases, finally, could we make choices among the many, many contenders for place within the limited confines even of two massive three-thousand-page volumes? On what basis might we decide—against the recommendations of most of our consultants—to stick with Frances Ellen Watkins Harper and not to include William Gilmore Simms? To keep Alice Cary and, at the last moment, after he had been set in type, excise James Russell Lowell? To include not only a large "Harlem Renaissance" minority contingent but also writers such as Anzia Yezierska, Mike Gold, John Joseph Mathews, Younghill Kang, and Saunders Redding?

It was, in fact, a part of Redding's *No Day of Triumph*, selected by Eleanor Tignor, which provided us the impetus toward that necessary reexamination of what most of us understood to be the standards defining the American literary terrain. We had gathered for our first meeting, in 1983, at the Seamen's Church Institute, a sailors' haven in New York near the Battery, built on the site of a place in which Melville had lived, and subsequently torn down for a fancy office building during the 1980s. We had read a few potential selections in common in order to begin the process of defining the grounds for making decisions. Now here was Redding's haunting autobiographical and social history, which only one or two of the fourteen of us had known before. Here was his evocation of family culture:

> Consciousness of my environment began with the sound of talk. It was not hysterical talk, not bravado, though it might well have been, for my father had bought in a neighborhood formerly forbidden, and we lived, I realize now, under an armistice. But in the early years, when we were a young family, there was always talk at our house; a great deal of it mere talk, a kind of boundless and robustious overflow of family feeling. Our shouts roared through the house with the exuberant gush of flood waters through an open sluice, for talk, generated by any trifle, was the power that turned the wheels of our inner family life. (*Heath Anthology*, 2:1713)

Here was his portrait of Grandma Redding, whose slavemaster had crippled her ankle by flinging a "hick'ry chunk" at her, who "hated white people," and about whom Redding puzzled: "I do not know how she managed to give the impression of shining with a kind of deadly hard glare, for she was always clothed entirely in black and her black, even features were as hard and lightless as stone" (p. 1714). How was it, we were forced to ask, that we had not known Redding's book? What did that say about our training? And how did it instruct us about what we were looking for in other works, in all of literature?

Answering such questions, constructing new organizational formats (rather than "The Rise of Realism"), choosing among writers known only to one or two of us stretched over three years and more, through meetings back at the Seamen's Church Institute, at the Dream Inn (where else?) in Santa Cruz, at Asilomar on the Monterey Peninsula, and at UCLA. I recall particularly that circular meeting room at Asilomar, the gentle surf offering a perpetual ostinato, a stray deer peering in at us as we tried to focus on the dozen sheets of newsprint filled with names of writers, famed, marginal, obscure, who might fit into our evolving narrative of the late nineteenth century. "Whoever was Sherwood Bonner," someone wearily asked, "and how did she differ from Gertrude Bonnin?" The question touched off hilarity—not because it was trivial but because it dramatized how near the furthest boundaries of our knowledge, of academic logic itself, this project was carrying us. And there was heat. "How could we, in good conscience, include someone as dull and racist as Thomas Dixon?" "Well, were we about 'conscience'?" Silence; tension. "Were we?" Where and how would we draw *our* lines between the elect and those consigned to whatever limbo remained even after our widespread revival campaign?

What we came to recognize was that no single standard—not even the elusive "aesthetic merit" that conservative critics are forever posing and never defining—is absolutely decisive. For example, to return to the *Times Literary Supplement* review, Edmundson poses "surprise" as a critical element in determining aesthetic merit. "Surprise" may indeed be essential to those forms of poetry which emphasize what he calls "intensity of verbal invention." But do such formal standards constitute the full measure of aesthetic value? Leni Riefenstahl creates surprisingly intense visual images in *Olympiad,* but does that make her film glorifying Nazi culture great art? And if it does, what does that say about theories that pose the creation of "great art" as the supreme accomplishment of human beings? Can we surrender the social values that produce nausea at that technically brilliant film, at antebellum racist writing, or at the anti-Semitism of Eliot and Pound? We came to feel, as I see it, that there were no clearly demarcated boundaries between what might be called "literariness" and politics or ideology. We were not, finally, willing to forgo either. Still, in practice, we might need to err on the side of the social values before we could come to balance formal and ideological criteria. We were not the first into that territory, of course, but we found surprisingly few guideposts to tell us where we had arrived. In fact, like the others we met out there, we became increasingly suspicious of the markers we uncovered: who had placed them? Under what auspices? To what ends?

We were able to answer such questions sufficiently well to place the *Heath Anthology* out in the field. But as need hardly be said, we did not arrive at definitive solutions. For example, the anthology was shaped by a conception of American culture as multiple and often contradictory. Yet in making and organizing our selections for the first edition, we were not always able to keep this fundamental idea before our eyes. Only when we began the process of revision were we able to confront some instances in which we had failed to foreground this central idea of conflicting narratives. I draw my example from the modern period, though I could point to similar instances elsewhere; but since a particular conception of modernism has been so influential in shaping the roles of literary academics, narratives of the "modern" are peculiarly bound up with ways of understanding our own work and status.

Implicit in the first edition's version of the modern period is a privileging of *modernism*—or, rather, a particular version thereof, whose cultural authority is in no way diminished by using, as I have often done in class, the term "high modernism." That cultural movement was effectively defined in the first edition of the *Heath* by the continued dominance of certain familiar writers and particular texts—Faulkner, "Hugh Selwyn Mauberly," "Prufrock"—contained in the central section of the period, then titled "Alienation and Literary Experimentation." It was given even greater weight by such seemingly minor details as the previous section title: "Toward Modernism," or by the fact that the "Alienation" section was begun by Pound, born after writers like Williams, E. M. Roberts, or Stein, who came later in the section. Similarly, Millay, younger than Pound and almost a generation later than Stein, appears in the prior, "Toward Modernism" section. Further, these sections contained in isolated splendor but one critical essay, Eliot's "Tradition and the Individual Talent." Finally, one omission in the first edition particularly told: that of Amy Lowell (corrected in the subsequent editions).

To be sure, I think our selection within this modernist framework was (and is) wider, more diverse with respect particularly to gender, than that provided by previous anthologies. We included, for example, a substantial selection of H.D. as well as work of Moore, Roberts, Barnes, and Bogan. Moreover, we consciously separated out the "New Negro Renaissance," as we have come to call it, in part as an effort to suggest the importance of a cultural movement alternative in many ways to the dominantly white (and often explicitly racist) modernism of Pound, Eliot, and their compatriots.

All the same, the narrative of the modern period constructed in the first edition of the *Heath*—albeit somewhat more equivocally—maintained the centrality of an established version of modernism. What it did not do is deconstruct the continuing hegemony of that narrative within American literary studies. Nor should that be surprising when one considers the centrality of the modernist narrative to the value and status of what we do as professors of literature. Historically, the formalist strategies that have constituted the intellectual and pedagogical core of our profession grew in response to the complex, allusive, symbolic artistic practices of writers like Eliot (I use him here to symbolize a cultural movement), as well as to his success—and that of his successors among the New Critics—in articulating and arguing for an aesthetic theory which privileged that practice. Eliot's theory—enunciated most clearly in his canon-establishing essay "The Metaphysical Poets"—and his practice, initially codified in the work of the New Criticism, rationalized our value as interpreters and validators of certain forms of culture. Sustaining a certain idea of modernism at the center of our narrative could thus be viewed as a consequence of the basic processes of our own literary novitiate and promotion. Until recently, that had patterned us as interpreters of texts that were, and from an Eliotic perspective necessarily should be, "complex," "comprehensive," "allusive," "indirect," and dislocated.

In revising the anthology, we made a number of changes, such as including Lowell just after Pound and adding a "sheaf" of "political poems," designed to complicate, indeed contest, that traditional narrative of modernism. Similarly, in the third edition, we added some objectivist poetry, partly for the same reasons and partly because of the ways in which it leads, in time, to more experimental contemporary poetry (like the "language poets," whom we have still not been persuaded to include). But my main aim is not to examine the ins and outs of revising successful anthologies. Rather, it is to illustrate how "re-learning the alphabet," as Adrienne Rich has described it, remains an ongoing necessity for cultural workers like anthologists, teachers, and critics.

As I have tried to suggest earlier, the creation of any anthology—and certainly one as revisionist as the *Heath*—is not simply a process of academic training guided by detached logic. Rather, it is ringed by un-certainty, speculation, argument. Like any significant collective proj-ect, it deeply engages our convictions as well as our knowledge. The final boundary that has become increasingly permeable in our process was that usually maintained in academe between strong feelings and intellectual training. In at least one respect (and probably only in this one), the hot right-wing attacks on the anthology were appropriate: boundaries, whether one is talking of neighborhoods, nations, gender, or culture, are not light abstractions but the stuff of battle.

What a pleasure therefore to find, when the third edition of the *Heath* hit the market in 1997, that the anthology retained the capacity to engage peoples' passion not only about what is included and what is not but about the fundamental principles of the enterprise.

CHAPTER TEN

MELVILLE CLIMBS THE CANON

When I began the project to which this chapter is devoted, I had a relatively simple objective. I wanted to explain somewhat more fully than had previously been done[1] how it was that Herman Melville was transformed during the 1920s from an obscure teller of South Sea Island tales into the preeminent American novelist—at least for many reputable critics. But I was derailed from that relatively clear historical path into murkier cultural terrain: I found myself asking what the critics who were reviving Melville in that period had at stake in constructing his image as they did; into what contest for cultural authority was Melville being conscripted? I want to begin with how that shift in focus came about because it raises certain questions about the meaning of "Herman Melville" in literary study.

When I talk about the literary canon or teach the course "Race, Gender, and the Canon" at Trinity College, I generally begin with an exercise. I ask the participants to write on a piece of paper the names of five or perhaps ten American books or writers they think an educated person should have read—"educated" being defined as having completed a B.A. degree. I collate the responses and we have a small sample literary canon. There are seldom many real surprises, though there are some local variations. One finds Mark Twain at or near the top, together with Fitzgerald—at least in the Northeast—Faulkner, Hemingway, and a couple of other men like Steinbeck. Then, trailing along, Emily Dickinson, Henry James, and nowadays Alice Walker or, more likely, Toni Morrison.

What I found altogether odd when I did the exercise to begin my class a few years ago was that the one writer left off, with not a single vote among the one hundred or more registered in my poll, the one writer whose stories some of the students had before them on the table—that one writer was Herman Melville. That gave me pause. After all, as one of my students later said, most of them had been assigned to read *Moby-Dick* in high school and had hated it. Didn't that definitively qualify Melville as a classic, canonical writer? Not, apparently, for these students. I began to wonder whether this omission had occurred in earlier such exercises, and I had just not noticed it or had attributed the void to chance. So I went back to the results of a similar poll of secondary-school teachers I had done about a year before and, sure enough, Melville had received but one vote there, along with everyone from Ira Levin to Lydia Sigourney.

Unscientifically, I took these results as straws in a wind. And I felt that I needed to understand when it had begun to blow, and from what quarter. I began by asking my students, and they gave me some interesting answers. "You really feel belittled when you're reading Melville," one said. "I know this is art, and I can't understand it." You feel, another added, that "something's wrong with you; that you're missing something." My students seemed actively to dislike Melville, to feel humiliated by the prose and ignorant before the dense web of Melville's allusive, syntactically intricate style and his convoluted plotting.

What were my students expressing? I want to suggest that in some sense Melville had become for them a representative of what they hated about their academic training. Or, to broaden out that remark toward the thesis of this chapter: precisely what it was in Melville that critics and professors of the twenties found enthralling, indeed, what critics and professors continue to find enthralling in Melville—it was just *that* that my students were most put off by. And that hostility, which they could seldom register directly, emerged in the results of my poll. Moreover, their accounts of the reasons they had omitted Melville were legitimated by the very unanimity of that response, so they could say what they had been taught it was not legitimate even to think, at least in college classrooms.

Before I proceed, I need to reassure my readers that this essay is not an effort to enlist Melville's texts for my own political program. Nor do I wish to join my students (and probably a long, long line of undergraduate readers) in attacking Melville as a writer. In a sense, this is not even an essay about Melville. It is, rather, about Melville's reputation and how it was constructed and deployed. For my own part, I agree with the majority of critics and professors who champion Melville's virtues. To be sure, academics may argue violently whether Captain Vere in "Billy Budd" is a godlike dispenser of even-handed justice or a nascent fascist pig, but unlike my students, most finally come to agree that, "Damn it all, sir, Melville ought to be read!" My concern is not with how academics dispute Melville's values, but with how we largely agree about his value. I will claim, in fact, that the rise of Melville's reputation in the 1920s may be taken to represent the ascent of the ideology we call "modernism" and of the academy and its adjuncts in the hierarchy of cultural authority.

In mid-February of 1919, the New York City newspapers began to run long stories announcing the imminent celebration of the centenary of James Russell Lowell, poet, man of letters, ambassador to the Court of St. James, and longest-serving president of the Modern Language Association (though I have to admit that that last fact was strangely omitted from any of the accounts and editorials I have found). Sponsors of the four-day celebration, the American Academy of Arts and Letters and the National Institute of Arts and Letters, wished to use the occasion to underline the unity of the English-speaking nations and thus invited distinguished representatives of the arts and letters from Great Britain and Canada to address one or another of the events held at Columbia University, the Ritz-Carlton Hotel and the University Club. In the major speech, reported the New York *World,* the British novelist John Galsworthy claimed that a country's most lasting good "comes from rectitude of conduct and the work of thinkers." "Perfected language," Galsworthy continued, in tones echoed throughout the events, "is the cement of the spirit, mortar linking the bricks of our thoughts into a single structure of ideals and laws, painted and carved with the rarities of fancy, the manifold forms of Beauty and Truth." Further, according to the *World*, Galsworthy told an audience including Mrs. Andrew Carnegie and Miss Carnegie, Admiral and Mrs. Albert Gleaves, Mrs. Schuyler Van Rensselaer, and Sir Richard and Lady Crawford, that England and America have reaped from the "grim years of war the promotion of our common tongue to the position of the universal language."[2]

Alas, the Lowell celebration did little to promote rectitude and magnanimity in national conduct, much less the peaceful and harmonious outlook for which celebrants eulogized Lowell. Nineteen nineteen was a year which seemed to confirm in shrill propaganda, conflict, and bloodshed precisely the anxieties of the Lowell celebrants that their old order was passing. American and British troops in Archangel were engaged in battle against the Bolsheviki, even while Allied leaders tried to impose a victory settlement on an increasingly socialist Germany, and Woodrow Wilson began the ultimately losing process of restraining Allied greed and senatorial jealousy. All Europe except the Western Front seemed "swept with confused alarms of struggle and flight"; in the American press, at least, Bela Kun was in and out of power almost daily, while the armies of Deniken and Kolcheck regularly announced the downfall of Bolshevik rule. At home, the Prohibition amendment was beginning to turn the normal social habits of middle-class Americans into petty lawlessness; the women's suffrage bill was finally passed by the whole Congress and sent to the states for ratification; the "Fighting Quaker," A. Mitchell Palmer, with the help of a network of federal agents and American Legionnaires, was busily deporting reds, blacks, and pinks; the city of Seattle was, for a week and more, closed down by a general strike; and—even as black regiments like New York's famed 369th returned from fighting—a series of pogroms in twenty-five U.S. cities, beginning in Washington, D.C., and rising to a climax of terror in Chicago, reduced many of the nation's urban black communities to smoking, bloody ruins. Meanwhile in Boston, on a lighter note, the Red Sox had traded Babe Ruth to the Yankees, the cops had gone out on strike, and the one-piece bathing suit had been banned from the city beaches. Even allowing for the generally hysterical tone of the nation's press, one must acknowledge that 1919 was a year of contention, indeed revolution, especially from the point of view of America's comfortable classes, largely including its intellectuals. As one businessman wrote to the attorney general, "There is hardly a respectable citizen of my acquaintance who does not believe that we are on the verge of armed conflict in this country."[3]

Moreover, in 1919 what many native-born Americans viewed as a "deluge" of immigration, interrupted by the war, resumed. Between 1901 and 1920 over 14.5 million immigrants came to these shores, particularly from Italy, the Austro-Hungarian Empire, and czarist Russia. Though the foreign-born and their children, together with African Americans, did most of the hard work in mining, manufacture, and construction, they remained—in their presumptively curious dialects, strange religions, and exotic cultures—alien if not positively menacing to established classes of Americans. Debating the first of a series of bills restricting immigration in 1921, Representative James V. McClintic of Oklahoma described practically every one of the arrivals at Ellis Island he had observed as "weak, small of stature, poorly clad, emaciated" and with "less than $50 to his credit."[4] This climate of fear and prejudice in the immediate aftermath of the war encouraged a variety of efforts to reassert the hegemony of Anglo-Saxon society: the Ku Klux Klan trumpeted the dominance of white, Protestant America; the trial and ultimately execution of Sacco and Vanzetti turned into a social imperative; the Immigration Acts of 1921 and 1924 excluded Japanese altogether and virtually halted immigration from Eastern and Southern Europe; Western Civilization requirements spread through the nation's major universities. Even Harvard discovered that it had a "Jewish problem" when, by 1920, second- and third-generation Jews came to constitute as much as 20 percent of its student body. "It is the duty of Harvard," President Abbott Lawrence Lowell wrote privately to the Board of Overseers, "to receive just as many boys who have come, or whose parents have come, to this country without our background as we can effectively educate; including in education the imparting, not only of book knowledge, but of ideas and traditions of our people."[5] The question was deciding the upper limit of those who could thus be assimilated. Communities, Congress, the courts, and the colleges became arenas wherein struggles for authority would be contested between the culturally powerful and those they saw as sources of opposition or even of chaos.

No wonder, then, that to a younger generation of intellectuals, the celebration of Lowell's centenary must have seemed as anachronistic as Lowell's beard. I imagine them looking back into the nation's earlier history for a new champion, someone who might uphold against British condescension American claims to an equality in culture that would be consonant with America's established title to military and diplomatic parity. A writer, too, who might stand in the cynical winds blowing from modern artistic horizons but who would, nevertheless, sustain certain established American values now at contest. Who would they choose? What qualities would professors desire and critics seek? Why might one writer be preferred to others? Answering such questions is the main task of this chapter.

A variety of candidates presented themselves in the centennial class of 1919: Pulitzer's *New York World* had, indeed, surveyed the field of writers born in 1819.[6] There was Walt Whitman, of course; but his very popularity among those of anarchistic and even German sympathies made him an inappropriate choice.[7] There was Susan Warner, but her books, as an *Evening Post* writer mentioned, while once wildly popular now "stood on one of the upper shelves of the small press that held the Sunday-school library."[8] Besides, like Mrs. E. D. E. N. Southworth and Julia Ward Howe, she was female and author of "many less famous writings than 'The Battle Hymn of the Republic.'" The rest of the 1819 roster, Samuel Longfellow, Josiah Gilbert Holland—the Timothy Titcomb of mid-century letters—and Thomas Dunn English, among others, inspired no one. Another obscure novelist, one Herman Melville, was not even included in the *World*'s list. But it was Melville, as we know, who fit the bill. The question here is why.

I want to advance a number of claims. They have to do with the impact of the centennial itself, with the South Sea Island connection and the involvement of Melville with that charmed locus of the "primitive," with the image of Melville as the archetypical misunderstood American genius, with the appeal of his complex texts to modernist and particularly academic predilections, with the continuing allure of his books to grown-up boys, and finally, when he had begun to achieve "classic" status, with how his canon could be reassessed to conform to changing critical priorities. I want to argue that, in the main, "Melville" was constructed in the 1920s as part of an ideological conflict that linked advocates of modernism and of traditional high cultural values—often connected to the academy—against a social and cultural "other"—generally, if ambiguously, portrayed as feminine, genteel, exotic, dark, foreign, and numerous. In this contest a distinctively masculine, Anglo-Saxon image of Melville was deployed as a lone and powerful artistic beacon against the dangers presented by the masses; creating such an image entailed overlooking issues of race, eroticism, democracy, and the like, which have become commonplaces of contemporary Melville criticism.

The centennial celebration of Melville, however small, helped propel the bibliographers, the bibliophiles, the editors and the biographers into motion. Melville's name began to get around. The *Bulletin of the Brooklyn Public Library* provided catalogues of Melville and Thomas Dunn English late in 1919. Bibliographers added to each other's lists and argued about omitted works.[9] Meade Minnegerode began assembling a group of Melville letters and a list of his first editions, as well as noting differences between the original and revised editions of *Typee*.[10] In 1920, new editions of *Typee*[11] and *Moby-Dick* appeared, the latter—with an introduction by Viola Meynell—the first American novel included in the important Oxford World's Classics series; and Everyman's Library reissued its editions of *Typee, Omoo,* and *Moby-Dick*. Two years later Oxford and Princeton University Presses followed up with separate collections of reasonably obscure Melville sketches and poems.[12]

Perhaps most important, late in the spring of 1919, Carl Van Doren, an established professor at Columbia, proposed to one of the English Department's instructors, Raymond Weaver, that he prepare a brief centennial account of Melville for *The Nation,* of which Van Doren was literary editor. "He was a wonderful old boy," Van Doren said, "and I'd like to do him myself. But if you'd try him, I'm willing."[13] The invitation led the rather unsuspecting Weaver into the research that would, at the end of 1921, produce the first book on Melville,[14] and, within a few years thereafter, the Constable edition of Melville's works. To anyone familiar with the reawakening of interest in nineteenth-century American women writers during the last three decades, the pattern is clear enough: locating the books, putting out bibliographies, publishing editions, talking about your finds—all help produce a kind of material base upon which a structure of serious criticism can be erected.

That criticism took as its point of departure the South Seas connection. As the *Literary Digest* commented, Melville "has come back to us on the tidal wave raised by the South Sea books of Frederick O'Brien, the art furor over Gauguin, and all the smaller writers and painters who hurry to adopt a new fashion."[15] Indeed, Brander Matthews's *New York Times* review of the Weaver biography and the Everyman reprints was titled "Teller of Sea Tales."[16] And Melville is prominently featured in an elaborate spread on "The Men That Found the South Seas" in *The Mentor*.[17] The story is headed with a Frederick O'Brien photograph called "Samoan Girl and Her Natural Mirror"—the character of which one can easily imagine. Melville's portrait appears on the first text page; the caption describes him as "Friend of Nathaniel Hawthorne, whose books first acquainted Americans with the South Seas. He is yearly gaining recognition as one of the foremost literary men America has produced."[18] Appropriately, the summary of articles on the Melville centenary in *Current Opinion* was followed by a piece on "Aboriginal Art in the Pan-American Garden."[19] No one was better aware of the commercial potential of the South Seas connection than Weaver's publisher, George H. Doran. In their publicity organ, *Literary News Notes,* for December 14, 1921, they say of Weaver's work that "he has been able to reveal for the first time the life of the man who is really the father of South Sea literature." And, later, "He introduces the Creator of South Sea Fiction in This Romantic Record." In their issue for January 11, 1922, they ask rhetorically "Who Started the South Sea Craze?" and, of course, answer with Melville.[20]

As is well known, this passion, not just for the South Pacific, but for all supposedly primitive places and peoples persisted throughout much of the twenties. Artists sought the vivid colors and striking forms of aboriginal life. Museums displayed primal African artifacts. Ordinary people wished to escape the pressures of "civilization" by imaginary, and sometimes real, visits to exotic spots like Nukuaheva . . . or Harlem. "The number of people is not small," pronounced a *New York Times* editorial, "who, with the choice of being translated to the unknown land of their desire, would pronounce for Tahiti."[21] And, observing Melville's centenary, the *Boston Herald* celebrated rather more his four "happiest months . . . among a people living close to nature, untroubled by social conventions, not advanced enough to know the meaning of money, and 'absolutely free from cares, griefs, troubles or vexations.' "[22]

Elaborate theories have been spun to explain the attractiveness of "primitive" cultures to white "civilization"—which is how the discussion was then structured. My concern is not with this phenomenon as such but with the role in it constructed for "Marquesan" Melville, as one newspaper called him at the time of his death.[23] That role develops *not* simply because Melville wrote about "primitive" places but because he could be appropriated to the needs of America's cultural elite to model a correct relationship *to* the "primitive." Almost all early twentieth-century accounts of Melville begin by mentioning that he came from "the best American stock, English, Scotch-Irish and Dutch."[24] In fact, no word appears more often in these biographical essays than the racially freighted term "stock." Weaver characterizes Melville's origins more fully in these terms: "Well-born, and nurtured in good manners and a cosmopolitan tradition, he was like George Borrow and Sir Richard Burton, a gentleman adventurer in the barbarous outposts of human experience."[25] The *Literary Digest* had gone further. Complaining in an article devoted to Melville of the "contempt . . . for our older literature," which had become "one of the notes of our modern life," the *Digest* wrote: "To this our younger school of writers with names that suggest much more recent ships than the *Mayflower* are the chief contributors. They would have us forget altogether our literary heritage and concentrate on Chicago as a center of all that is worth conserving. Even our academic research, which must embrace more than the present to give the tone of scholarship, is frightened away from our literary past and forages in the well-cropped fields of foreign letters."[26] Study of New England's Herman Melville, the *Literary Digest* suggests, would prove an antidote to this disease; thus the value of Melville as an exemplar of "our literary heritage" is linked, in a fashion become customary among conservative critics, to the traditional values signified by the *Mayflower.* A preference for Melville emerges as a defense against the immigrant ship, the "Hog Butcher for the World," polyglot culture, the dangerous fodder of foreign fields.

Carl Van Doren takes a further step in defining the importance of Melville to a time troubled—and intrigued—by the darker and "primitive" peoples of the world. In *The American Novel* he characterizes Melville as "thoroughly sensitive to the felicities of the exotic life." However, he continues, Melville "never loses himself in it entirely as did later men, like Lafcadio Hearn and Pierre Loti, but remains always the shrewd and smiling Yankee."[27] Or, as another of Melville's partisans had put it: "He had no particular desire to become decivilized. His stay in the Valley of Typee was in the nature of exile and he took the first opportunity to get among his own kind. To his credit also it should be said that he never, in after life, sentimentalized over the joys of barbarism. . . . [I]n the earlier narratives the happy riot of untrammelled folk among the cocoa palms and bread-fruit trees of the Pacific archipelagoes symbolize to him a triumph over the tribulations and complexities which beset civilized races."[28] In other words, neither Melville himself, nor his narrators—nor, properly instructed, his readers—are about to abandon "civilization" for the South Seas, assuming that option were still truly available. Even Gauguin's sojourn might be too extended. To taste of the primitive, to make art of the primitive, to consume the primitive is one thing—quite another to lose oneself among "irresponsible natives hovering between cannibalism and a half-comprehended Christianity" (the language is Van Doren's). One might appropriate the freer rhythms of primitive culture, its sexual immediacy, its exotic sounds, just as one might visit the Cotton Club, but a well-born gentleman will guide us with Yankee shrewdness through such alien scenes. In short, Melville comes to be seen as evincing the correct relationship of a true American artist to "primitive" life and peoples, precisely at a time in which the United States is developing its career of imperial expansion among the darker people of the world and thus deeply in need of an appropriate ideology. And at a time, too, when white American artists, from Carl Van Vechten to George Gershwin, are trying to discover the means for assimilating the domestically exotic into their work. Ironically, of course, what twenties critics discovered in Melville was not the democratic, much less homoerotic, "squeeze of the hand," the bonding of Ishmael with Queequeg, but the presumed distance that Herman Melville, of good New England stock, placed between himself and the felicities of "primitive" life.

Initially, then, Melville is constructed as the shrewd Yankee gentleman guiding us through dangerous—if seductive—encounters with the primitive; soon, however, in a variant of this bipolar structure of cultural authority, he emerges as the exemplary artist, masculine and compelling, posed against a dull, feminized Philistine herd. Indeed,

Melville's major role for 1920s (and 1930s) critics is the artist as hero, standing apart from, in fact above, his society. The contrast between Melville's genius and the previous lack of appreciation comes to stand more generally for the plight of artists in crass materialistic societies, like those of America in the 1850s and 1920s.

Modernist mythology enshrined this view of the relationship between artists and their society, glorifying phrases like Joyce's "silence, exile, and cunning." "The age demanded an image / Of its accelerated grimace," Pound had written in "Hugh Selwyn Mauberley (Life and Contacts)":

> The "age demanded" chiefly a mould in plaster,
> Made with no loss of time,
> A prose kinema, not, not assuredly, alabaster
> Or the "sculpture" of rhyme.

In this degraded environment, Melville emerges as "the blinded Samson set to grind chaff for the Philistine,"[29] "a jungle lion chained by the leg, burning out his soul in rage, powerless save for his roar,"[30] and thus a figure of even more heroic proportions than his own extraordinary characters. Weaver's biography was undoubtedly the primary force in establishing as critical gospel this drama of the sensitive artist whose "warring and untamed desires were in violent conflict with his physical and spiritual environments." He cites both Freud and Plato to refute the charge that Melville's supposed "decline" was attributable to insanity:

> "From insanity," said Plato, "Greece has derived its greatest benefits." But the dull and decent Philistine, untouched by Platonic heresies, justifies his sterility in a boast of sanity. The America in which Melville was born and died was exuberantly and unquestionably "sane." Its "sanity" drove Irving abroad and made a recluse of Hawthorne. Cooper throve upon it. And of Melville, more ponderous in gifts and more volcanic in energy than any other American writer, it made an Ishmael upon the face of the earth. With its outstanding symptoms of materialism and conformity it drove Emerson to pray for an epidemic of madness. . . . From this it would appear that a taste for insanity has been widespread among poets, prophets and saints: men venerated more by posterity than by their

neighbors. . . . The herd must always be intolerant of all who violate its sacred and painfully reared traditions. . . . Openly to harbor convictions repugnant to the herd is still the most unforgivable sin against that most holy of ghosts—fashionable opinion. . . . Melville sinned blackly against the orthodoxy of his time.[31]

By the easy transition of shifting verb tense, Weaver links Melville's time to his own; Melville's career thus becomes a contemporary archetype of the "poets, prophets and saints" betrayed by a callous or indifferent mob. Moreover, among those "men venerated" by posterity, poets emerge as foremost; Melville's new disciples, then, implicitly become the interpreters of a modernist secular writ, Platos refashioning the strangeness of modern art as true sanity in a "dull and decent" bourgeois world.

The drama constructed by Weaver became the commonplace of Melville scholarship. "It is not difficult," the *Times Literary Supplement*'s reviewer of Weaver's book writes of *Typee*, "to see why it was so bitterly assailed in the Puritan New England of 1846. It ran atilt at every convention: the picture of Fayaway using her only garment as a sail and, more terrible still, the profligate suggestion that women look their best while smoking were more than enough to shock the conscience of the early Victorians."[32] No Melville quotation emerged as more popular than that from one of his letters (June 1, 1851?) to Hawthorne: "Dollars damn me; and the malicious Devil is forever grinning in upon me, holding the door ajar. . . . What I feel most moved to write, that is banned,—it will not pay. Yet, altogether, write the *other* way I cannot. So the product is a final hash, and all my books are botches."[33] In time, other quotations from Melville family members came to the surface as evidence to support this portrait. For example, there is Mrs. Melville's remark in 1859: "Herman has taken to writing poetry. You need not tell any one, for you know how such things get around."[34] This romantic myth of the artist defeated by society persists right through the 1920s. Thus, Lewis Mumford concludes his 1929 biography with this peroration, interesting for the underlying masculine sexual metaphor and for the romantic picture of the artist as visionary, both characteristic of 1920s criticism: "Whatever Melville's life was, his art in *Moby-Dick* exhibits that integration and synthesis which we seek. Through his art, he escaped the barren destiny of his living: he embraced Life; and we who now follow where his lonely courage led him embrace it, too. This embrace was a fertile one; and in each generation it will bring forth its own progeny. The day of Herman Melville's vision is now in the beginning. It hangs like a cloud over the horizon at dawn; and as the sun rises, it will become more radiant, and more a part of the living day" (p. 368). Mumford's fundamental scenario differs from Weaver's only in that he differentiates the provincialism of antebellum America from the crass materialism of the Gilded Age and significantly modifies Weaver's notion that Melville's capacities as a writer declined seriously after *Moby-Dick*.

In fact, this romantic construction of Melville as thwarted artist became pervasive. In one of the first scholarly articles on him, written in 1928, Horace Scudder of the University of New Hampshire discusses the textual origins of "Benito Cereno" and interprets its final conversation between the gloomy Don Benito and the American captain, Amasa Delano. That dialogue, as readers will recall, includes this famous exchange:

> "You are saved, Don Benito," cried Captain Delano, more and more astonished and pained; "You are saved; what has cast such a shadow upon you?"
> "The Negro."
> There was silence, while the moody man sat, slowly and unconsciously gathering his mantle about him, as if it were a pall.
> There was no more conversation that day.

Professor Scudder's take on this conversation typifies much Melville criticism even unto our own time: "This dialogue which darkens the whole tale is the voice of Melville himself crying out against the injustice which has been done him, charging his critics with a misrepresentation which had brought his work to a premature close, and ruined his life. . . . Melville himself is Benito Cereno, and Babo is the personification of malicious criticism."[35] The construction of Melville as spurned artist and prophet overwhelms all other ways of thinking about his texts. Scudder's interpretation of "Benito Cereno," altogether typical of his time, suggests, in fact, a certain *need* among upper-middle-class white intellectuals of the day to ignore the racial texts that open before them in this story, or in Melville's works generally. That should not be surprising, given the ways in which 1920s critics used

Melville to mark "civilization" off from "savagery." Not the least of the ironies in this situation—one Melville might himself have enjoyed—is how Captain Delano, in all his racial blindness and condescension, continues to be the appropriate model of Melville's modernist champions. For them, as for Delano, the roots of the story remain mysterious; as Henry Seidel Canby writes, "Benito Cereno" is a "mystery in which the impending weight of a barbarous black power gradually comes to realization."[36] This is as close to a recognition of the story's racial content as critics come until 1936, when Arthur Hobson Quinn, an older and somewhat traditional scholar, writes that "the test of such a story is the effect upon the reader, of course, and so real is the atmosphere Melville creates that each time Delano sends his boat back to his own ship without him we feel a strong desire, as though he were living, to warn him to go with it. It is the picture of one man, of our own race, alone amid the hostile strangers who are waiting to strike, that appeals so strongly. . . . Benito and Delano are both surrounded by human beings whose only hope of freedom lies in mutiny and murder."[37] But for most other critics both of the 1920s and 1930s, regardless of their politics, Melville's dramatization of American racism remains altogether hidden behind their construction of Melville's biography as an archetype of the limits and frustrations of their own class position.

Rarely are the grounds of this portrait of Melville as prophet betrayed brought into question. Vernon Louis Parrington emphasizes Melville's democratic outlook, even in *Pierre*[38] but this is not a widely shared perception even, perhaps surprisingly, among progressive critics of the thirties like Granville Hicks. Most sharply, perhaps, the anonymous reviewer of Weaver's biography for the *Catholic World* excoriates both his failure to account for Melville as "a religious man" and for his view of humanity as "the herd." "The white whale," the reviewer argues, "is the heart of humanity. . . . He who loves not humankind and the heart of humankind, wicked, faithless, ungrateful, treacherous as it is—he who turns upon it in disdainful hate—will be destroyed by it."[39] Thus the reviewer, speaking from a traditional religious position, attacks Weaver's myth as at once supercilious and sacrilegious.

But such views are rarely articulated. The appeal of the myth of the misunderstood, exiled artist to modernist intellectuals, however differently articulated in *Portrait of the Artist as a Young Man* or "Hugh Selwyn Mauberly," in *The Education of Henry Adams* or "The Waste-

Land," can hardly be exaggerated. The myth had enormous explanatory—and consolatory—power for members of a class whose status had been brought into question and whose authority had seemed to be eroding. It set at immediate discount the complaints about the difficulties of modern art: not to understand it marked you as Philistine, rather than the artist as obscurantist. It elevated writers to positions of moral primacy and their priests, the critics and professors, to cultural dominion.

Embodied in Melville, moreover, this myth took a particularly potent shape. E. H. Eby insists in a review of one of the new editions of *Pierre* that "this destruction of certainties alienated Melville from his generation just as it brought him close to the moderns."[40] One such modern was Archibald MacLeish; reviewing Lewis Mumford's biography of Melville, he dramatizes the conflict between the mass and the modernist:

> In our time one world is broken, has been broken for a hundred years. Another is building, has been built to the eye-height of the great majority of men so that they believe their heads are covered, or will soon be covered—Science will know it all soon: it will soon be known. A few, and those the men most characteristic of our time, are still unhoused. . . . [A]ll of them are naked to the air, and to these men, like a written stone on the promontories of an uninhabitable land, the voice of Melville comes with almost unendurable meaning. The knowledge of evil in the world. The stumbling malice. The brute chance. They, too, have known it and spoken and been spat upon by the new-roofed fellows with their plaster facts and their watts and kilos and their safe, sure incomes from their six percents. The cosmopolitan, Semitic pseudo-Gallicized, ironical, sophisticated, giggling spirit of our time knows nothing of that terror and shrieks with spiteful laughter when the words are said.[41]

Melville could thus be deployed against those twin—and perhaps, as Andreas Huyssen suggests,[42] fundamentally identical—enemies of high modernism: the (giggling) feminine and the (Semitic) mob. Around Melville, men—Anglo-Saxon, poetic, prophetic—critics and intellectuals, could bond in true masculine style.

No one presents this conception of Melville so starkly as Fred Lewis Pattee, perhaps the very first professor of American literature. He portrays Melville as a thundering naysayer, Byronic, Nietzschean, displaying his "contempt for the herd," his characters "supermen who flaunt their defiance even in the face of the Almighty."[43] This heroic being he poses against "the feminine fifties with their 'Wide Wide World,' their 'Lamplighter,' their Uncle Tom's Cabin" (p. 381). The modernist battle against gentility and the popular, against mass culture and the feminine, is thus provided with historical precedent and mythological incarnation. And the study of American literature, so constructed, becomes an ideological vehicle to pursue the modernist project of separating art that is true—read masculine, autonomous, experimental—from art that is false—read feminine, referential, traditional. Pattee's reading of Melville, with its barely suppressed misogyny and triumphal elitism, is, after all, offered in a book concerned, to quote its title, with *The New American Literature, 1890–1930.*

Interestingly, leftist critics of the 1930s accept this fundamental drama of Melville in combat with his world, but see that as representing not the triumph of the artist but his flaw. Both Granville Hicks and V. F. Calverton, for example, present Melville (quite briefly) as heroic but failed. Hicks insists that he could not find ways to come to terms with the evil embodied in the "concrete economic phenomena" with which men were "wrestling" after the Civil War.[44] Calverton claims that Melville could only turn and flee from the "industrialism of the east" and the "commercial cunning of his own land": "The more serious, the more significant task of changing that civilization, staying with it to transform it, did not inspire him. Like Thoreau, he preferred to desert it, to build his fantasies where he could be free of it. All his novels, including his masterpiece *Moby-Dick,* in which, in symbolic form, our whole capitalist society was indicted, advanced no further in its solution."[45] But these represent minority views, even during the "progressive" thirties. In any case, they reenforce the basic drama of the great artist posed against *his* society.

In time, the dominant critical position became *not* to test Melville's values or his prose against traditional standards of merit, but to test a reader's worthiness by his or her responses to Melville. Melville's difficulties appear not as problems to be overcome, but as virtues which place him in the camp of modernist poets. Most earlier enthusiasts had assumed that "to love Melville was to join a very small circle. It was like eating hasheesh." To be sure, an interest in Melville marked one as "extraordinary . . . for no ordinary person loves Melville."[46] But that was hardly matter for remark for those bred to such comfortable distinctions. Culture, after all, came of class. But by the end of 1921, Carl Van Vechten would begin his aggressive review of Weaver's biography by quoting a passage from H. S. Salt's unusual 1892 article on Melville:

> Has America a literature? I am inclined to think it a grave mistake to argue seriously with those afflicted persons who periodically exercise themselves over this idlest of questions. It is wiser to meet them with a practical counter-thrust, and pointedly inquire, for example, whether they are familiar with the writings of Herman Melville. Whereupon confusion will, in most cases, ensue, and you will go on to suggest that to criticise 'Hamlet' with the prince's part omitted would be no whit more fatuous than to demonstrate the non-existence of an American literature, while taking no account of its true intellectual giant.[47]

Not to know Melville, here, "argues yourself unknown." A couple of months earlier, H. M. Tomlinson had posed *Moby-Dick* as "a supreme test. If it captures you, then you are unafraid of great art. You may dwell in safety with fiends or angels and rest poised with a quiet mind between the stars and the bottomless pit."[48] A taste for Melville, which had been the emblem of a gentlemanly coterie on "both sides of the seas," has now become the index to a reader's poetic sensibilities, a token of admission to the precincts of modern intellectual respectability. This should be no surprise, for the pleasure of the modernist text is in many ways the pleasure of initiation, of separation from the ordinary, of difference insisted upon.

The alteration in valuing Melville as an artist that took place during the first decades of the twentieth century registers three fundamental changes in the construction of his image, having to do with audience, style, and the texts focused for the critical eye. In her 1894 primer on *American Literature*, Mildred Cabell Watkins expresses directly a widely held view of Melville's audience: "Four wildly exciting tales of adventure might be named here; they are of just the kind to please the boys. They are *Typee, Omoo, White Jacket*, and *Moby Dick, or the White Whale*, all by Herman Melville."[49] Similarly, in its 1919 centennial article on *Moby-Dick*, the *New York Tribune* suggested that the book "has been read all these years by that thin but unending line of boys and men to whom the sea is home and heaven, and the one great adventure, whether seen and known or only dreamed of and imagined."[50] Summarizing Moby-Dick, the New York Evening Post asserted that "no boy, no matter how grown up, ever tired of this. By way of compensation to oldsters, the book is full of that philosophy which makes Melville unique among sea writers."[51] The implication of the Evening Post's editorial, that at some level Moby-Dick always remains a boys' book, underlies Percy Boynton's account of Melville: "Two thirds of the chapters," he writes, "might be culled to present this relentless sequence in the form of a so-called boys' book. Yet even so presented the story would contain more than meets the eye."[52] Without being derogatory, I want to suggest that much of Melville's appeal, and especially in the critical period during which he was being established as a "classic" writer, had precisely to do with the validation of boys' tastes in men's criticisms. I suspect that continues to be true, for what is more powerful than the confirmation of youthful enthusiasm in the language of mature reflection?

There is, obviously, a kicker here. Mildred Cabell Watkins knew whereof she spoke: to the extent that they appeal to adolescents, Melville's earlier works do speak almost exclusively to boys. Girls seldom, indeed, take a place in the Tribune's "thin but unending line" of seaward-yearning youth. But that masculinity was precisely part of Melville's appeal to twenties critics. As I have argued elsewhere,[53] and as many of the quotations I have used suggest in image and word, nothing was more important to that postwar generation of literary intellectuals than masculinizing American culture. And surely their boyhood enthusiasm helped fill that bill. As Frank Jewett Mather put it, "Out of his [Melville's] loins grows the recent 'strong school.' They have nothing in common with him but his emphasis."[54] And, perhaps, as Mather goes on immediately to say, his "witchery of words."

Nothing in the views of Melville as artist changed so fully as the accounts of his language, his imagery, his style: at the beginning of his revival Melville is valued despite his mannered style; by the end of a decade, his value lies precisely in the appeal of his style to a modernist reader. To be sure, some early critics, notably Archibald MacMechan, praised Melville's style, at least in Moby-Dick, as "distinctly American."[55] But the conventional wisdom had it that "his style suffered a complete and disastrous change from the directness of *Typee* and *Omoo*."[56] One of the more senior professors at Columbia interested in American literature, William P. Trent, thought *Moby-Dick*'s "inordinate length, its frequently inartistic heaping up of details, and its obvious imitation of Carlylean tricks of style and construction" limited the value even of Melville's "masterpiece."[57] But it was precisely in Melville's irregularities and difficulties of style that the newer generation of critics, like Carl Van Doren and Van Wyck Brooks, took pleasure. "The style" of *Moby-Dick,* Van Doren wrote, "is mannered but felicitous, warm, insinuating, pictorial, allusive, and witty."[58] Still, in the early twenties Van Doren continued to accept the judgment that *Pierre* is "hopelessly frantic" and the later novels and tales "not markedly original." Brooks claims Melville as a "word-master" and celebrates precisely those qualities which Trent had deplored: "If Melville's learned loquacity takes one back three hundred years, so does his use of language. He can carry an apostrophe to the length of a page, and his words have the strong natural flavour of Shakespeare's prose, or of Southdown mutton."[59] Shakespeare, Dekker, Webster, Carlyle, Sir Thomas Browne, Robert Burton, Smollett, Rabelais—of such were constructed the touchstones to validate Melville's mature style. Increasingly, thus, Melville comes to be seen not as a transparently approachable chronicler of sea tales, but as a densely allusive composer whose most precious treasures would be yielded up, as with other modernist texts, only to learned initiates.

In fact, by the late 1920s, Melville's style is being portrayed as exactingly "poetic." In 1927, Percy Boynton prints a passage from *Pierre* in verse form.[60] The following year, John Erskine presents *Moby-Dick* as a kind of *symboliste* "prose poem": "[W]hen we say that this story is a poem rather than a novel, we mean that its art consists not in reproducing pictures of the outside of life, such as we can call faithful, but rather in preparing our minds for an effect of emotion, so that at the end there will be a powerful catharsis, or release of feeling. . . . No detail is lost in the ultimate effect."[61] By the following year, the characterization of Melville's prose as "poetic" has become a critical commonplace, endlessly recycled in reviews of Lewis Mumford's biography.[62] Thus Melville's books emerge from the twenties garbed in the metaphysical designs valorized by his modernist and academic champions.

Still, for murkier later texts like *Pierre,* critics began to turn toward an even more powerful domestic analogy, Henry James. Early in the re-assessment of Melville, Arthur Johnson, who saw the enormous influ-ence of James on the work of the "Younger Generation," imagines what he doubts can ever be established: that in his boyhood James might have been "irresistibly attracted by things in stray Melville vol-umes he chanced to espy standing dusty on the shelves of libraries he was brought up among." The Melville strays Johnson evokes are, inter-estingly, "Bartleby," "Benito Cereno," and ultimately *Pierre*. The issue for Johnson is not plot or theme—"advanced," he says, even for today—but rather "sentences," that is, style. And he quotes two long columns worth from the then out-of-print *Pierre* to illustrate how "their thor-oughness . . . involved devices and idiosyncrasies grotesquely alike," and how "their methods of presentation . . . may appear rather to tally."[63] What Johnson is about here, I think, is drawing to the support of Melville, and especially his disregarded later works, the increasing critical prestige of James. At the same time, he is offering Melville as an older historical precedent for the modernist obsession with the more complex formal qualities of art. That paragon of the avant-garde, Carl Van Vechten, takes the process one step further in a few years. "I think it highly probable," he insists, "that the day may come when there will be those who will prefer the later Melville just as there are those who prefer the later James, those who will care more for the metaphysical, and at the same time more self-revealing works, than for the less subtle and more straightforward tales."[64]

Van Vechten did, in fact, call the turn. By the end of the decade, it is *Pierre* that is being reprinted in more than one new edition, and is being widely discussed by critics indifferent to South Seas adventures but attuned to the new insights of Freudian psychology.[65] And to how *Pierre* can be seen to enact yet another version of the artist's struggle against the feminized conventional. Weaver, irrelevantly but tellingly, uses the opportunity of introducing Melville's shorter novels to de-velop precisely such a reading of *Pierre*.[66]

I think my students' distaste for Melville needs to be understood in this context. For them, the modernist preference for difficult, indeed obscure, texts is no virtue; it may, in fact, reflect a process, deeply in-flected by class standards, whose effect is to marginalize them cultur-ally. Moreover, the high modernism of the 1920s has until recently—and still, in secondary schools—shaped literary study in the United

States, embodying in the New Criticism the theory and practice of writers like Eliot and Pound—and, thanks to many of those who promoted him seventy years ago, Melville as well. However my students might position themselves with respect to "Yankees" and "Redskins," masculine individual artists and feminized "others," few if any perceive virtue in obscurity of subject or density of style. My point here is not to validate my students' tastes but to understand how they shed light on the way Melville was constructed as an icon of modernist values in the 1920s and therefore as well, an icon of an academic reading community toward which my undergraduates feel deep suspicion.

The shifts in critical attention during the 1920s are suggestive not only of how Melville was used during that time but also of the workings of academic culture since. The movement from *Typee* and *Omoo*, the dominant texts (and the only ones steadily in print) prior to the First World War, through *Moby-Dick*, the book discussed by almost every critic in the early twenties, and to *Pierre* illustrates one of the points Jane Tompkins has made about Hawthorne in *Sensational Designs*. Over the years, he remained a "classic" author, but many of the texts on which that judgment was based changed with changing conceptions of literary value and the changing needs of literary intellectuals. So it happened, in a more compressed time frame, with Melville.

Challenges to established cultural values, as the modernist attacks on the genteel tradition suggest, often involve a process by which the authority of certain institutions declines while that of others rises. Melville's initial usefulness to the modernist project of the 1920s involved the roles constructed for him within the cultural contests I have been sketching: gentlemanly guide through the primitive, misunderstood heroic genius, modernist poet and icon. Essentially in one decade, he was transformed from the treasure of a small coterie of gentlemen into a form of cultural capital deployed by the advanced writers, critics, and professors and their disciples, who were exerting ever more cultural authority in the post–World War I period. He became important in their struggle against alternative sources of social power, whether these were defined as the exotic, the herd, or the genteel. As is, perhaps, always the case, what the critics of the 1920s made of Melville tells us more about them than about him. By the same token, the persistence of Melville as an academic cultural icon, however much our own tastes and our readings of him have altered, also tells us something about the nature of the academy in twentieth-century American life. Once Melville, by the processes I have been describing, began to achieve classic or canonical status, it has been far easier to reconstitute his values (or meaning) than his value (or canonicity). But tracking that process, how and why Melville has remained atop the academic canon, is yet another essay.

CHAPTER ELEVEN

**AND NOW, LADIES
AND GENTLEMEN,
MAY I PRESENT
MISS AMY LOWELL**

How does one account for Amy Lowell? Why would one wish to do so? To the extent that such questions have been posed in our time, they have been answered primarily in terms derived from queer theory. Just as that term, "queer theory," turns on its head an earlier derogatory valence, so with accounts of Lowell. In the twenties and thirties, especially after her death, Lowell was denigrated in significant measure because she was seen as lesbian; today, her recuperation is often a function precisely of her sexuality. There is a charming irony in that reversal and some critical truths as well. But to understand Lowell herself as a poet, and particularly to perceive how she stands in the gateway between earlier forms of nineteenth-century verse and high modernism requires an excursion both into late-twentieth-century constructions of gender and into nineteenth-century conceptions of the nature of and venues for poetry. What is necessary is an examination of her boundary-challenging qualities, her ways of bringing into question gender assumptions and borders as well as the categories by which we have learned to sepa-

rate "poet" from "entrepreneur," "lesbian writer" from "wealthy pa-
tron."

The term "Imagism" served for Lowell as a name for the literary movement with which she identified. But what did that term mean? Ezra
Pound had in 1913 explained "imagisme" primarily by "A Few Don'ts,"[1]
describing an image as "that which presents an intellectual and emotional complex in an instant of time." William Carlos Williams defined
imagism with the rubric "No ideas but in things," and he famously
illustrated it with the example

> so much depends
> upon
>
> a red wheel
> barrow
>
> glazed with rain
> water
>
> beside the white
> chickens.
>   (*Spring and All*)

Lowell shared something of these views of the movement. But in time
she extended the concept of imagism; for example, she writes to poet
and fellow imagist Richard Aldington (February 5, 1916) in connection
with plans for the second imagist collection:

> I am afraid it is quite impossible for me to confine myself within the
> strict Imagist tenets originally set down by Ezra [Pound]. You remem-
> ber that last year, when we severed our connection with Ezra, we
> decided to become broader, and we have certainly done so. In the
> main, I think Fletcher and I both agree with your interpretation of
> Imagism, but we are both intensely dramatic in our work, and I think
> both of us are willing to sacrifice some of the more stringent Imagis-
> tic rules for the sake of vividness and life. I think we should, within
> reason, allow such variations of type, as I am sure it tends to make the
> movement more interesting, not only to the public, but in itself as art,
> and I feel sure that there is in Imagism something very vital and real,
> which can withstand differences and yet remain itself.[2]

Here she is characteristically pushing beyond Pound's conception toward a more theatrical idea of verse. Indeed, Lowell's most interesting definition of imagism occurs in her introduction to the first imagist anthology she edited, *Some Imagist Poets*,[3] where she says that imagism is "presentation, not representation." She is consistent in that focus on "presentation." For example, she writes to a questioner, Ethel Harris (November 2, 1921): "I hoped I had made it clear in my 'Tendencies in Modern American Poetry' that Imagism has very little to do with the image, as that term is usually employed, but is a manner of vision and presentation. There is no such thing as this particular kind of vision and presentation in Shakespeare; his vision and presentation were utterly different."[4] It seems to me that Lowell's concept of "presentation" must be taken in at least three different but overlapping senses. Presentation implies, first of all, an oral/aural framework for the circulation of poetry. Second, and related, it points to a distinctive presentational role for the imagist poet, an active and, of course, gendered role performed within the world in which poetry was produced and consumed. Finally, Lowell's phrase suggests that poetic statement derives its value not from the "truths" it is taken to represent but from its distinct presentation of experience and of material reality. I want to look at each of these senses of the concept "presentation" as a means for better situating Lowell's poetic practice as well as her modes for problematizing gender and the boundaries of literary movements.

Lowell was very insistent on poetry as a performative medium. To Thomas Hardy, for example, she wrote (May 8, 1923): "I am sorry that you cannot get the hang of free verse. Some day you must let me read you a little; I think you will find that its rhythms come out with reading aloud. You know I make long lecture trips every year in this country, or rather readings, and I find that quantities of people understand these free verse poems better when they hear them read than they do when they read them off the page, so that I shall be grateful if you will let me have five minutes some time to give you an example of what they can be made to sound like."[5] As early as 1915, she had begun composing what she called "polyphonic prose"; to William Rose Benet, she had written enclosing such a work, "It looks like prose, but that it is not prose you will find if you read it aloud" (June 9, 1915).[6] The next year she had written to *The Dial* (August 21, 1916) "Of course poetry is a spoken art." And she commented to Mary Reynolds Aldis (February 5, 1916) about her poem "The Grocery," which was about to be published in *Masses*: "Please remember that it was not written intentionally as a play, but when I got it done, it seemed to me eminently actable."[7] In 1919, she was reading her poem "Bronze Horses," which took an hour and a half without breaks, to audiences across the nation, and such was the venue she preferred. In fact, as she explained to Hardy, polyphonic prose "has given me a vehicle which I did not seem to find in the other forms, and when I read it aloud to my audiences (for I have been acting the part of John the Baptist, going all over the country and giving readings and talks to stimulate interest in poetry) I have no difficulty in making them apprehend it" (May 14, 1919).[8] She even thought of her prose in similar terms; to Helen Bullis Kizer she wrote (October 23, 1917): "My prose writing is subjected to the same test which I use in my poetry, the test of oral rendering. To me all writing, whether poetry or prose, is merely a symbol for the spoken word."[9]

This oral conception of poetry connects Lowell to a nineteenth-century world, wherein poems were read aloud, not only from the lecture platform but in the parlor, not only at the fireside but at the graveside as well. One thinks here of Lydia Sigourney reading poems commissioned for public occasions as well as for private funerals, or Frances Ellen Watkins Harper, creating a character like Aunt Chloe as part of her platform repertoire. Twain hilariously satirized the verse of Emmeline Grangerford in *Huckleberry Finn,* but accurately conveys her public role in the local economy of death: "The neighbors said it was the doctor first, then Emmeline, then the undertaker." This significantly oral conception of poetry persists well into the twentieth century in the work of writers like Lowell, Frost, and Lindsay, all of whom were quite successful from the platform. But high modernism shifts the venue for poetry more toward the private study. It is not that Eliot's work, for example, fails to reward oral recitation—quite the contrary, as his own renditions of parts of *The Wasteland* show. But in many respects, his work, like that of Pound, is a poetry of allusion and diagnosis, a poetry of conscious difficulty designed to resist casual apprehension. Other modernists, like cummings, Moore, and Williams, create visual designs altogether lost in recitation. To some extent, the shift I am describing involves a change in the primary space for the circulation of poetry from various public and domestic venues to more academic locales. But I also want to argue that the change involves an analogous conversion in the persona of "the poet," a matter critical to Lowell's approach to literature.

Fairly early in her career, certainly soon after meeting Pound and others active in the imagist movement in England in 1913, Lowell undertook the construction of a quite distinctive literary role for herself: a poetic impresario. She took effective control of the imagist anthologies from Pound, who huffily withdrew, threatening lawsuits. As the primary editor of three collections (1915, 1916, 1917), and effectively the business agent for the group (including Richard Aldington, H.D., John Gould Fletcher, F. S. Flint and D. H. Lawrence), Lowell negotiated contracts, oversaw production, reviewed the publisher's accounts, and distributed royalties. In a sense, she was taking on little more than other female editors of that early modernist moment, like Harriet Monroe at *Poetry* or Margaret Anderson at the *Little Review*. But Lowell did not sit quietly in an office reviewing, editing, and soliciting contributions, literary and pecuniary. Rather, she created a very public role for herself, as performer, publicist, polemicist. She carried on a two-front war: on the one hand against Pound and his apostles, who viewed her as a "demon saleswoman" of poetry; and, on the other, against the conventions of American poetry societies, who viewed her as, at best, a disturber of the peace.

She was, of course, both. But more to my point, she was engaged in constructing a complex persona that, in the poetry as in the life, she performed at the edges of then contemporary definitions of gender. My language here is calculated to evoke recent theories of gender as performance, a kind of metaphor implying that since gender is constituted by matters like dress, carriage, speech, gesture, it can, imprecisely stated, be seen, like most of these, as what we "put on" each day when we rise and face the world. The metaphor implies that gender is very unstable, since performances change day by day—even if only in small and subtle ways, and as performers meet other performers and act out on the stage of everyday life. There is implicit in this metaphor, as appears from the phrase "gender bending," a considerable element of play. The form of play necessarily engages individual choice, since performance hinges on selection among alternatives by the performer. By "choice" here I do not refer to the question of sexual orientation but rather to the forms in and through which that orientation is—to introduce yet another performative image—"expressed." But "bending" also implies a certain constraint upon gender formation. As Judith Butler has put it in a passage often cited but oddly neglected: "*Gender* is not a noun, but neither is it a set of free-floating attributes, for we have seen that the substantive effect of gender is performatively produced and compelled by the regulatory practices of gender coherence. . . . There is no gender identity behind the expressions of gender; that identity is performatively constituted by the very 'expressions' that are said to be its results."[10] What gets marginalized in this passage, I think, is the phrase "regulatory practices of gender coherence," as if gender were an arena of free play and all of us able to don whatever costumes we find in the closet. But that is not the case, nor has it ever been, an acknowledgment critical to understanding the real dimensions of Lowell's work.

Lowell has sometimes been portrayed as something of a pathetic figure, upon whom male modernists like Pound and Eliot were able to act out their scorn–or anxiety. Pound was supposed to have brought a tin tub to a dinner party given by Lowell, presumably humiliating her by proposing that, as a "nagiste" (and, not incidentally, as a fat woman), she take a public bath. There is no question that Lowell was angered by such puerile joviality at her expense, as she made clear to Louis Untermeyer once she had gotten to know him. On the other hand, one of her favored ways of tweaking the good poetic fathers of the American poetry societies was by reading her poem "Bath,"[11] a work that necessarily evokes images of the speaker at her ablutions:

> Little spots of sunshine lie on the surface of the water and dance, dance, and their reflections wobble deliciously over the ceiling; a stir of my finger sets them whirring, reeling. I move a foot, and the planes of light in the water jar. I lie back and laugh, and let the green-white water, the sun-flawed beryl water, flow over me.

No doubt, Lowell was self-conscious about her size and personally resented gestures like Pound's that called attention to her body; yet she herself did precisely that in her reading. The seeming contradiction dissolves once one recognizes that Lowell's desire was, on one hand, to avoid being incorporated into Pound's increasingly masculinist project, a project capsulized in relation to Lowell by his term for her work,

"Amygism." In fact, Lowell was quite consistent in refusing *not* to meet, read, or even compliment Pound, but in avoiding any and all association with him: she would not appear in an issue of *Poetry* containing his work and rejected participation in *The Little Review* once Pound became a presence in that journal.[12] The issue is not, it seems to me, her corporeal self but how and by whom it would be deployed: she was indeed willing to assert her physicality as part of her own project, that is, breaking through gendered poetic and social constraints embedded in the Victorian culture of the poetry societies.

The line she is walking—or, more properly, creating—can be plotted from other sets of connections. For example, Lowell's letters reveal that she was a great champion of D. H. Lawrence, promoting him in America, occasionally helping support him, and insisting on including him in the imagist anthologies of which she was prime mover, though his poetry hardly fit even the most capacious definition of imagism. On the other hand, she never tired of disparaging James Joyce, whose work she regarded in much the same light as some ostentatious dirty joke. Explaining to Bryher (Winifred Ellerman) why her poems were not likely to be published in the United States in 1922, Lowell writes:

> You see you have gone off on rather a tangent in regard to poetry, and fallen into a curious malodorous strain which does not fit very well with your usual delicate and beautiful style, and it is just that kind of thing which publishers shy at. I like a great many of these poems very much, but others worry me by what I consider a slight lack of taste, a sort of jar in the feeling. I think one can say anything, no matter how peculiarly revealing, if one says it in keeping with the setting of the rest of the poem. For instance, D.H. Lawrence's eroticisms never strike me as otherwise than beautiful because of his point of view in regard to them. On the other hand, James Joyce's attempts in that line are as disagreeable as putrified meat. (March 20, 1922)[13]

Looking backward eighty-some years and through the lens constructed by a dominantly masculine high modernist narrative, it is hard to evoke the sources of Lowell's taste. Was it that she apprehended the sexual ambiguity of the earlier Lawrence, the Lawrence, as Eve Kosofsky Sedgwick has pointed out, heavily attracted to the equivocal sexuality of J. M. Barrie?[14] And at the same time that she saw Joyce as one of the Boys of 1914, forever caught up in rituals of male bonding and that kind of masculine self-assertion that construes women either as available or as antagonists?[15] Bryher was, at that 1922 moment, married to Robert McAlmon, whose efforts to be part of the expatriate, French circle of American and Irish writers are well known; did Lowell sense Bryher's puzzling, and quite temporary, drift away from her long-term lover, H.D., and toward that boy's world? There are no definitive answers, but the line Lowell draws between Lawrence and Joyce, between Bryher in relationship with H.D. and Bryher in relationship with McAlmon seems to me constituted by a project of gender definition.

A slightly different instance, having to do with clothing. To Bryher at an earlier moment, when the younger woman is contemplating travel to the American West, Lowell writes: "As to you dressing up in boys' clothes, I cannot help smiling. Do you think that we are a pioneer country? Alas, we are quite as civilized as England in those ways and have more prejudice. You would stand a better chance walking through the streets of London in men's clothes than in one of our small Western towns. The speed with which you would find yourself in the lock-up would really astonish you (January 7, 1919)."[16] Is Lowell simply being, as she writes later in the same letter, an "old fogy"? Consider one of the central image patterns of Lowell's somewhat later poem, "The Sisters" (1925). In this poem, how one treats clothing becomes central both to relationships and self-definition. Of Emily Dickinson Lowell writes:

> She hung her womanhood upon a bough
> And played ball with the stars—too long—too long—
> The garment of herself hung on a tree
> Until at last she lost even the desire
> To take it down. Whose fault? Why let us say,
> To be consistent, Queen Victoria's.
> But really, not to over-rate the queen,
> I feel obliged to mention Martin Luther,
> And behind him the long line of Church Fathers
> Who draped their prurience like a dirty cloth
> About the naked majesty of God. (lines 154–164)

Dickinson's problem arises (like her "sister's"?), one thus discovers, from the work of Martin Luther and the line of church fathers. A more

harmonious and fruitful program had earlier been posed in relationship to Sappho:

> I wish I could have talked to Sapho,
> Surprised her reticences by flinging mine
> Into the wind. This tossing off of garments
> Which cloud the soul is none too easy doing
> With us to-day. But still I think with Sapho
> One might accomplish it, were she in the mood
> To bare her loveliness of words and tell
> The reasons, as she possibly conceived them,
> Of why they are so lovely. (lines 19–27)

Again, it seems to me, Lowell is in life and in poetry crafting a way of
being in the world, a performance, that is at once practical, complicated, and heavily determined by her effort to construct a particular
gender definition. To don masculine garb is too simple—and, in Boston, U.S.A., too dangerous. To allow oneself to be draped by the Fathers leads to "hoarding" and "a gaunt maturity." Flinging off obscuring garments and baring words may lead to embracing a "leaping
fire." But the "mood" has to be right, for intimacy is "none too easy" in
the world the speaker inhabits, much less a more than "sisterly" clasp.
The "mood," the feelings toward which Lowell's imagery points, helps
determine—as recent psychiatric study suggests—what it becomes
possible to think.

A final instance having to do with reticence and display: Lowell
writes to one of the many young male poets, Donald B. Clark, for
whom she served as mentor, "in true Imagistic poetry, the method
more often than not points like a weather-cock to the emotion it both
reveals and conceals" (August 23, 1918).[17] She is at the moment completing the sequence of love poems that includes the well-known "Ve-
nus Transiens" and "Madonna of the Evening Flowers." Lesser known
is "The Weather-Cock Points South":

I put your leaves aside,
One by one:
The stiff, broad outer leaves;
The smaller ones,
Pleasant to touch, veined with purple;

The glazed inner leaves.
One by one
I parted you from your leaves,
Until you stood up like a white flower
Swaying slightly in the evening wind.

Lowell's problem with Joyce and with e. e. cummings (another young mentee she came to disapprove of) was not, this poem demonstrates, their sexual playfulness nor the generation of double-entendres. It was, rather, the direction in which the weathercock pointed. For them, it signified the strut of masculine play in which the female body passes as sexual currency. For her, it pointed "south," down, toward what was hidden, and yet revealed, concealed and yet performed. Toward, in short, the carefully-shaped gender identity Lowell embodied in her person and in her verse. The poem also vividly illustrates one of Paula Bennett's points about the tradition of women's poetry in the late nineteenth and early twentieth centuries: that they used floral imagery as a (relatively) safe way of encoding otherwise not publicly discussable—at least by them—matters of sexuality and desire.[18]

Bennett has also convincingly demonstrated that early modernist poets like Lowell and H.D. were drawing upon the development, particularly among women writers of the later nineteenth century, of a poetry whose meaning resided *not* in the text's "reference to a transcendent vision or an explanatory metaphysic" but only in itself, in the particular details the poem itself embodies.[19] It seems to me Lowell's formulation points to this distinction, to the systematic rejection of the idea, enamored by the poetry societies, that decent verse necessarily adumbrated decent values. For example, she writes to Edward Marsh of Macmillans (May 22, 1914) about the preface to her second book: "I find that people are not only interested in the form, they are startled, surprised, by the vividness of the images, upset by the obvious lack of the moral tag."[20] A few years later she picks up the theme with Ethel Harris (November 2, 1921): "The type of imagination you call Wordsworthian is as far at variance from the Imagist type of imagination as could well be. Wordsworth's vision may have started as simply as the Imagist vision starts, but his imagination instantly suggested significances beyond the mere vision. This is an unimagistic way of proceeding."[21]

All the same, there are values at contest in Lowell's verse, and not just those connected to the innovative aesthetics of Imagism. Rather, what Lowell is constructing is a world more widely open to the dramatic enactment of a queer variety of personalities. She never tired of mocking those who insisted on identifying the speakers of her poems with the writer—a common enough error, of course, seriously absurd when it came to a poem like "Appuldurcombe Park," which begins "I am a woman, sick for passion." But what is at stake is more than establishing the central nature of the dramatic monologue and related forms, so long after Browning. Lowell's project, it seems to me, is an effort to break down gender walls that largely confined writers to the consciousness of characters of their own sex. To be sure, this is not an altogether unique project: Cather, for example, essays it in *Death Comes for the Archbishop*, Wharton in *The Children*, and Joyce, with ambiguous success, in the Molly Bloom chapter of *Ulysses*. But this effort is much more central to Lowell, in terms both of her dramatic aesthetic and her desire to reconstruct gender definitions. For example, she writes to Mitchell S. Buck (April 12, 1922):

> One thing in which I disagree with you . . . is the question of men and women being different. I do not believe they are different; I think men and women are exactly alike. I have read Havelock Ellis's book "Man and Woman," and, like most of Havelock Ellis's things, it is special pleading; but, as far as psychological attributes are concerned, my experience has been that people are divided more by type than by sex, that the artistic man is more like the artistic woman than either is like the practical man or woman, for instance. I think, if you regard the matter dispassionately for a moment, you will find that we overstress the differences of the sexes.[22]

There is in this statement a certain conventionality within her unconventionality, but, as I have been suggesting, the gender play emerges more clearly in her poetry.

A large number of her poems, especially in the early years, take the form of what appear at first to be conventionally defined lyrics. Looked at more closely, however, these turn into a rather different form. For example, consider "A Petition":

I pray to be the tool which to your hand
   Long use has shaped and moulded til it be
   Apt for your need, and, unconsideringly,
You take it for its service. I demand
To be forgotten in the woven strand
   Which grows the multi-coloured tapestry
   Of your bright life, and through its tissues lie
A hidden, strong, sustaining, grey-toned band.
   I wish to dwell around your daylight dreams,
The railing to the stairway of the clouds,
   To guard your steps securely up, where streams
A faery moonshine washing pale the crowds
   Of pointed stars. Remember not whereby
   You mount, protected, to the far-flung sky.[23]

I think the sensibility expressed in this poem is butch and bottom; but more conventionally in our culture, masculine: gestures of abasement but a reality of control, praying "to be the tool . . . apt for your need," but still asserting "Remember not, whereby / you mount, protected." Lowell thus persistently turns the lyric form into a dramatic endeavor, a form of narration into a performance; many of her poems are indeed, as she wrote, "intensely dramatic." She thereby enables herself to try on a variety of personae, of ambiguous and it sometimes seems of multiple gender possibilities. Andrew Parker and Eve Kosofsky Sedgwick argue that "the performative has . . . been from its inception already infected with queerness."[24] They are referring to the 1962 work of J. L. Austin and to Derrida's critique of him, but it seems to me that the play across gender lines is precisely what, in 1918, interested Lowell in the lyric form. Certainly it is the form she adopted to produce her most successful—and ambiguously gendered—love poems, as in "Two Speak Together," the formal title of which, seldom noted, is "Planes of Personality."

One might argue further that Lowell's project is in some sense subversive. Butler argues against the idea of constructing identity utilizing "standards of narrative coherence."[25] Rather, she proposes, "performance may preempt narrative as the scene of gender production" (p. 339). Performatively subverting fixed narratives of gender, she argues, might allow "cultural configurations of sex and gender . . . to proliferate" and thus a "new configuration of politics to emerge" (p. 149). Perhaps. On the other hand, while Lowell's queer performativity certainly opened a certain gender space in her poetry and her life, the narrowness of that space, and the rapidity with which it closed when her voice was silenced, underlines the power of the "regulatory practices of gender coherence" against which such performances were pursued.

I have been endeavoring here to tease out the implications of Lowell's assertion that imagism is "presentation not representation." I want to return in concluding to Lowell's real life situation. Bound up by conventions of class, family, and regional provincialism, and unwilling to jettison privilege, she nevertheless played out on the elaborate stage of her Brookline home a serious and often outrageous drama of gender bending: living in a "Boston marriage," describing herself in Ada's absence as a "widow,"[26] smoking her Cuban cigarillos, running a household and a poetry business, even turning night to day in her working habits. Her life and her poetry are thus quite continuous, the one with the other, both aspects of the performance of what never was: a queer normativity, wherein the authority of class, like the authority of poetic theory, can be deployed as cultural capital to clothe in conventional Boston dress the "naked majesty" of Lowell.

CHAPTER TWELVE

**COLD WAR CULTURE
& THE CONSTRUCTION
OF MODERNISM**

One of the valuable services of the late and unlamented "culture wars" was to remind us that such contentions over artistic and cultural authority take place in every period distinguished by literary historians. Indeed, naming and establishing the boundaries of a "period" are among the means deployed in the struggle for preeminence within it. Cultural preeminence, moreover, even when achieved, is never writ in stone; or, rather, it is like the pedestal of Ozymandias, though subject not so much to time and tide as to human struggles over values and power. Not only do writers and critics contend for domination in their own moments, but long thereafter, other writers and critics reconstruct, reinterpret such conflicts as part of their own efforts to establish hegemony.

American "modernism" provides a case in point for this process. I and others have argued that a close look at literary culture during and after the First World War offers a far more conflicted landscape than one might have seen from the vantage points of classrooms and anthologies of the 1960s and 1970s.[1] The view offered then amounted to a chronicle of the triumph of experimental or "high" modernism, as exemplified by T. S. Eliot, Ezra Pound, Gertrude Stein, Wallace Stevens, e. e. cummings, William Faulkner, William Butler Yeats, James Joyce, and occasionally even Virginia Woolf, among others. It is much more clear today that the cultural terrain of the first decades of the twentieth century was inhabited by a far greater assortment of literary practitioners, including those of the New Negro Renaissance, including writers on the Left, and including many women, some of whom, like Amy Lowell and Woolf, consciously engaged in a kind of guerrilla warfare with the increasingly dominant male and largely white modernists.

But, I want to argue, it was less the contests that took place *in* the twenties that shaped later views of what constituted literary "modernism" than the conflicts that emerged from and helped underwrite the cold war. "Modernism"—a valued title though not a single style particularly of the post–World War One period—became the terrain upon which battles over cultural values, so central to the cold war, were fought. Now, with the petering out of the cold war, its totalizing narratives have also begun to deteriorate, and the processes which set them in place have come more clearly into view. I want to sketch here one of those processes, concentrating on American literature of the "modern" period, particularly poetry, and on some of the critics and institutions responsible for constructing what became for half a century the hegemonic view of that literature.

It is important to remember that in the mid- and late-1930s quite different conceptions of literary development and value during the two previous decades jostled one another for attention. Those differing views can be observed, among other places, in the many textbooks and anthologies published in the years immediately preceding and following the Second World War. Indeed, the changes in such books marks a process of cultural constriction characteristic of the cold war. The rather inclusive definition of modernism, or at least of the modernist period, prevailing in the 1930s may be represented by the contents of part 7 of Alfred Kreymborg's 1930s *Lyric America: An Anthology of American Poetry*.[2] Part 7 of the 1935 edition contains thirty-three poets, many of them familiar: Pound, Eliot, Lowell, Stevens, Sandburg, Moore, H.D. But it also contains many who would likely be unknown to most of us: James Oppenheim, Lola Ridge, Arturo Giovannitti, Walter Arensberg, Jeanne D'Orge, Evelyn Scott, Wallace Gould (whose work occupies almost as much space as Eliot's), Maxwell Bodenheim, Emanuel Carnevali, and Isidor Schneider, to choose some not quite at random, for I'm struck by the ethnic names, types not usually associated with the literary modernism of the Eliots, Stevenses, or even Lowells. Part 8, I should mention, includes southern writers, a full third of them African American.

I want to look more closely at a few of these collections, particularly *This Generation* (1939 and 1949), edited by George K. Anderson and Eda Lou Walton; *Understanding Poetry* (1938 and 1950), edited by Cleanth Brooks and Robert Penn Warren; and *The Democratic Spirit* (1941), edited by Bernard Smith.[3]

All of these were mainstream literary texts, not efforts by some small presses to call attention to marginalized writers. Anderson was a professor at Brown University and Walton at NYU; their book was published by one of the major textbook houses, Scott, Foresman and Company. Brooks and Warren were faculty members at Louisiana State University when they began the project of which *Understanding Poetry* is a part; by the time of the second edition they were professors at Yale and Minnesota, respectively. Their publisher was Henry Holt and Company, and their book was sufficiently popular that it was reprinted frequently in the intervening years between first (1938) and revised (1950) editions, despite wartime restrictions on paper. Though largely forgotten now, Smith was a critic, editor, and popularizer of some reputation, particularly in the late thirties: Smith contributed an essay on Van Wyck Brooks to Malcolm Cowley's 1937 volume called *After the Genteel Tradition,*[4] and with Cowley, he edited in 1939 *Books That Changed Our Minds,* a collection of essays on works by Freud, Henry Adams, Turner, Beard, Lenin, Spengler, and others.[5] Smith's contribution was on V. L. Parrington's *Main Currents in American Thought.* Smith's own *Forces in American Criticism: A Study in the History of American Literary Thought* had also come out the same year, 1939 (Harcourt, Brace). Smith's anthology was published by Alfred Knopf, another significant house, more oriented to the trade market than Scott, Foresman or Holt. It was never reissued after its first printing, though in 1947 Smith did publish a popular collection, *The Holiday Reader* (Simon and Schuster), which he edited with Philip Van Doren Stern.

To be sure, these anthologies were different in kind as well as in their cultural politics. In their preface Anderson and Walton state that their book "attempts . . . to show the dominant moods, manner, and content of British and American literature from about 1914 to the present" (p. v); in fact, they are less interested in "manner," that is form and style, than in content and, particularly, social and political outlook. Their 1939 organizing categories, which include units titled "The Waste Landers," "American Revolutionists," and "British Revolutionists," suggest further that *This Generation* located itself politically somewhere on the Left.

Understanding Poetry, by contrast, was, to quote its introductory "Letter to the Teacher," "conceived on the assumption that if poetry is worth teaching at all it is worth teaching as poetry" (1938, p. iv). On the surface, it makes no political statement at all; indeed, as Brooks and Warren wrote in a 1950 "Postscript" to their "Letter to the Teacher," "A decade ago the chief need was for a sharp focus on the poem itself. At that time, it seemed expedient to provide that focus, and to leave to implication the relation of the poem to its historical background" (1950, p. xxi).

Smith does not present his book as a "comprehensive anthology of American literature," primarily because "there are other sides to our literature than the single side represented here" (p. xxxv). His book is, rather an "effort to gather together the truly influential and characteristic works of the democratic writers of this country. The latter phrase," he continues, "alludes to most of the writers of genuine stature that we have produced. We possess an aristocratic tradition too, but even though it includes several of our most distinguished writers, it is a minor tradition" (p. xxvii). Smith's choices of writers—to which I shall return—as well as his discussion of ways in which socialism is as characteristic of American as of other nation's ideas, mark his work as emerging from a specifically socialist context, one characteristic of the popular front period of the late thirties and the forties.[6]

While such differences are, I think, interesting in themselves, what I find particularly striking about these three collections, taking them together and in relation to many other such books, is that in 1940 or so there was cultural space for the full range of what these volumes contain in terms of authors, styles, and politics. Indeed, in 1946, in the immediate aftermath of the war, in the period of the Progressive Party, at a moment in which Left-led unions were struggling to redefine how the economic pie might be baked, there remained space for conflict over cultural values. That is usefully illustrated by a 1946 volume called *A New Anthology of Modern Poetry*, edited by Selden Rodman and published by the prestigious Modern Library, a new version of a volume Rodman had compiled in 1938.[7] In 1946, Rodman's section 3 included those who would become the usual modern experimentalist suspects—Pound, Eliot, Moore (the volume begins with her "Poetry"), cummings, and their British equivalents. But Rodman also prints in section 2 "A Group of Negro Songs," spirituals as well as "John Henry" and "Ah Hate to See De Evenin' Sun Go Down," though not a single identified black poet. Here is also Bartolomeo Vanzetti's "Last Speech to the Court," printed as a poem, as well as work by, among others, Sarah Cleghorn (she of "The golf links lie so near the mill"), Josephine Johnston, and Kay Boyle. Later sections include other politically conscious poets like José Garcia Villa, and Muriel Rukeyser. Rodman's choice of individual poems is similarly inflected by a certain "progressive" outlook: for example, Edwin Markham's "The Man with the Hoe," Dylan Thomas's "The Hand That Signed the Paper Felled a City," Karl Shapiro's "Nigger," and William Carlos Williams's highly class-conscious "The Yachts." Rodman includes as "modernists" only poets who lived in the twentieth century (except for Lewis Carroll), though he rejects Kipling who, as he says, "for all the recent efforts to trim his imperial feathers, belongs with the great Victorians" (p. xxviii). But part of what exemplifies modernism for him emerges in a low-keyed attack on his rival anthologists, Louis Untermeyer and Conrad Aiken, whose choices are, he thinks, too influenced by the "New Poetry" and by "that of the Lost Generation." "Neither of these anthologists," Rodman writes, "showed much favor in the thirties to the significant new poetry of social protest," or, he adds, "in the forties to the religious counter-current stimulated by the war" (1946, p. xxxi). It is not that Rodman is himself especially a partisan of the Left or, in fact, of the religious revival. My point, rather, is that his definition of modernism remains, in 1946, open to such contrary cultural pulls.

By 1949, however, when the second edition of *This Generation* emerged, that cultural space had significantly dwindled; by the next decade, it was virtually gone. What, then, did these books, particularly *This Generation* and *Understanding Poetry*, contain both by way of canon—that is, inclusion of literary writers—and in terms of the theoretical ground on which such choices were made and recommended to readers?

The first edition of *This Generation* (1939) is divided into three sections: 1) "Carrying on the Tradition," 2) "The War and the Waste Landers," 3) " 'Chorus for Survival' "; the revised edition (1949) added a fourth section titled " 'The Age of Anxiety.' " These major sections are, in turn, divided into somewhat smaller units. To some extent, the sections are tied to historical events: prewar America, the twenties, the Great Depression. However, the writers included in these sections are not placed chronologically; rather, they are situated primarily on the basis of their ideologies and social outlooks. Eliot, of course, is at the center of the unit called "The Waste Landers": although copyright restrictions, or perhaps the reluctance of his own publisher, kept his poems out of the 1939 first edition of *This Generation,* his essay "Tradition and the Individual Talent" is included, and his influence is discussed at length in introductions to the section and to him as author and critic. He is joined in the "Waste Landers" unit by poets Edith Sitwell, a very little of Pound, Robinson Jeffers, e. e. cummings, Wallace Stevens, John Crowe Ransom, Malcolm Cowley, Frederick Mortimer Clapp, and Archibald MacLeish, as well as prose writers such as Dreiser, Anderson, Cather, Fitzgerald, Hemingway, and O'Neill, just to mention the Americans. Section 3 of the book, called the " 'Chorus for Survival,' " is divided into five units, the first of which, "Forerunners," includes Carl Sandburg, Randolph Bourne, Bertrand Russell, and, interestingly, Hart Crane. The largest unit, accurately titled "American Revolutionists," contains poetry by Horace Gregory, William Carlos Williams, Sterling Brown, Muriel Rukeyser, Kenneth Fearing, Alfred Hayes, Sol Funaroff, Edwin Rolfe, David Schubert, Reuel Denny, and Ben Belitt, as well as prose, perhaps surprisingly, by Faulkner and, more predictably, by Albert Halper, Irwin Shaw, and Kenneth Burke. The unit also contains the full text of Paul Green's "Johnny Johnson," for which Kurt Weill wrote music in 1937. I should add that one of the more interesting units of the first section, "Carrying on the Tradition," is called "Emotionalism and Intellectualism in American Verse" and contains poetry by Millay, Wylie, Bogan, Léonie Adams, and Gertrude Stein, among others; "emotionalism," clearly, was a feminine quality here.

I have outlined the contents of Anderson's and Walton's first edition of *This Generation* in such detail, first, to illustrate something of the fluidity of categorization that existed in 1939: neither a canon nor an altogether defining set of ideological criteria of modernism had yet been fixed. By emphasizing social values, for example, writers like Hart Crane, Williams, and Faulkner, who would in later accounts largely be assimilated to the practice of formalist experimentation, here join in the "Chorus for Survival." I have examined the 1939 contents at length also to mark out the limits of what was acceptable a decade later, when the second edition came out. Categories like "American Revolutionists" have quieted down into "American Writers and the Social Scene." Most of the left-wing writers, such as Rukeyser, Hayes, Funaroff, Rolfe, and Halper, have disappeared. A unit called "The Religious Revival" has introduced Robert Lowell, George Barker, and Roy Campbell. Stein has migrated to "The War and the Waste Landers," Marianne Moore has appeared therein, together with Katherine Mansfield, Virginia Woolf and, of course, Eliot's poetry.

In the altered cultural context reflected by these changes, a book like Smith's *The Democratic Spirit* stood no chance of survival. His 1941 version of modern American literature had omitted people like Eliot, Pound, and Stevens. But it included Randolph Bourne, Masters, Dreiser, James Weldon Johnson, Claude McKay, Countee Cullen, Parrington, Sacco and Vanzetti, Heywood Broun, Mike Gold, Millay in her political modes, Erskine Caldwell, James T. Farrell, Leane Zugsmith, Langston Hughes, Richard Wright, Genevieve Taggard, Dorothy Parker, Albert Maltz . . . well, I could continue, but the picture is clear. Or, rather, the picture is clearer, or at least beginning to be so to a twenty-first century reader, for whom many of these names are once again becoming if not familiar at least recognizable. By contrast, a 1950 Prentice-Hall book entitled *Modern Poetry*, and edited by solid academicians, Maynard Mack of Yale, Leonard Dean of Connecticut, and William Frost of Wesleyan, contains major selections from Hopkins, Yeats, Frost, Eliot, and Auden, and briefer choices of Dickinson, Housman, Stevens, Pound, Ransom, MacLeish, Tate, MacNeice, and Dylan Thomas. In short, the familiar modernist canon is by this time already in place, particularly in the academic environs of New Haven, wherein, as William Epstein has brilliantly shown, one version of cold war culture was being richly elaborated in and around the "Walpole factory."[8]

The narrative of what could emerge from a mainstream publisher in 1941 and largely disappear in the decade following is, of course, relatively familiar, though not always in its details. The question I want to address, however, has more to do with how these changes were brought about. To be sure, in a general way they were functions of the accelerating cold war. In the context of rising tension with the Soviet Union, the House Un-American Activities Committee and the Senate Internal Security Committee investigations, loyalty oaths, Truman's campaign against subversives, security purges of supposed leftists and homosexuals, and a general suspicion of dissent, much less anything categorizable as "deviance," socially engaged writing (or even thought) became suspect, and intellectuals or poets "guilty" of harboring it dispensable.[9] But such an answer really avoids any precise description of what Lionel Trilling called the "bloody crossroads where literature and politics intersect." To fill in some of that description, I want to turn to the anthologists who not only survived but absolutely thrived in the cold war period, Brooks and Warren.

Mr. Brooks was not only a Southern gentleman but also a shrewd organizer of cultural politics. In retrospect his work over the two decades or so from 1935 to 1955 can be seen as a kind of campaign, the success of which might well be envied by yesterday's conservative campaigners like William Bennett and Lynne Cheney. Brooks and Warren compiled three anthologies; apart from *Understanding Poetry,* they issued *Understanding Fiction* in 1943, and *Modern Rhetoric* in 1949. In addition, Brooks compiled with Robert Heilman in 1945 a collection called *Understanding Drama; Twelve Plays,* put together a book called *An Approach to Literature* with Warren and John T. Purser in 1952, and a 755-page volume called *Literary Criticism: A Short History* with William K. Wimsatt in 1957. That apart, Brooks published two collections of his own critical writing in this period, *Modern Poetry and the Tradition* in 1939 and *The Well-Wrought Urn* in 1947, as well as an edition of John Milton's poems with John Edward Hardy.[10] His productivity is stunning, especially when one considers that the anthologies all contain extensive critical commentaries and many went through significant revisions in this period. Leaving admiration aside for the moment, one needs to ask what were the major elements of Brooks's project that made it so successful.

Any project of cultural reconstruction will involve not only ideological elements but also those familiar to organizers: a political base, an identifiable opposition, and a target population. In a market economy, moreover, one either needs products that meet the demands of potential consumers or one must manufacture the demands for the products one has—what one might call the Honda and the General Motors approaches to marketing.

Brooks, at any rate, did them all. He had, first, a strong political base, especially in certain universities, among the southern Agrarians, who had by the late 1930s pretty much given up their political aspirations, such as these ever were, and settled back into more familiar, and accessible, cultural domains. These were men whose outlooks and partialities Brooks and Warren shared, and whose works they helped promote in their collections. So it is no surprise that of the approximately ninety poets in the revised and expanded 1950 version of *Understanding Poetry,* none is African American, and of some twenty-four twentieth-century American poets, four—Ransom, Tate, Bishop, and Davidson—are associated with the southern group, others are the group's students, and Delmore Schwartz is about as far as one gets toward the Left, or toward ethnicity for that matter.

Similarly, in his essay "The Modern Poet and the Tradition," Brooks briefly attacks Lindsay, Masters, and Sandburg—no surprise there— while devoting most of the essay's forty pages to close readings of poems by Ransom, Warren, and Tate, presumably his prototypical "modern" poets.[11] Again, in "Metaphysical Poetry and Propaganda Art," Brooks mobilizes I. A. Richards, as well as Ransom, Tate, and Eliot as critic to attack Marxist writers in general and the poetry of Langston Hughes and Genevieve Taggard in particular.[12] Brooks argues, somewhat obviously, that "the truth of the doctrine enunciated in a poem cannot in itself make the poem good," and that the "propagandist poet," "preoccupied with the inculcation of a particular message," incurs the additional risk of "leaving out of account the elements of experience not favorable to the matter in hand" (p. 49). Taggard, Hughes, and others in the collection of *Proletarian Literature,* then just published, are "sentimental," he insists, because "these poems demand a sympathetic audience upon which they may rely for a sympathetic context. . . . The experience established involves illegitimate exclusions and a special posing in a special light" (pp. 50–51). "The point is not whether or not the poet 'believes' in something, but that, though dealing with beliefs, he has not depended illegitimately on our emotional attachment to them as beliefs" (p. 53, note). As these remarks make clear, the identifiable opposition remained for Brooks, as for the Agrarians, communists, and other writers on the Left, whose poems fail to display the "toughness," "maturity," (p. 49) and ironic detachment critical to Brooks's model, the "metaphysical poets," and to those modernists he admires.[13]

But what is more interesting is Brooks and Warren's definition of their target population, identified at the very outset of *Understanding Poetry* in their prefatory letter as "Teachers." I doubt that they anticipated in 1938 the enormous expansion of higher education in postwar America, and its increasing authority over certifying and valuing cultural productions. Rather, I suspect, they saw culture as a province of the elite, largely male, and white people who would have been able, in Depression America, to become their students and those of the "Teachers" they addressed. But as the huge postwar expansion of higher education blossomed, Brooks and Warren's texts were as ideally positioned to take advantage of a thriving market as were manufacturers newly converted from tanks and bombs to producing Kaisers and Fridgidaires. And in the process, they helped install a set of cultural and social outlooks as surely and perhaps more systematically than did Charles Wilson in proclaiming that "what's good for General Motors is good for America."

For Brooks and Warren had a commodity—or perhaps it should be called a service—much in demand among those who would teach the still unacculturated people flooding into colleges after 1945. Assimilating these veterans, the sons and daughters of white ethnics, farmers' children, and others seeking to move upward in the postwar—and, more importantly perhaps, post-Depression economy—was central to federal policy in housing, in building suburban infrastructure, in supporting consumer industries and, vitally, in promoting higher education. Moving upward—being acculturated to upper-middle-class American norms—meant learning, in good Arnoldian fashion, at least a modicum of the best that had been thought and said. Here, of course, is where poetry came in, *Understanding Poetry,* in fact. What Brooks and Warren offered was not precisely a recipe for becoming "poetic"; rather, they provided practical, down-to-earth guidance for those wishing to figure out how such a cultural machine operated. To make it go one did not need to know anything much about history, biography, philology, or criticism, much less politics or ideology. Politics, ideology, immediate social issues probably got in the way, in fact. A dictionary and a little practice with language would do. It all seemed, at one level, so very . . . well, democratic, exactly what the new generation of students and their teachers needed. Indeed, in certain respects this "New Criticism," as it came to be called, *was* a progressive force vis à vis the often thoroughly academic philology that constituted the staple of university English departments, and the appreciative biographical gossip that made up much of what passed in secondary schools as the teaching of literature. At the same time, of course, Brooks and Warren were posing just what it was in the way not only of poetry, but of fiction, nonfiction, and drama, that a cultivated person *ought* to possess, like the appropriate Beethoven LP, the Picasso Pierrot print, the Russell Wright dishes. In this sense, they were not simply fulfilling demand, *à la* Honda, but helping to create it, like G.M.

Still, their own persuasive analyses, their readerly sensitivity, their ease before allusion and myth made it clear that however democratic the entryway to the domains of poetry, full citizenship in that world did not come quickly nor with ease. Indeed, full citizenship, it turned out, entailed not only perfecting the capabilities for close reading, but rather more importantly, developing that central quality of a mature "sensibility" (to use T. S. Eliot's term): irony. And here we return to the question of ideology. For if the surface of *Understanding Poetry* seems—and was seen—as remarkably free from the oppressive hand of political obligation, in fact its anti-ideological stance, as is clear today, constituted not an escape from politics but a shift of the ground upon which the cultural politics of the cold war would be fought.

We can observe the promotion and elaboration of what I might call the "politics of irony" by comparing comments on Eliot's "The Love Song of J. Alfred Prufrock" by George Anderson and Eda Lou Walton, on one hand, and by Brooks and Warren, on the other. The former's quick summary in the second edition of *This Generation* is contained in a note at the beginning of the poem, in part a summary of its action, in part their view of its content: "With death forever in mind, love and intellectual inquiry grow empty; life is an ironic picture, a meaningless pattern endlessly repeated everywhere. The epigraph indicates Eliot's view of life's futility, since death is inevitable. Since man no longer imagines he can conquer death, no longer believes he can bend the universe to his will, he is, for all his contemplation of death . . . or of life, mediocre, and his actions and decisions are therefore inconsequential" (p. 234). Today's reader might well regard this take on "Prufrock" as simplistic, but it is of a piece with Anderson and Walton's generally negative view of the character and influence of Eliot. They admire his formal innovations, his variations on neoclassical models. But they see strong romantic elements in him, a "nostalgia for the past." They also picture him as a man driven by concern with "modern morals and modern spiritual emptiness," but desiring to "avoid contact with ordinary people." "Although he gives no direct political advice," they write, "his argument seems to be that only by repentance and by acceptance of our fate, and perhaps by the martyrdom of our spiritual leaders, can this world be saved" (p. 229). Value for Eliot, they assert, "lay in the residue of art which the spiritual man has created. And the only retreat, therefore, was the retreat to great books, by the reading of which human nobility may be recalled" (p. 192). In short, Anderson and Walton present Eliot, the archetype of the "Waste Landers," as bored and driven, methodologically clever but bookish, a backward-looking chronicler of chaos and old night. They are focused on questions of value, of a writer's argument, of the social implications of poetic tropes like the "waste land." And if their tendency to identify Eliot's outlook with those of his characters, like Prufrock, is critically naive, they are nevertheless trying to sustain, even in 1949, some sense of the cultural work that literary texts in fact perform. If literature is no longer for them simplistically a weapon, they nevertheless see it as socially engaged even if, as in the case of Eliot, that form of engagement is hostile to their political agenda.

By contrast, Brooks and Warren's discussion of "Prufrock" occupies eleven full pages (*Understanding Poetry,* 2nd ed., pp. 433–444; cf. 1st ed., pp. 589–596). It begins by comparing Eliot's use of the dramatic monologue with that of Tennyson in "Ulysses" and Amy Lowell in "Patterns." What follows is an exemplary *explication de texte* of this exemplary modernist poem. Brooks and Warren are not content, however, to leave us at the level of close analysis. After six pages the discussion focuses on the nature and quality of irony as the fundamental method of this particular poem and as a central "instrument" of the skillful poet. It is worth quoting Brooks and Warren at some length here:

> As for "Prufrock," first, the irony is in keeping with the character. Prufrock is intelligent; he does see around and beyond himself; he sees his own failure in a perspective. Furthermore, Eliot the poet, as distinguished from the dramatic character in the poem, wants to make the point that the modern damnation is not a grand damnation: Prufrock is not to be taken too seriously, he is comic as well as tragic. It is easy to be self-pitying and over-serious about one's damnation, and Eliot would deprive the modern "you" of that satisfaction.
>
> There are many shades of irony, and sometimes the direct statement or presentation that is meant to be taken with full seriousness may be accompanied by some irony, perhaps the merest flicker, to indicate that the poet, in making his statement, is still aware of other possible attitudes toward the subject. . . . Irony . . . is not to be taken as indicating merely the negative and destructive attitudes, but as an indication of the complication and depth of experience. (2nd ed., p. 442)

This passage, and the ones that follow on the uses of allusion, illustrate nicely the direction, so different from that of Anderson and Walton, of Brooks and Warren's pedagogy. The lesson to be read here is *not* one having to do with a poet's social outlook but rather with a reader's cultural values. The capacity for irony, in particular, marks one's sophistication, one's ability to value complication, embrace contradiction. Irony, as I have argued at some length elsewhere,[14] the ability to hold contradictory ideas in balance rather than becoming committed to any dominant outlook, comes to represent the primary quality of the mature modern temper. It is supposedly what marks the American intellectual, unlike ideologues of Soviet persuasion. Indeed, the ironic point of view emerges as the defining feature of cold war liberalism.[15] For it enables intellectuals to disengage from the compulsions of earlier politically driven, and especially left-wing, analytic categories and the programs of social activism they underwrite.

What Brooks and Warren are promoting, in short, is a "structure of feeling" (to use Raymond Williams's phrase), irony, peculiarly suited to the cultural priorities of the cold war. Cultivating irony enabled many of us comfortably to discard the cultural imperatives of popular front or even mildly socialist politics in favor of a presumptively more "mature" and certainly more passive—and safe—way of being in the world, a way of being whose superiority was attested and promoted by our very admission to the house of poetry. Or rather, to that particular poetic house being constructed by Eliot, Brooks, Warren, and the other New Critics who came to dominate conceptions of literary value, and study, in the postwar years.

The ideological dimensions of this struggle over cultural authority emerges clearly in a chapter of William K. Wimsatt and Brooks's 1957 *Literary Criticism*: "Eliot and Pound: An Impersonal Art." Here Wimsatt and Brooks focus on Eliot's notion, articulated in his essay "Tradition and the Individual Talent," that "the poet has, not a 'personality' to express, but a particular medium, which is only a medium and not a personality." Indeed, Eliot goes on to talk about the need for the poet to "extinguish" personality to write significant verse. Wimsatt and Brooks comment that Eliot's passage "focuses attention, 'not upon the poet but upon the poetry.' It thus emphasizes the art object as such."[16] Returning later in their essay to Eliot's conception—after examining and criticizing Yvor Winters's ideas on the subject—Wimsatt and Brooks write:

> [Allen] Tate, rejecting Winters' conception of a poem as a *statement* about something, would define it as an action rendered in its totality. This action is not prescriptive of means (as science is) nor of ends (as religion is). The reader is left to draw his own conclusions. . . . There can be no *external* verification: the reader grasps it by an act of the imagination or not at all. (The didactic poet, the rhetorician in the service of a cause, the advertising man—all do appeal to some "truth"—some authority, scientific or unscientific—as proof of the case being made.) (p. 677)

Like Emerson, Wimsatt and Brooks are here confronted with the problem that a reader's imagination may prove whimsical, idiosyncratic. And also like Emerson, they are therefore drawn to the view that "the imagination obeys laws implicit in the human psyche" (p. 677). That, in turn, leads them to the universalist "assumption that man exists and that his fundamental oneness transcends the innumerable differences that set apart individual men and set apart men of various cultures and periods of history" (p. 678). Such an assumption is obviously antagonistic to the Marxist insistence on fundamental distinctions between human beings predicated upon their class positions, their relations to the means of production and distribution.

What remains unstated here are precisely the class-based conceptions of culture against which Wimsatt and Brooks have implicitly been arguing. To emphasize "the art object as such" is to marginalize anything that the work is presumed to represent or embody, whether the personality of the writer or, importantly in cold war terms, the social conflicts operating within the writer's society and culture. Read in this light, Brooks and Wimsatt's theoretical prescription can be seen as serving a function analogous to that performed by contemporary art critics like Clement Greenberg, who insisted upon the nonreferentiality of postwar American painting as central to its force and influence— disregarding, of course, how well a style like abstract expressionism, with its colossal individualism and utter marginalization of the social critique implicit in earlier social realist and expressionist styles, fit into the ideological needs of American cold war doctrine.[17] What Brooks and Wimsatt offer here theoretically is the other side of the same coin that Brooks and Warren offer as practice: a way of reading art which removes it from the practices of representation, either those of romanticism, with its emphasis upon the artist's personality, or those of marxism, with its emphasis upon the artist's world.

By way of contrast, consider a passage written by Leo Marx in 1953 on the problem of the ending of *The Adventures of Huckleberry Finn*. Marx is arguing against the efforts by figures like Eliot and Lionel Trilling to present Twain's novel as *the* quintessential American text. Marx wrote:

> To minimize the seriousness of what must be accounted a major flaw in so great a work is, in a sense, to repeat Clemens' failure of nerve. This is a disservice to criticism. Today we particularly need a criticism alert to lapses of moral vision. A measured appraisal of the failures and successes of our writers, past and present, can show us a great deal about literature and about ourselves. That is the critic's function. But he cannot perform that function if he substitutes considerations of technique for considerations of truth. Not only

248 ★ From Walden Pond to Jurassic Park

will such methods lead to errors of literary judgment, but beyond that, they may well encourage comparable evasions in other areas. It seems not unlikely, for instance, that the current preoccupation with matters of form is bound up with a tendency, by no means confined to literary quarters, to shy away from painful answers to complex questions of political morality.[18]

It took about thirty years to vindicate Marx's views over against those offered by Brooks, Wimsatt, Warren, and their confederates.

I do not want to exaggerate the influence of one set of texts or of one group of critics in the complex process of constructing cold war culture or of establishing a particular idea of the character and canon of American modernism. Brooks and Warren are, one might say, more characteristic than defining. And yet, cultural moments have a way of crystallizing in particular books, objects, art works, which do not only "represent" but help define such moments. The "understandings" Brooks and Warren's texts enable—and disable—constituted a very powerful set of learnings having to do with what is of value in literature, in cultural study, and thus in society. They are learnings that, even today, retain real power in the academy and therefore among those shaped by it, including, particularly, secondary school teachers of literature and many of their students. In a way, the most striking testimonial to the impact of Brooks and Warren's work is the silent grip it has retained upon ideas of a modernist canon and the appropriate approaches to its study.

1. Reconfiguring Academic Disciplines:
The Emergence of American Studies

1 The critique is that of George E. Marcus in "Repatriating an Interpretive Anthropology: The American Studies/Cultural Criticism Connection," *American
Anthropologist* 85 (December 1983): 859–865. Marcus attributes this limitation
to the focus of anthropologists upon small-group ethnography. As a consequence, he writes, "anthropology has largely failed to portray the cultural
meanings of its subjects—most often the disadvantaged, or marginally integrated ethnics—in the full context of a thoroughly penetrating culture of capitalism against which or in terms of which all small-group cultural life must be
created" (p. 862). Some more recent anthropological work seems to me to
transcend such limitations and therefore represents a fruitful addition to the
eclectic repertory of American studies methodologies.

2 See, for example, William E. Cain's opinion piece in the *Chronicle of Higher
Education*, December 13, 1996, p. B5, which argues that English departments
are, or should be, the domains for close reading of literary texts; and Stanley
Fish, who argues that English has lost its identity, its sense of coherent mission,
and thus a good deal of its public support in "Them We Burn: Violence and
Conviction in the English Department," *English as a Discipline: Or, Is There a
Plot in This Play?*, ed. James C. Raymond (Tuscaloosa: University of Alabama
Press, 1996), pp. 160–173.

3 Richard Ohmann, *Selling Culture: Magazines, Markets, and Class at the Turn of
the Century* (London: Verso, 1996); Rob Kroes, *If You've Seen One, You've Seen
the Mall: Europeans and American Mass Culture* (Urbana: University of Illinois
Press, 1996).

4 As is done, for example, in Alan Trachtenberg, "Myth, History, and Literature
in *Virgin Land*," *Prospects* 3 (1997): 125–133. Perry Miller, *Errand into the Wilderness* (Cambridge: Harvard University Press, 1956; Henry Nash Smith, *Virgin
Land: The American West as Symbol and Myth* (Cambridge: Harvard University
Press, 1950).

5 At the conclusion of "Common Sense," Paine speaks of "Freedom" in these
terms: "Freedom hath been hunted round the Globe. Asia and Africa have long
expelled her. Europe regards her like a stranger, and England hath given her
warning to depart. O! receive the fugitive, and prepare in time an asylum for
mankind." He thus constructs manliness in terms of a competition between a
new, legitimate suitor and the illegitimate authorities who have maltreated
Freedom in the past. By contrast, Hamilton concludes two early historical para-
graphs about the failures of Pericles, Cardinal Wolsey, and King Louis XV with
this sentence: "The influence which the bigotry of one female, the petulancies
of another, and the cabals of a third, had in the co[n]temporary policy, ferments

and pacifications of a considerable part of Europe are topics that have been too often descanted upon not to be generally known." The passage helps set up the gendered imagery employed toward his conclusion: "From this summary of what has taken place in other countries, whose situations have borne the nearest resemblance to our own, what reason can we have to confide in those reveries, which would seduce us into an expectation of peace and cordiality between the members of the present confederacy, in a state of separation? Have we not already seen enough of the fallacy and extravagance of those idle theories which have amused us with promises of an exemption from the imperfections, weaknesses and evils incident to society in every shape?" Thus for Hamilton, manly conduct is constructed against feminized utopianism. *The Heath Anthology of American Literature*, 3rd ed., vol. 1 (Boston: Houghton Mifflin, 1998), pp. 890, 1243–1244, 1247.

6   Leo Marx, *The Machine in the Garden: Technology and the Pastoral Ideal in America* (New York: Oxford University Press, 1964), p. 365. Marx writes: "To change the situation we require new symbols of possibility, and although the creation of those symbols is in some measure the responsibility of artists, it is in greater measure the responsibility of society. The machine's sudden entrance into the garden presents a problem that ultimately belongs not to art but to politics." To take those sentences with full seriousness, it seems to me, calls into question the project of devoting oneself to the analysis of art, writing books about high culture, especially if that entails—as it largely did in the cold war—placing politics, at best, on a back burner.

7   Priscilla Wald, "Terms of Assimilation: Legislating Subjectivity in the Emerging Nation," in *The Cultures of U.S. Imperialism*, ed. Amy Kaplan and Donald Pease (Durham, N.C.: Duke University Press, 1993), pp. 59–61.

8   Amy Kaplan, " 'Left Alone with America': The Absence of Empire in the Study of American Culture,' " in Kaplan and Pease, *The Cultures of U.S. Imperialism*, pp. 3–21.

9   As is done in Robert F. Berkhofer Jr., "A New Context for a New American Studies?" *American Quarterly* 41 (1989): 588–613.

10 Donald Pease, "Preface," *Revisionary Interventions into the American Canon*, ed. Donald Pease (Durham, N.C.: Duke University Press, 1994), pp. 4–7.

11 Pease, "Preface," p. 16.

12 Lisa Lowe, "Heterogeneity, Hybridity, Multiplicity: Marking Asian American Differences," *Diaspora* 1 (1991): 33.

13 Michael Denning's approach to the 1930s and 1940s "Cultural Front" offers an excellent contrary example. Denning argues against the usual accounts of the popular front and its cultural manifestations, which emphasize affiliation ("Are you now, or have you ever been . . . ?") and ideology. Rather, Denning emphasizes the importance of the 1930s social movements that helped construct the Congress of Industrial Organizations and combat fascism and racism, and also the material factors having to do with the changing constitution of the working class, especially in the newly emergent industries that pro-

duced and distributed mass culture. See *The Cultural Front* (London: Pluto Press, 1997).

14 Some overseas associations for "American" studies have pioneered such comparative strategies, notably the Brazilian Association for American Studies, within which the term "American" almost never refers solely to *North* America.

15 I examine this approach in greater detail in the chapter on American studies at the borders. A veritable explosion of work developing such paradigms has followed the pioneering approaches of Gloria Anzaldúa (see particularly *Borderlands/La Frontera—the New Mestiza* [San Francisco: Aunt Lute Books, 1987]); Néstor García Canclini (see particularly *Hybrid Cultures: Strategies for Entering and Leaving Modernity*, trans. Christopher L. Chiappari and Silvia L. López, foreword by Renato Rosaldo [Minneapolis: University of Minnesota Press, 1995]); and José David Saldívar (see particularly *Border Matters: Remapping American Cultural Studies* [Berkeley: University of California Press, 1997]), among others.

16 See also Paul Lauter and Ann Fitzgerald, "Introduction," *Class, Culture and Literature* (New York: Addison, Wesley, Longmans, 2001).

17 Particularly the group in the University of California system organized by John Carlos Rowe at UC-Irvine, and others.

18 T. J. Jackson Lears's, "The Concept of Hegemony," *American Historical Review* 90 (June 1985): 567–593, and Michael Denning's critique of Lears in "'The Special American Conditions': Marxism and American Studies," *American Quarterly* 38 (1986): 356–380, illustrate some of the tensions about the usefulness of such terms and the problems of the contexts from which they derive. See Antonio Gramsci, *Selections from the Prison Notebooks of Antonio Gramsci*, ed. and trans. Quintin Hoare and Geoffrey Nowell-Smith (New York: International Publishers, 1971).

19 For three (among many) striking instances of how ideas of hegemony are deployed, see Lisa Lowe, "Heterogeneity, Hybridity, Multiplicity: Marking Asian American Differences," *Diaspora* 1 (1991): 29–30, 41–42; Richard Ohmann, *Selling Culture: Magazines, Markets and Class at the Turn of the Century* (London: Verso, 1996), pp. 44–47; and Michael Denning, *The Cultural Front* (London: Verso, 1997), pp. 6, 63.

20 I have made some of this argument in "A Call for (At Least a Little) American Studies Chauvinism," *American Studies Association Newsletter* 18, no. 2 (June 1995). 1–3.

21 Claire Goldberg Moses, "Made in America: 'French Feminism' in Academia," *Feminist Studies* 24 (summer 1998): 261.

22 A case in point is at least some of the peculiarly harsh response to Janice Radway's 1998 American Studies Association (USA) presidential address. It may be that the discourse context Radway constructs in her paper, which consists largely of work by people in or from literary or discourse-oriented departments, has struck at least some historians and social scientists as exclusionary. See "What's in a Name? Presidential Address to the American Stud-

ies Association, 20 November 1998," *American Quarterly* 51 (March 1999): 1–32, and the responses to it posted on the American studies listserv, H-AMSTDY ⟨H-AMSTDY@H-nct.msu.edu⟩ in the weeks immediately following its delivery. Cf. David Simpson, *The Academic Postmodern and the Rule of Literature: A Report on Half-Knowledge* (Chicago: University of Chicago Press, 1995).

23 Michael Denning, " 'The Special American Conditions': Marxism and American Studies," *American Quarterly* 38 (1986): 360.

24 Robert F. Berkhofer Jr., "A New Context for a New American Studies?" *American Quarterly* 41 (1989): 593.

25 Trilling's classic formulation of the capacity of the rare artists to "contain within themselves . . . the very essence of the culture" appears in *The Liberal Imagination: Essays on Literature and Society* (New York: Viking, 1950), p. 9.

26 It is important to emphasize, as I do in chapter 3 ("Versions of Nashville, Visions of American Studies") that the discipline has been around in nonacademic form for a considerably longer period of time. One might argue, in fact, that "American studies" is coterminous with the construction of "America."

27 See, for example, Robin W. Winks, *Cloak and Gown: Scholars in the Secret War, 1939–1961*, 2nd ed. (New Haven: Yale University Press, 1996).

28 See, for example, Leo Marx, "Text vs. Context," talk given at the annual meeting of the American Literature Section of the Modern Language Association, Toronto, Canada, December 28, 1993.

29 Fully half the writers I mentioned above as contributing to a distinctive American studies reading list would, I think, characterize themselves as socialists of one kind or another, as is illustrated by, among other things, their emphasis on material conditions, their use of conceptual frameworks like that of "hegemony," and their focus on the dialectics of power in cultural analyses.

30 Michael Denning, " 'The Special American Conditions': Marxism and American Studies," p. 357.

31 Bill Readings, *The University in Ruins* (Cambridge, Mass.: Harvard University Press, 1996).

32 Norman Yetman, director of American studies of the University of Kansas, commented to me "that for students, it is precisely the American Studies' critique of consumer culture and the extent to which it pervades the university . . . that is both fascinating and attractive. Even the most unconscious of them seem intrigued by analyses that critique the institutions that they've been taught to regard with at least some semblance of reverence." Personal correspondence, June 16, 1999. I think Yetman is right, though my observation is that that reverence has been eroding, more or less rapidly.

33 Melani Budianta, response to Carl Pedersen essay, on Interroads discussion page, *Crossroads*, January 14, 1997 ⟨http://www.georgetown.edu/crossroads⟩ (American studies Crossroads Project, a project of the American Studies Association, sponsored by Georgetown University).

34 Steven Mintz, response to Pedersen essay, Interroads, January 15, 1997.

35 The syllabus is attached to this chapter.

36 Some have asked as a practical matter how I would deal with the fact that many local American studies programs list virtually any course that deals with the United States as part of the major or minor. Am I not here proposing a kind of ideological test for what "counts" as American studies? I do not actually think that is the case, for I am trying to report on what I observe.

As to the issue of what should count in terms of course credit, my approach to that is to raise the question with colleagues of how their course in history or English or another traditional discipline would be different were it cross-listed in American studies and thus counted toward an American studies major or minor. I do not think that colleagues are obligated to answer such questions; on the other hand, I do not think that American studies programs are obligated to accept any and all courses dealing with the United States as parts of an American studies program. It does not seem to me that there is any single answer to the question of how a course listed in American Studies would be different from one not so listed. My only contention, at this point, is that such a question needs to be raised . . . and answered.

37 Needless to say, the course has changed somewhat over the years. In the current (2000) version, I have dropped a few items and added, among other things, readings from *Exhibiting Cultures: The Poetics and Politics of Museum Display*, ed. Ivan Karp and Steven D. Lavine (Washington: Smithsonian Institution Press, 1991); articles about the exhibition "The West as America," notably William Truettner, "Ideology and Image: Justifying Westward Expansion," in *The West as America*, ed. William Truettner (Washington: Smithsonian Institution Press, 1991): 27–53, and Steven Dubin, "A Matter of Perspective," in *Displays of Power* (New York: New York University Press, 1999): 152–185; and a piece by Eric Lott on minstrelsy as an arena for staging working-class identity, "White Kids and No Kids at All," *Rethinking Class*, ed. Wai-chee Dimock and Michael Gilmore (New York: Columbia University Press, 1994): 175–211. These and other changes reflect, in part, the interest of our master's degree students in a new concentration on museums and archives and, in part, my sense that the study of exhibitions and museums represents an increasingly important area of work in American studies.

2. American Studies, American Politics, and the Reinvention of Class

1 Elliott Abrams, "Why Are There Neoconservatives?" *American Spectator* (November 1979): 10–11.

2 The 1999 report of the mayor's commission on CUNY included in an appendix information indicating that New York State's funding had, in constant dollars, decreased by 40 percent since 1980 while the city's funds had been cut by 90 percent! Cf. Nathan Glazer, "What the CUNY-Bashers Overlook," *New York Times*, July 11, 1999, sec. 4, p. 17. It has not been unusual for students to be closed out of required courses, to register in courses where they must sit in the aisles of lecture halls, or for whole categories of curricular offerings to be cycled down to a once-in-three-years basis.

3   The full text of the memorandum, GPO 899-125, July 1, 1965, is reprinted, among other places, in Paul Lauter and Florence Howe, *The Conspiracy of the Young* (New York: World Publishing, 1970), pp. 184–191.

4   Here, for example, is George F. Will on the subject (in "The Education Bubble," *Washington Post*, March 30, 1997, C7): "But, then, the market for college graduates is saturated: an estimated 20 percent work in jobs that do not really require a degree. Says [Anne] Matthews [in *Bright College Years*], 'A third of Domino's pizza-delivery drivers in the Washington, D.C., area have B.A.s.' A help wanted ad seeking a warehouse supervisor for The Gap reads: 'Bachelor's degree required, and the ability to lift 50 pounds.' Matthews's book refutes the premise of President Clinton's plan for tuition tax credits and deductions."

5   The first report, *Breaking the Social Contract*, is available from the Council for Aid to Education (Santa Monica: Rand Corporation, 1997). The second, by the National Commission on the Cost of Higher Education, *Straight Talk about College Costs and Prices*, is available from Oryx Press, Phoenix, Ariz.

6   It is perhaps useful in assessing the council's prescription to keep in mind a figure cited by Bill Fletcher Jr., the education director of the AFL-CIO. Fletcher put it this way: "358 people, on this planet of ours, have a total combined wealth greater than the poorest 45% of the world's population. That's right . . . 358 people have a combined wealth greater than 2.3 billion people!" Speech to the University and College Labor Education Association, San Jose, Calif., May 1, 1998.

7   Three of the commission members were appointed by Newt Gingrich and three by Trent Lott. They included a senior fellow at the Hoover Institution, a lobbyist for banks, another lobbyist for U.S. West, Inc., and a number of middle-America college and university presidents. Needless to say, no faculty (or student) organizations were represented among the commissioners, much less organizations of the many others who work in higher education.

8   National Commission, *Straight Talk*, p. 14. The statistics it provides are striking: "The proportion of part-time faculty and staff employed by colleges and universities increased from 33 percent of all instructional faculty and staff in 1987 to 42 percent in 1992. In the same period, the percentage of instructional faculty and staff with tenure declined from 58 to 54 percent. And, the reported number of student contact hours at all institutions increased from 300 in 1987 to 337 in 1992."

9   Bill Readings, *The University in Ruins* (Cambridge, Mass.: Harvard University Press, 1996).

10   Of course, this immediately raises a generally unasked question: "Who is most ready for higher education?" That is precisely the question addressed in a research project being carried out by Richard Flacks and Scott L. Thomas, "Students in the Nineties: Report on a Project in Progress." Photocopy in possession of author. I shall have more to say about this research below.

11   A lively debate on the subject took place at ⟨H-AMSTDY@H-net.msu.edu⟩, August 7–14, 1997.

12 For a succinct example, see the entry on the "Frontier" by Patricia Nelson
    Limerick in *A Companion to American Thought*, ed. Richard Wightman Fox
    and James T. Kloppenberg (Oxford: Blackwell, 1995), pp. 255–259.

13 F. O. Matthiessen, "The Education of a Socialist" (excerpted from his *From the
    Heart of Europe* [New York: Oxford, 1948] in *F. O. Matthiessen (1902–1950): A
    Collective Portrait*, ed. Paul M. Sweezy and Leo Huberman (New York: Henry
    Schuman, 1950), p. 5.

14 Paul M. Sweezy, "Labor and Political Activities," in Sweezy and Huberman,
    F. O. Matthiessen, pp. 61–63.

15 Sweezy, "Labor and Political Activities," pp. 73–74.

16 F. O. Matthiessen, "The New Mexican Workers' Case," *New Republic* 82 (1935):
    361–363.

17 The best account of the virtues and contradictions in Matthiessen's political
    activities and cultural writings is, I think, to be found in William Cain, *F. O.
    Matthiessen and the Politics of Criticism* (Madison: University of Wisconsin
    Press, 1988), especially chapter 4 and "Conclusion."

18 A trenchant analysis is provided by Micaela di Leonardo in "White Lies, Black
    Myths: Rape, Race, and the Black 'Underclass,' " *The Gender/Sexuality Reader:
    Culture, History, Political Economy*, ed. Roger N. Lancaster and Micaela di
    Leonardo (New York: Routledge, 1997), pp. 53–68.

19 Kathy Newman, "Poor, Hungry, and Desperate? Or, Privileged, Histrionic,
    and Demanding? In Search of the True Meaning of 'Ph.D.,' " *Will Teach for
    Food: Academic Labor in Crisis*, ed. Cary Nelson (Minneapolis: University of
    Minnesota Press, 1997), p. 88.

20 From H. H. Lewis's book, *Thinking of Russia* (1932), reprinted by Cary Nel-
    son in *Repression and Recovery: Modern American Poetry and the Politics of Cul-
    tural Memory, 1910–1945* (Madison: University of Wisconsin Press, 1989),
    p. 49.

21 See Ann Fitzgerald and Paul Lauter, "Introduction," *Class, Culture and Litera-
    ture* (New York: Addison, Wesley, Longman, 2000).

22 Karl Shapiro, *Collected Poems, 1940–1978* (New York: Random House, 1978),
    p. 10.

23 Jules Henry, *Culture against Man* (New York: Random House, 1963), pp. 289–
    290.

24 A useful and easily accessible analysis of some of the negative policy implica-
    tions of student evaluations is to be found in Robert E. Haskell "Academic
    Freedom, Tenure, and Student Evaluation of Faculty: Galloping Polls in the
    21st Century," *Education Policy Analysis Archives: A Peer-Reviewed Electronic
    Journal* 5, February 12, 1997, ⟨http://www.bus.lsu.edu/accounting/faculty/
    lcrumbley/educpoly.htm⟩. Haskell's article is primarily concerned with the
    issue of academic freedom, but he cites a number of other studies dealing with
    the impact of student evaluations, particularly on job retention decisions.
        See also Robin Wilson, "New Research Casts Doubt on Value of Student
    Evaluations of Professors," *Chronicle of Higher Education* 44 (January 16,

1998): A12(3) (an article summarizing studies published, among other places, in *Change Magazine* 29, no. 5 (September–October 1997): 12ff: [Wendy M. Williams and Stephen J. Ceci, "'How'm I Doing?' Problems with Student Ratings of Instructors and Courses"] and *American Psychologist*).

25 On the *New York Times* op-ed page for August 6, 1998, Sheila Schwartz, a retired professor of English education at SUNY/New Paltz related how one of her unhappy students arrived at her office with a West Point husband decked out in full uniform, including a galaxy of medals. Schwartz, of course, laughed, but for a younger faculty member or a part-timer such a display, and an assistant dean's complaint about her hard standards, would be no laughing matter but the preliminary to joblessness.

26 The locus classicus of this swill is probably to be found in Peter Brooks's endpaper "Graduate Learning as Apprenticeship," in the *Chronicle of Higher Education* 20 (December 1996): A52. I remember when I was an undergraduate coming on a book titled, as I recall it, *How to Lie with Statistics*. I suppose a collection of these paeans to mentoring could be collected in a volume called "How to Lie with Panache." While the Brooks article would no doubt be a star attraction, form letters, written in the wake of the TAS' grade strike, from Yale's president Richard Levin and from senior members of its English department would no doubt provide excellent filler.

27 Micaela di Leonardo, "Patterns of Culture Wars: Place, Modernity, and the Contemporary Political Economy of Difference," *Exotics at Home: Anthropologies, Others, American Modernity* (Chicago: University of Chicago Press, 1998), for example, pp. 319–324.

28 Sandra Patton, "Producing '(Il)Legitimate' Citizens: An Interdisciplinary Ethnographic Approach to Public Policy," photocopy of paper presented at 1996 American Studies Association convention, Kansas City, p. 3. An updated version of Patton's research appears in her book, *Birth Marks: Transracial Adoption in Contemporary America* (New York: New York University Press, 2000). The M. H. Agar article is "Stretching Linguistic Ethnography over Part of a State," *Journal of Linguistic Anthropology* 1, no. 2 (1991): 131–142.

29 Di Leonardo, "Patterns of Culture Wars," p. 319.

30 It is interesting to speculate in this connection what combination of informed testimony and political pressure apparently moved the National Commission on the Cost of Higher Education from what initially appeared to be a very conservative agenda to its relatively restrained report.

31 Patton, "Producing '(Il)Legitimate' Citizens," p. 8. The articles referred to include Charles Murray, "The Coming White Underclass," *Wall Street Journal*, November 17, 1994; David W. Murray, "Poor Suffering Bastards: An Anthropologist Looks at Illegitimacy," *Policy Review* 68 (spring 1994): 9–15.

32 Guilt is not, of course, the operative category. As George Lipsitz has pointed out (*The Possessive Investment in Whiteness* [Philadelphia: Temple University Press, 1998]), all whites in the United States, have what he calls a "possessive investment in whiteness," a product of the construction of all racial categories.

That investment includes not only income advantages, but the probably greater advantages accruing from discrepancies in wealth. These derive in significant measure from differential access to owning property—most often in the form of a private home—the primary way by which ordinary people in this country have accumulated meaningful wealth.

33 Richard Flacks and Scott Thomas, "Students in the Nineties," p. 13. Flacks and Thomas are careful to qualify these generalizations by pointing out, first, that the majority of white students do not "identify with the party culture," and that they need to conduct more research to clarify the outlooks and behaviors of such students as well as of Asian American students, since their sample contained too few of the last to draw meaningful conclusions (p. 20).

3. Versions of Nashville, Visions of American Studies

1 Janice Radway has raised some interesting issues regarding both the name and the conception of American studies in her 1998 presidential address, "What's in a Name?" *American Quarterly* 51 (1999): 1–32. There have, on occasion, been efforts to change the name of what we do; for example, the international fellowship program at the University of Iowa directed by Jane Desmond and Virginia Domínguez is called "International Fellowships in United States Studies," but more often IFUSS, the acronym to some extent absorbing the politics of the changed name.

2 See "Talk Concerning the First Beginning," in Ruth Bunzel, "Zuni Origin Myths," *Forty-Seventh Annual Report of the Bureau of American Ethnology* (Washington, D.C.: Government Printing Office, 1930). A slightly abbreviated version is included in Paul Lauter, et al., *The Heath Anthology of American Literature,* 3rd ed., vol. 1 (Boston: Houghton Mifflin, 1998), pp. 27–41.

3 See, for example, Cary Nelson and Michael Bérubé, eds., *Higher Education under Fire: Politics, Economics and the Crisis of the Humanities* (New York: Routledge, 1994).

4 Richard Gray, *Writing the South: Ideas of an American Region* (Cambridge: Cambridge University Press, 1986), pp. 122–164; Alexander Karanikas, *Tillers of a Myth: Southern Agrarians as Social and Literary Critics* (Madison: University of Wisconsin Press, 1966); Louis D. Rubin Jr., *The Wary Fugitives: Four Poets and the South* (Baton Rouge: Louisiana State University Press, 1978); Lewis P. Simpson, *The Fable of the Southern Writer* (Baton Rouge: Louisiana State University Press, 1994), pp. 13–23; Thomas Daniel Young, *Waking Their Neighbors Up* (Athens: University of Georgia Press, 1982), and "The Fugitives: Ransom, Davidson, Tate" and "The Agrarians," in *The History of Southern Literature,* ed. Louis D. Rubin Jr., et al. (Baton Rouge: Louisiana State University Press, 1985), pp. 319–332, 429–435.

5 John Gould Fletcher, "Education, Past and Present," in *I'll Take My Stand: The South and the Agrarian Tradition* (New York: Harper, 1930), p. 117.

6 Lyle H. Lanier, "A Critique of the Philosophy of Progress," in *I'll Take My Stand,* p. 146.

7   See, for example, Young, *Waking Their Neighbors Up*, pp. 6off., and Rubin, *Wary Fugitives*, pp. 237–240.

8   This phrase appears as part of the foreword to the first issue of *The Fugitive*. In view of the backward directions in which the Agrarians' ideas seemed to lead, some of the rest of the statement bears repeating: "Official exception having been taken by the sovereign people to the mint julep, a literary phase known rather euphemistically as Southern Literature has expired, like any other stream whose source is stopped up. The demise was not untimely: among other advantages, THE FUGITIVE is enabled to come to birth in Nashville, Tennessee, under a star not entirely unsympathetic. THE FUGITIVE flees from nothing faster than from the high-caste Brahmins of the Old South."

9   George Core argues, correctly I think, that "to say that Ransom, Tate, and Warren simply transferred their energy from Agrarianism to the New Criticism is simplistic at best, and it denies what one knows not only of these men but of artists in general." "Agrarianism, Criticism, and the Academy," *A Band of Prophets: The Vanderbilt Agrarians after Fifty Years*, ed. William C. Havard and Walter Sullivan (Baton Rouge: Louisiana State University Press, 1982), p. 128. As I suggest below, no simplistic theory can account for this shift in direction. Still, the fundamental views of the men involved persist. As Core himself points out, "The leading Agrarians wrote criticism not only in a positive response to Eliot and the others [like I. A. Richards, William Empson, and F. R. Leavis, for example] but in a negative reaction against Marxism and Marxist criticism (one remembers the alternative title that was proposed for *I'll Take My Stand—Tracts against Communism*)" p. 129.

10 See, for example, Ransom's "Introduction" to *I'll Take My Stand*, p. xv; his "The Aesthetic of Regionalism," *American Review* 2 (January 1934): 290–310; and Donald Davidson, "A Mirror for Artists," in *I'll Take My Stand*, pp. 40–50.

11 Gray, *Writing the South*, p. 145.

12 See particularly, Clayborne Carson, *In Struggle: SNCC and the Black Awakening of the 1960s* (Cambridge, Mass.: Harvard University Press, 1981), pp. 21–25, 34–35; and James H. Laue, *Direct Action and Desegregation, 1960–1962: Toward a Theory of the Rationalization of Protest* (Brooklyn: Carlson, 1989), passim. The only publication I have found wholly devoted to the Nashville movement is James E. Jackson, *Three Brave Men Tell How Freedom Comes to an Old South City* (New York: Publisher's New Press, 1963), which is a twenty-eight-page pamphlet mainly devoted to interviews with John Lewis, the Reverend J. Metz Rollins, and the Reverend C. T. Vivian.

13 The first statement of purpose for what was to become the Student Nonviolent Coordinating Committee, prepared for the Raleigh meeting of sit-in leaders, April 15–17, 1960, was written by the Reverend James Lawson, the primary organizer of the Nashville student movement. It emphasized the transformative power of nonviolence: "By appealing to conscience and standing on the moral nature of human existence, nonviolence nurtures the atmosphere in which reconciliation and justice become actual possibilities." Quoted in Laue,

Direct Action and Desegregation, p. 7. Nashville participants in SNCC continued to stress nonviolence as a fundamental philosophy of life both during the southern movement and afterward in venues like Chicago. In 1961, when people from Nashville took up the freedom rides, the city became the site of nonviolent training for participants.

14 The "Negro Students' Code" is reprinted in full in Harrison E. Salisbury, "Negro Cleric Sets Nonviolent Aims," *New York Times*, March 2, 1960. A flier containing the code in a slightly altered version, among other materials, is in the Swarthmore College Peace Collection, Fellowship of Reconciliation Race Relations Files, DG 13, series E, box 5, file for John Nevin Sayre. In the margin is written, perhaps by Sayre or another Fellowship of Reconciliation (FOR) staff person, "James Lawson worked this out."

15 "Annual Report of Howard Kester, Southern Secretary to the Annual Conference of The Fellowship of Reconciliation, October 1933." FOR Race Relations Files, DG 13, series E, box 1.

16 See letterhead for Fellowship's Southern Advisory Committee, FOR Race Relations Files, box 1.

17 See variety of materials in FOR Race Relations Files, box 2.

18 Paul Laprad, "Nashville: A Community Struggle," *Sit-Ins: The Students Report*, CORE pamphlet, May 1960, FOR Race Relations Files, box 5. Laprad was a student at Fisk University. See also William V. Shannon, "Sitdowns in the South," *New York Post*, March 30–31, 1960.

19 See "Violence, Non-Violence and the Struggle for Social Justice," undated [1969?] FOR flier, and J. Robert Nelson, "Vanderbilt's Time of Testing," *Christian Century*, August 10, 1960, p. 4, reprinted in *The Lawson-Vanderbilt Affair: Letters to Dean Nelson* (Nashville: privately printed, August 1960), FOR Race Relations Files, box 2.

20 J. M. Lawson Jr., "Evaluation, Institute on Nonviolence, Spelman College, Atlanta Georgia, July 22–24, 1959," FOR Race Relations Files, box 2.

21 "Report of the SNCC Meeting, Atlanta, May 13–14, 1960," FOR Race Relations Files, box 5.

22 James Laue quotes Diane Nash as saying, "The feeling of right, the moral rejuvenation is the only thing that carries you over," *Direct Action and Desegregation*, p. 205. Laue's comment, as both a participant and observer of the southern movement, is also of interest here: "The research of others as well as my own interviews indicate that most sit in participants in 1960 felt that for the first time they were actually *doing* something to help bring social reality in line with their ideals" (p. 205).

23 James Laue twice quotes the Reverend James Lawson as follows: "Most of us work simply for concessions from the system, not for transforming the system. . . . But if after 300 years, segregation is still a basic pattern rather than a peripheral custom, should we not question the 'American way of life' which allows segregation so much structural support?" *Direct Action and Desegregation*, p. xviii.

24 H. D. Thoreau, "A Plea for Captain John Brown," *The Works of Thoreau*, sel. and ed. Henry Seidel Canby (Cambridge, Mass.: Houghton Mifflin, 1937), p. 833.

25 Pauline Knight, "Notes from Prison," *Southern Patriot*, September 1961, FOR Race Relations Files, box 6.

26 Gerard Plecki, *Robert Altman* (Boston: Twayne, 1985), p. 77.

27 See William H. Epstein, "Counter-Intelligence: Cold-War Culture and Eighteenth-Century Studies," *ELH* 57 (1990): 63–99; and Paul Lauter, "Little White Sheep, or How I Learned to Dress Blue," *Yale Journal of Criticism* 8 (fall 1995): 103–129.

28 So, very persuasively, argued Christopher Newfield in "Corporate Pleasures for a Corporate Planet" and Avery F. Gordon, "The Work of Corporate Culture: Diversity Management," at the convention of the American Studies Association, Nashville, Tenn., October 30, 1994.

29 See Malcolm W. Browne, "What Is Intelligence, and Who Has It?" *New York Times Book Review*, October 16, 1994, pp. 3, 41, 45; and *New Republic* 211 (October 30, 1994), especially pp. 27–37.

4. Culture and Conformity in Wartime America:
My Junior High School Songbook

1 See Clifford Geertz, *The Interpretation of Cultures; Selected Essays* (New York: Basic Books, 1973).

2 See Joel Pfister, "The Americanization of Cultural Studies," *Yale Journal of Criticism* 4 (1991): 199–229.

3 See, for example, Andrew Ross, *No Respect: Intellectuals and Popular Culture* (New York: Routledge, 1989).

4 Such policies are usefully discussed in Micaela di Leonardo, "Black Myths, White Lies," *Village Voice* 37 (September 22, 1992): 30ff.

5 See, for example, Marjorie Garber and Rebecca Walkowitz, eds., *Secret Agents: The Rosenberg Case, McCarthyism, and Fifties America* (New York: Routledge, 1995).

6 The songbook could also be an index to the ideas of music teachers as a group. Others of my generation with whom I have spoken about music classes had similar experiences, including the compiling of the kind of songbook I describe below. But I have not been able to determine whether the process reflected a citywide curriculum.

7 See Robert A. Caro, *The Power Broker: Robert Moses and the Fall of New York* (New York: Knopf, 1974).

8 See John Costello, *Virtue under Fire* (Boston: Little, Brown, 1985).

5. Dinosaur Culture: From Mansfield Park *to* Jurassic Park

1 Dwight Macdonald, "A Theory of Mass Culture," *Diogenes* 3 (summer 1953): 1–17.

2   Lionel Trilling, "*Mansfield Park*," *The Opposing Self* (New York: Viking Press, 1955), pp. 181–202.

3   When I gave the material in this essay at the College of William and Mary, Robert Gross suggested to me that the path I am charting had been laid out some time before by writers affiliated with the Frankfurt school of social and cultural thought. No doubt that is historically accurate, and perhaps my account reflects less a general set of experiences than those particular to academics initially trained in earlier forms of English studies. Nevertheless, I think my narrative may accurately capture a certain widely shared learning curve for those interested in American studies. But that, I suppose, I must leave to my readers to decide.

4   Editorial, "Jurassic Jitters," *Los Angeles Times*, June 16, 1993, p. B6.

5   Many of these details are drawn from the book produced to capitalize on the interest in the film's production, Don Shay and Jody Duncan, *The Making of Jurassic Park* (New York: Ballentine Books, 1993), especially pp. 28–32.

6   "Should We Revive the Dinosaurs?" *New York Times*, June 13, 1993, p. E18.

7   See, for example, Stephen Jay Gould, "Dinomania," *New York Review of Books* 40 (August 12, 1993): 52–53.

8   Elizabeth Ross, "Din-O-Mite Exhibit on the Prowl," *Christian Science Monitor*, November 17, 1993, p.17.

9   Kate Fitzgerald and Marcy Magiera, " 'Jurassic Pk.' Blitz: It's (Pre)historic," *Advertising Age* 64 (May 17, 1993): 1.

10 Fitzgerald and Magiera, " 'Jurassic Pk.' "

11 Lisa Marie Petersen and Matthew Grimm, "Big Mac Execs' Fretful Walk in Jurassic Park," *Brandweek* 34 (May 3, 1993): 1.

12 Leonard Klady, "Billion-Dollar Dinos' Merchandising Mania," *Variety* 352 (October 4, 1993): 11. See also Jeff Giles, "Coming to a Toy Store Near You," *Newsweek* 121 (June 14, 1993): 64.

13 Leonard Klady, "Dino-soars to $100 Mil," *Variety* 351 (June 28, 1993): 5.

14 Kathleen O'Steen, " 'Park' Gooses Nerve," *Variety* 352 (September 20, 1993): 7.

15 *New York Times*, July 1, 1996, p. D7.

16 Stephen J. Dubner, "Steven the Good," *New York Times Magazine*, February 14, 1999, p. 41.

17 Klady, "Billion-Dollar Dinos," p. 11. Dubner's estimate is $294 million.

18 Don Groves, "Dino Dub Rubs Coin in India, Pakistan," *Variety* 354 (April 25, 1994): 27.

19 Don Groves and Uma da Cunha, "India's Dino-Size Legacy," *Variety* 356 (August 15, 1994): 41.

20 Stuart Elliott, "Marketers Rush to the Television Premiers of a Hollywood Behemoth," *New York Times*, May 5, 1995, p. C5.

21 See also Jefferson Graham, "A Wild, Wet Jaunt to Jurassic Park," *USA Today*, June 21, 1996, p. D10.

22 O'Steen, " 'Park' Gooses Nerve," p. 7.

23 See Shay and Duncan, *Making of Jurassic Park*, pp. 40, 56, passim.

24 Shay and Duncan, *Making of Jurassic Park*, p. 15.

25 Justine Tally pointed out that another source of anxiety about technology might be centered in the masculine effort to control reproduction—in the film, of dinosaurs, to be sure, but such "experiments" are always in some sense testing grounds for human application.

26 Shay and Duncan, *Making of Jurassic Park*, p. 57.

27 Shay and Duncan, *Making of Jurassic Park*, p. 56.

28 Shay and Duncan, *Making of Jurassic Park*, p. 4.

29 This very neat speculation was suggested to me by Scott Nelson.

30 It is worth pointing to some of the uncanny parallels between *The Lost World* and *Amistad*. Both involve separations of tropical families, a fierce desire to return home to family and freedom rendered in terrifying action, and the ambiguities of Americans toward both family and freedom—at least when it comes to "others." Of course, we have seen these elements in Spielberg before. In a way, he can be thought of as focusing on what are, at least to many white Americans, progressively more unfathomable avatars of the "other": an E.T., a T-Rex family, and finally a group of Africans. That may help to explain some of the critical ambivalence toward *Amistad*, at least among commentators not otherwise troubled by the film's problematic handling of African agency and abolitionist politics, among other matters.

31 See particularly, Andrew Ross, *No Respect: Intellectuals and Popular Culture* (New York: Routledge, 1989).

32 Paul J. DiMaggio, "Cultural Entrepreneurship in Nineteenth-Century Boston, part II: The Classification and Framing of American Art," *Media, Culture, and Society* 4 (1982): 303.

6. American Studies and Ethnic Studies at the Borderlands Crossroads

1 Chapter 3, "Versions of Nashville, Visions of American Studies," first appeared in *American Quarterly* 47 (June 1995): 186.

2 I want to express my appreciation to Laura Wexler for calling my attention to Woodville's painting.

3 I am trying here to offer a metaphorically spatial version of something related to what Donald Pease has called the "field-Imaginary" of a discipline. I would not claim for my metaphor the dramatic psychic orientations Pease argues are effected by the "field-Imaginary." On the other hand, I do think that such spatial orientations deeply shape what we are able to construct as the "common sense" of a discipline. See Donald Pease, "New Americanists: Revisionist Interventions into the Canon," in *Revisionary Interventions into the Americanist Canon*, ed. Donald Pease (Durham, N.C.: Duke University Press, 1994), especially pp. 11–15.

4 Henry Nash Smith, *Virgin Land: The American West as Symbol and Myth* (1950; Cambridge, Mass.: Harvard University Press, 1978), p. 4.

5 As well, of course, as Smith's conception of the continent as "vacant," a metaphor which remarkably illustrates the invisibility of some of the same folks
   who fall outside Woodville's painting.

6 Toni Morrison, *Playing in the Dark: Whiteness and the Literary Imagination*
   (Cambridge, Mass.: Harvard University Press, 1992), p. 5.

7 Christopher Newfield and Avery F. Gordon provide a nuanced and useful
   account of relationships between assimilationist and pluralist ideologies in
   "Multiculturalism's Unfinished Business," *Mapping Multiculturalism*, ed.
   Newfield and Gordon (Minneapolis: University of Minnesota Press, 1996),
   pp. 76–115.

8 Analogous processes of erasure in the Supreme Court decisions in *Cherokee
   Nation v. Georgia* (1831) and in the *Dred Scott* case (1857) are examined by
   Priscilla Wald in "Terms of Assimilation: Legislating Subjectivity in the
   Emerging Nation," *The Cultures of U.S. Imperialism*, ed. Amy Kaplan and
   Donald Pease (Durham, N.C.: Duke University Press, 1993), pp. 59–84.

9 Randolph Bourne, "Trans-National America" (1916), in *The Heath Anthology
   of American Literature*, 3rd ed., ed. Paul Lauter et al., vol. 2 (Boston: Houghton
   Mifflin, 1998), pp. 1732–1733.

10 Michael Geyer, "Multiculturalism and the Politics of General Education," *Critical Inquiry* 19 (spring 1993): 528.

11 See, for example, Mike Davis, "Dark Raptures: a Consumers' Guide to the
   Destruction of Los Angeles," *Grand Street* 15 (winter 1997): 7–17, and Davis's
   articles on Los Angeles in the *New Left Review* nos. 197 and 199 (1993).

12 Duster's figures were given in a teleconference between Berkeley and the USIA
   center in Tokyo in June 1994.

13 "State demographers predict that by 2015 the county's [Santa Clara] population
   will be about one-third Asian, one-third Hispanic and one-third white. And by
   2025 whites will fall to the third-largest racial group." Ariana Eunjung Cha
   and Ken Mclaughlin, "A Majority of None," *San Jose Mercury News*, April 14,
   1999, and on line at ⟨http://www.mercurycenter.com/local/majority/day1/
   change.htm⟩.

14 Karl Kahler, charts for "A Majority of None," *San Jose Mercury News*, April 14,
   1999, and on line at ⟨http://www.mercurycenter.com/local/majority/day1/
   change.htm⟩.

15 David M. Halbfinger, "Immigrants Continue to Reshape the City," *New York
   Times*, December 1, 1997, p. B3. The same analysis of federal Census Bureau
   figures by New York University's Taub Urban Research Center indicates that
   in that decade and a half the black, Latino, and Asian populations have expanded somewhat from 24.0, 20.2, and 3.9 percent respectively, to 26.2, 26.6,
   and 8.7 percent. A more recent *Times* report suggests that in 1997 36.1 percent
   of New Yorkers were foreign born, compared with 19.0 percent in 1970.
   Deborah Sontag and Celia W. Dugger, "The New Immigrant Tide: A Shuttle
   between Worlds," *New York Times*, July 19, 1998, I, p. 28.

16 A *New York Times* series phrased it this way: "So fluid is the exchange between the homeland and New York that it alters both places. People move back and forth, money moves back and forth, ideas move back and forth." Sontag and Dugger, "The New Immigrant Tide: A Shuttle between Worlds."

17 Lourdes Portillo and Rosa Linda Fregoso, "Screening Resistance," in Newfield and Gordon, *Mapping Multiculturalism*, p. 189.

18 Thomas J. Ferraro, *Ethnic Passages: Literary Immigrants in Twentieth-Century America* (Chicago: University of Chicago Press, 1993), p. 10.

19 And yet, I had initially included the Hmong in this paragraph only to learn that, in fact, they are spread across Southeast Asia, Australia, and Canada, as well as the United States. Precision in applying these terms requires detailed study of each group.

20 Gloria Anzaldúa, *Borderlands/La Frontera* (San Francisco: Spinsters/Aunt Lute, 1987); Cherríe Moraga and Gloria Anzaldúa, eds., *This Bridge Called My Back: Writings by Radical Women of Color* (New York: Kitchen Table/Women of Color Press, 1981); José David Saldívar, *The Dialectics of Our America* (Durham, N.C.: Duke University Press, 1991); Néstor García Canclini, *Hybrid Cultures: Strategies for Entering and Leaving Modernity*, trans. Christopher L. Chiappari and Silvia L. López, foreword by Renato Rosaldo (Minneapolis: University of Minnesota Press, 1995); George Sánchez, *Becoming Mexican American: Ethnicity, Culture and Identity in Chicano Los Angeles, 1900–1945* (New York: Oxford, 1993).

21 John E. Bodnar, *The Transplanted: A History of Immigrants in Urban America* (Bloomington: Indiana University Press, 1985). Cf. Sucheng Chan, *Asian Americans: An Interpretive History* (Boston: Twayne, 1991), and Ronald Takaki, *Strangers from a Different Shore: A History of Asian Americans* (Boston: Little, Brown, 1989).

22 As, for example, in Roberto Fernández Retamar, *Caliban and Other Essays*, trans. Edward Baker; foreword by Fredric Jameson (Minneapolis: University of Minnesota Press, 1989), and Consuelo López Springfield, ed., *Daughters of Caliban: Caribbean Women in the Twentieth Century* (Bloomington: Indiana University Press, 1997).

23 Paul Gilroy, *The Black Atlantic: Modernity and Double Consciousness* (Cambridge, Mass.: Harvard University Press, 1993); *"There Ain't No Black in the Union Jack": The Cultural Politics of Race and Nation* (London: Hutchinson, 1987).

24 Maria Diedrich and Werner Sollors, eds., *The Black Columbiad: Defining Moments in African American Literature and Culture* (Cambridge, Mass.: Harvard University Press, 1994).

25 Carl Pedersen and Fran Hopenwasser, eds., *Voices from the African-American Experience* (Copenhagen: Munksgaard, 1995).

26 I have in mind, for example, Sau-ling Wong's critique of Sollors's *Beyond Ethnicity: Consent and Descent in American Culture* (1986) in *Reading Asian*

American Literature: From Necessity to Extravagance (Princeton: Princeton University Press, 1993), and the problems that arise in Walzer's very useful essay "What Does It Mean to Be 'American'?" when he, too, resurrects American exceptionalism—for example, "There is also an idea of America that is itself distinct, incorporating oneness and manyness in a 'new order' that may or may not be 'for the ages' but that is certainly for us, here and now." In *The American Intellectual Tradition*, vol. 2, ed. David Hollinger and Charles Capper (New York: Oxford, 1993), p. 396.

27 Guillermo Gómez-Peña, "Documented/Undocumented," *The Graywolf Annual 5: Multi-cultural Literacy*, ed. Rick Simonson and Scott Walker (Saint Paul, Minn.: Graywolf Press, 1989), pp. 128–129.

28 I use this formulation because Gómez-Peña and Sifuentes performed when the piece was initially mounted and afterward substituted for their living bodies elaborately costumed manikins.

29 Guillermo Gómez-Peña and Roberto Sifuentes, *Temple of Confessions: Mexican Beasts and Living Santos* (New York: powerHouse Books, 1996). The performance piece/installation was held at the Detroit Institute of Arts, the Corcoran Gallery of Art, and the Scottsdale Center for the Arts beginning in 1994 and running into 1996.

30 The CD itself is something of a borderland product. It contains two tracks, the "Temple of Confessions" and "Menage-A-Trade." The first, funded in part by a National Endowment for the Arts grant, was produced in San Francisco, though gathered from places elsewhere. The second, funded by the United States Information Agency, was recorded at the Banff Center for the Arts, Alberta, Canada.

31 Margaret Fuller, "Woman in the Nineteenth Century" (1844), in *Heath Anthology of American Literature*, vol. 1, pp. 1726–1727.

32 Some of the most useful and interesting work in this connection was done by Claudia Sadowski-Smith in her University of Delaware dissertation, "Transnational Border Crossings: Theorizing Difference for the Twenty-First Century." She presented part of that work in a paper for the Modern Language Association, entitled "Global Borderland Difference (Under Construction)." I want to express my appreciation to Ms. Sadowski-Smith for sharing her work with me.

33 In fact, in October 1996, the Center for Lesbian and Gay Studies (CLAGS) at the City University of New York convened a conference precisely on this set of intersections. It was titled "Crossing National and Sexual Borders: Lesbian and Gay Sexualities in Latin/o America."

34 Gómez-Peña, "Document/Undocumented," p. 127. He does not argue, though I think it the case, that the image of gender as performance is preferred by academic intellectuals, particularly in theatrical centers like New York and Paris. That may be because their sense of self is generated by the forms of performance in which they engage in classrooms, meetings, stages,

and other intellectual forums. And it is distinctively urban, a phenomenon of cities in which the range of forms available for breaking out of what Judith Butler describes as "regulatory practices," the opportunity for gender bending, is much wider than in the provinces. The metaphor's attraction to urban intellectuals becomes clearer if we consider that the flow of the image is toward self-expression, a mode of behavior enabled and stimulated in first-world societies, though envied and imitated across much of the globe, especially by adolescents.

35 For example, Jim Sleeper, *The Closest of Strangers: Liberalism and the Politics of Race in New York* (New York: Norton, 1990); Arthur Schlesinger Jr., *The Disuniting of America* (Knoxville, Tenn.: Whittle Direct Books, 1991); Todd Gitlin, *The Twilight of Common Dreams: Why America Is Wracked by Culture Wars* (New York: Metropolitan Books, 1995). These are, it needs to be said, very different books in political origin and largely in tone and outlook, but they do share a certain profound angst over the rise of ethnic particularisms.

36 For example, Lisa Lowe, *Immigrant Acts: On Asian American Cultural Politics* (Durham, N.C.: Duke University Press, 1996).

37 See particularly Michael Omi and Howard Winant, *Racial Formation in the United States: From the 1960s to the 1990s* (New York: Routledge, 1994).

38 Then not your deeds only O Voyagers, O scientists and inventors, shall be
        justified,
    All these hearts as of fretted children shall be sooth'd,
    All affection shall be fully responded to, the secret shall be told,
    All these separations and gaps shall be taken up and hook'd and link'd
        together,
    The whole earth, this cold, impassive, voiceless earth, shall be completely
        justified,
    Trinitas divine shall be gloriously accomplish'd and compacted by the true
        son of God, the poet,
    (He shall indeed pass the straits and conquer the mountains,
    He shall double the Cape of Good Hope to some purpose,)
    Nature and Man shall be disjoin'd and diffused no more,
    The true son of God shall absolutely fuse them.
        (Walt Whitman, "Passage to India," sec. 5, lines 26–35)

39 Coco Fusco and Guillermo Gómez-Peña, "Bilingualism, Biculturalism, and Borders," in Coco Fusco, *English Is Broken Here: Notes on Cultural Fusion in the Americas* (New York: New Press, 1995), p. 153.

40 Alvina E. Quintana, " 'Borders Be Damned': Reconfiguring 'The Multicultural,' " in *Cultural Studies,* ed. Angie Chabram (New York: Routledge, 1994).

41 See Elizabeth Cook-Lynn and Craig Howe, "The Dialectics of Ethnicity in America: A View from American Indian Studies," photocopy, p. 9.

42 David A. Hollinger and Charles Capper, eds., *The American Intellectual Tradition: A Sourcebook,* 2nd ed. (New York: Oxford University Press, 1993); Rich-

ard Wightman Fox and T. J. Jackson Lears, eds., *The Power of Culture: Critical Essays in American History* (Chicago: University of Chicago Press, 1993); Philip Fisher, ed., *The New American Studies: Essays from* Representations (Berkeley: University of California Press, 1991); Ralph Cohen and Michael S. Roth, eds., *History and . . . —Histories within the Human Sciences* (Charlottesville: University Press of Virginia, 1995); Donald E. Pease, ed., *Revisionary Interventions into the Americanist Canon* (Durham, N.C.: Duke University Press, 1994).

43 Amy Kaplan and Donald E. Pease, eds., *Cultures of United States Imperialism* (Durham, N.C.: Duke University Press, 1993).

44 I am very slightly misquoting here from "New Americanists: Revisionist Interventions into the Canon," in Pease, *Revisionary Interventions,* p. 16.

45 One of the most useful analyses of Proposition 187 is Kitty Calavita, "The New Politics of Immigration: 'Balanced-Budget Conservatism' and the Symbolism of Proposition 187," *Social Problems* 43 (August 1996): 284–305. Calavita sees Proposition 187 primarily as a "symbolic statement of fear, anger, and frustration emanating from the economic uncertainty" that, over the past quarter century, has produced "workers' stagnant wages and increasing insecurity, and the dismantling of the welfare state" (p. 285)—to summarize in something of a crude way her quite subtle and detailed argument.

It is interesting to contrast the tone of Calavita's argument with that of the *New York Times* series (July 19–21, 1998) on the "new immigration." While the latter does mention in passing "current debates about immigration, multiculturalism and bilingualism" (p. I.28), it primarily celebrates the advent of "binational society" and its binational inhabitants, at home and empowered both in the United States and in another land. Calavita's article offers a much more apprehensive view of the changing terrain of immigration, citizenship, and the polis. That may, in part, be a function of the differences between New York City and California, or between a journalistic approach almost devoid of historical or class analysis and a social scientist's analysis rooted in accounts of earlier outbreaks of American nativism. At a more fundamental level, the difference may reflect a sharp division of view over the state of the American economy and who is and is not benefiting from its much touted "restructuring."

46 I particularly wish to express appreciation to Marco Portales of Texas A&M University for his strong editorial hand in improving this chapter.

7. *Of* Chadors *and Capital*

1 In my talk, I should say, I reexamined the critical assumptions and practices by which people like Eliot and Pound—with whom my audience is familiar— effectively marginalized writers like Countee Cullen, Sterling Brown, and Amy Lowell—mostly unknown to my listeners.

2 David Hollinger takes up what may be an uncommon position in this regard: "A postethnic perspective invites critical engagement with the United States as a distinctive locus of social identity mediating between the human species and its varieties, and as a vital arena for political struggles the outcome of

which determine the domestic and global uses of a unique concentration of power." "How Wide the Circle of 'We'? American Intellectuals and the Problem of the Ethnos since World War II," *American Historical Review* 98 (April 1993): 335.

3   Or, as press reports (June 1997) have suggested, lining their own pockets in good capitalist fashion—even to the point of forcing USAID to cancel its contract with Harvard University.

4   Cf. Sara Suleri, "Woman Skin Deep: Feminism and the Postcolonial Condition," *Critical Inquiry* 18 (summer 1992): 339.

5   The fullest and most convincing analysis of these processes in the United States is provided by Richard Ohmann, *Selling Culture* (London: Verso, 1996).

6   As Ohmann points out, in the United States such changes took place relatively rapidly, during the 1890s mainly. But as he shows, a long prehistory involving basic changes in production, distribution, communications, and the elaboration of advertising had set the stage for such rapid consolidation of the culture of consumer capitalism.

7   "Manufacturing consent" is a term coined by Walter Lippman but given substantial contemporary content in the book of that title by Edward Hermann and Noam Chomsky (New York: Pantheon, 1988).

8   I am not attempting here to construct some crude alternative to the subtle understandings of hegemony developed by contemporary Marxist thinkers. Nor am I arguing that the present, post-Soviet (no breakfast food that) moment is altogether distinct from earlier processes of colonization. Nevertheless, "hegemony" as an explanatory theory has generally been deployed to understand developed or developing capitalist societies, which Russia—much less other formerly Soviet states—may or may not be. It remains empirically obscure whether, or how, the forms either of earlier capitalist or of colonial development function, or even apply at *this* particular historical juncture, in distinctive situations overseas. It seems likely to me, however, that any explanatory paradigm will need to deal with at least four conflicting forces: the logic of local capitalist development—and constraint; the continuing power of authoritarian structures of enforcing consent; the passion of politics turned not just against repressive regimes but, potentially, against exploitative economic arrangements; and, to return to our central subject, the role—what does one call it?—of U.S. culture as it is carried abroad by Americans, whatever their ostensible political persuasions.

9   See, for example, Rob Kroes, *If You've Seen One, You've Seen the Mall: Europeans and American Mass Culture* (Urbana: University of Illinois Press, 1996).

10 I am indebted to Carl Pedersen of the University of Odense for this insight. Working-class studies, for example, which in most places in the United States are viewed as exotic are, in Denmark, much more conventional, whereas issues of race, in that ethnically homogeneous society, can be obscure to students.

11 See, for example, John Bodnar, *The Transplanted: A History of Immigrants in*

Urban America (Bloomington: Indiana University Press, 1985); and George Sánchez, *Becoming Mexican American: Ethnicity, Culture and Identity in Chicano Los Angeles, 1900–1945* (New York: Oxford, 1993).

12 See Lisa Lowe, "Heterogeneity, Hybridity, Multiplicity: Marking Asian American Differences," *Diaspora* 1 (1991): 24–44.

13 *IWW Songbook*, 1970 edition, p. 12.

8. Fiction as Exploration: The Novels of Charles Chesnutt

1 See, for example, J. Noel Heermance, *Charles W. Chesnutt: America's First Great Black Novelist* (Hamden, Conn.: Archon Books, 1974). The most fully developed account of Chesnutt's motives and practices is in William Andrews, *The Literary Career of Charles W. Chesnutt.* (Baton Rouge: Louisiana State University Press, 1980).

2 Richard Brodhead, "The Reading of Regions," *Cultures of Letters: Scenes of Reading and Writing in Nineteenth-Century America* (Chicago: University of Chicago Press, 1993), pp. 116–141.

3 Journal entry for May 29, 1880, *Journals of Charles W. Chesnutt,* ed. Richard H. Brodhead (Durham, N.C.: Duke University Press, 1993), pp. 139–140.

4 John Hope Franklin and Alfred A. Moss Jr., *From Slavery to Freedom: A History of Negro Americans,* 6th ed. (New York: Knopf, 1988), pp. 230–231.

5 Franklin and Moss, *From Slavery to Freedom,* pp. 235–236.

6 Paul Lauter, "The Literatures of America—A Comparative Discipline," *Canons and Contexts* (New York: Oxford, 1991), pp. 61–64.

7 Charles W. Chesnutt, *The Conjure Woman* (Ann Arbor: University of Michigan Press, 1969), p. 159. *The Conjure Woman* is also available in a volume containing other of Chesnutt's conjure tales, edited by Richard H. Brodhead (Durham, N.C.: Duke University Press, 1993).

8 For example, in *Looking Backward* (1888), *The Jungle* (1906), *The Story of Avis* (1877), "The Yellow Wallpaper" (1892), and *A Woman of Genius* (1912), respectively.

9 I shall be referring to the following editions: *The House behind the Cedars* (London: Collier Books, 1969); *The Marrow of Tradition* (Ann Arbor: University of Michigan Press, 1969); *The Colonel's Dream* (New York: Doubleday, Page, 1905; facsimile reprint by Mnemosyne Publishing, 1969).

10 SallyAnn H. Ferguson, "Chesnutt's Genuine Blacks and Future Americans," *MELUS* 15 (fall 1988): 111. The same issue of *MELUS* contains the full text of Chesnutt's three "Future American" articles, published in the Boston *Evening Transcript,* August 18 and 25 and September 1, 1900.

11 This is precisely the argument made by SallyAnn H. Ferguson in "Rena Walden: Chesnutt's Failed 'Future American,'" *Southern Literary Journal* 15 (fall 1982): 74–82, especially p. 82: "When Rena Walden retains her black qualities after complete acceptance in the white world, she is set at odds with Chesnutt's theory of racial development. Her ignorant bungling of the opportunity

to marry white and well retards the evolutionary process that leads to higher black status in society. Rena, therefore, commits a crime against society when she fails to pass, because racial suffering continues when miscegenation does not. Her crime—refusal to miscegenate—makes her elimination inevitable. Because Rena does not stop being black, she dies."

12   See Robert Sedlack, "The Evolution of Charles Chesnutt's *The House behind the Cedars*," *CLA Journal* 19 (December 1975): 125–135. Basically, Sedlack argues that successive versions of the story increasingly shift responsibility for the catastrophe from intraracial color prejudice to white racism.

13   William Andrews, "Chesnutt's Patesville: The Presence and Influence of the Past in *The House behind the Cedars*," *CLA Journal* 15 (March 1972): 294.

14   Charles W. Chesnutt, *Mandy Oxendine*, was brought into print and edited by Charles Hackenberry (Urbana: University of Illinois Press, 1997).

15   Hackenberry, "Introduction," *Mandy Oxendine*, p. xviii.

16   This is essentially William Andrews's reading in *The Literary Career of Charles Chesnutt*, pp. 197–201.

17   *Independent* 13 (1902): 582.

18   Andrews, *The Literary Career of Charles W. Chesnutt*, p. 253.

9. *Reflecting on the* Heath Anthology of American Literature

1   The somewhat droll formal title emerged when we became what the MLA calls an "allied organization." As such, MLA sessions, many of them on that still-marginalized area of literary study, working-class culture, have been organized for almost all of the intervening thirty years by the Radical Caucus—or, frankly, by me for the most part, until the last five years.

2   Frances Ellen Watkins Harper, *Three Novels*, ed. Frances Smith Foster (Boston: Beacon Press, 1995).

3   María Amparo Ruiz de Burton, *The Squatter and the Don*, ed. and introduced by Rosaura Sánchez and Beatrice Pita (Houston : Arte Público Press, 1992).

4   Karen Kilcup, ed., *Nineteenth-Century American Women Writers* (Oxford: Blackwell, 1997); Paula Bennett, ed., *Nineteenth-Century American Women Poets* (Oxford: Blackwell, 1997).

5   Paul Lauter, ed., *Reconstructing American Literature* (Old Westbury, N.Y.: Feminist Press, 1983).

6   Essentially the argument made by Glen M. Johnson in "Anthologies and Marketing," paper delivered at the meeting of the American Literature Section, Modern Language Association, December 1990.

7   See Paul Lauter, "Race and Gender in the Shaping of the American Literary Canon: A Case Study from the Twenties," *Canons and Contexts* (New York: Oxford, 1991), pp. 22–47.

8   Mark Edmunson, "Dangers of Democracy," *Times Literary Supplement*, October 19–25, 1990, p. 1133; Richard Ruland, "Art and a Better America," *American Literary History* 3 (summer 1991): 337–359.

10. Melville Climbs the Canon

1   Most usefully in Michael P. Zimmerman, "Herman Melville in the 1920's: A Study in the Origins of the Melville Revival, with an Annotated Bibliography," Ph.D. dissertation, Columbia University, 1963; and Hershel Parker, ed., *The Recognition of Herman Melville* (Ann Arbor: University of Michigan Press, 1967). See also O. W. Riegel, "The Anatomy of Melville's Fame," *American Literature* 3 (May 1931): 1–9, which debunks some of the early myths about Melville's reception in the nineteenth century.

2   *New York World,* February 21, 1919, p. 13.

3   Quoted in John A. Garraty, *The American Nation: A History of the United States,* 3rd ed. (New York: Harper and Row, 1975), p. 681.

4   *Congressional Record,* December 10, 1921, p. 177.

5   March 29, 1922, quoted by Ronald Takaki, *A Different Mirror: A History of Multicultural America* (Boston: Little, Brown, 1993), p. 305. "Experience," Lowell went on, "seems to place that proportion at about 15%."

6   Editorial, *New York World,* February 9, 1919, p. 2.

7   See, for example, "Topics of the Times," *New York Times,* June 15, 1919, and an editorial, "Walt as a Cult," *New York Times Review of Books,* June 1, 1919, p. 308.

8   George S. Bryan, "Two Minor Literary Centenaries," *New York Evening Post Books,* July 12, 1919, p. 1.

9   See, for example, H. M. T[omlinson], "The World of Books," *Nation and Athenaeum* 29 (June 4, 1919): 363; Michael Sadleir and James Billson, "Letters to the Editor: The Works of Herman Melville," *Nation and Athenaeum* 29 (June 11, 1919): 396–397. See also Sadleir's "Herman Melville," in *Excursion in Victorian Bibliography* (London: Chaundy and Cox, 1922), pp. 217–234.

10 Meade Minnegerode, ed., *Some Personal Letters of Herman Melville and a Bibliography* (New York: Brick Row Book Shop), 1922.

11 Herman Melville, *Typee,* ed. Sterling A. Leonard (New York: Harcourt, Brace, 1920).

12 Herman Melville, *The Apple-Tree Table and Other Sketches* (Princeton: Princeton University Press, 1922), and *John Marr and Other Poems* (London: Oxford University Press, 1922), both ed. Henry Chapin.

13 Quoted from Weaver's account in Raymond Weaver Papers, Special Manuscript Collections, Columbia University. In significant ways, Van Doren represents the kind of masculine academic intellectual who brought Melville to prominence during the 1920s. He held an academic appointment and did teach and carry out academic research. But he also wrote for a general public, not only in the pages of the *Nation* and other periodicals, but in his books, which were clearly directed to a general literate audience.

14 Raymond M. Weaver, *Herman Melville: Mariner and Mystic* (New York: George H. Doran, 1921).

15 "A Neglected American Classic," *Literary Digest* 70 (July 16, 1921): 26.

16 *New York Times Book Review and Magazine,* December 25, 1921, p. 5.

17 *Mentor* 10 (February 1, 1922): 17–31.

18 *Mentor* 10 (February 1, 1922): 18.

19 *Current Opinion* 67 (September 1919): 186.

20 Copies in Raymond Weaver Papers, Special Manuscript Collections, Columbia University. Weaver himself had evidently clipped reviews of Frederick O'Brien's *White Shadows in the South Seas* and Somerset Maugham's *The Moon and Sixpence*, both published the previous year.

21 *New York Times*, October 10, 1920, editorial page, summarizing an article by Paul Gooding in the October *National Geographic*.

22 "Today's Centenary of Herman Melville," *Boston Herald*, August 1, 1919.

23 *New York World*, Oct. 11, 1891.

24 Brander Matthews, "Teller of Sea Tales," *New York Times Book Review and Magazine*, December 25, 1921, p. 5. Matthews had used similar phrases in his earlier work.

25 Raymond M. Weaver, "Herman Melville," *Bookman* 54 (December 1921): 318. The magazine was issued by Weaver's publisher, and this article was clearly designed to whet readers' appetites for the biography about to appear.

26 "A Neglected American Classic," p. 26.

27 Carl Van Doren, *The American Novel* (New York: Macmillan, 1921), p. 70.

28 Holbrook Jackson, "Herman Melville," *Anglo-French Review* 2 (August 1919): 63. Something of this view persists even in F. O. Matthiessen's *American Renaissance* (New York: Oxford, 1941), p. 374. Commenting on the remark "I am myself a savage," Matthiessen writes: "But there were many senses in which Melville was not. Of the same racial mixture as Whitman, English on his father's side, Dutch on his mother's, his ancestors had risen far above the Whitmans' plebian class."

29 The phrase is that of F. L. Lucas, "Herman Melville," *Authors Living and Dead* (New York: Macmillan, 1926), p. 109; this is actually a reprint of a 1922 review of Weaver's biography.

30 Fred Lewis Pattee, *The New American Literature, 1890–1930* (New York: Century, 1930), p. 372.

31 Raymond M. Weaver, "Herman Melville," *Bookman* 54 (December 1921): 320–321.

32 "Herman Melville," *Times Literary Supplement* 1051 (March 9, 1922): 151.

33 *The Melville Log*, ed. Jay Leyda (New York: Harcourt, Brace, 1951), 1:412. Only one of the writers who cites this passage bothers to point out that when it was written Melville was, in fact, completing *Moby-Dick*.

34 Quoted in Lucas, "Herman Melville," p. 110.

35 Horace Scudder, "Melville's *Benito Cereno* and Captain Delano's Voyages," *PMLA* 43 (1928): 531. "Benito Cereno" was reprinted in 1927 by the Nonsuch Press in a particularly handsome illustrated edition. Reviewers discuss, in the main, the qualities of the edition and present the story primarily as a sea mystery, never really suggesting that it concerns a slave revolt. See also "Affable Hawk," "Books in General," *New Statesman* 28 (March 5, 1927): 635;

Herbert L. Matthews, "Another Melville Tale Is Rescued from Oblivion," *New York Times Book Review,* May 15, 1927, p. 6.

36 Henry Seidel Canby, "A Fragment of Genius," *Saturday Review of Literature* 3 (May 28, 1927): 864.

37 Arthur Hobson Quinn, "Herman Melville and the Exotic Romance," *American Fiction: An Historical and Critical Survey* (New York: Appleton-Century, 1936), pp. 154–155.

38 Vernon Louis Parrington, *The Romantic Revolution in America, 1800–1860* (New York: Harcourt, Brace, 1927), p. 265.

39 "New Books," *Catholic World* 114 (February 1922): 686–687.

40 *American Literature* 2 (1930): 321. Cf. Grant C. Knight, "The Literature of Romanticism," *American Literature and Culture* (New York: Ray Long and Richard R. Smith, 1932), p. 221: "The large claims made for him now arise in some part from the demands of post-war disillusionment which found in Melville a similar revulsion from platitudes, from the acceptance of things as they are. His tone pleases well the dismayed 'intelligent minority' of the 1920's and 1930's."

41 Archibald MacLeish, "A New Life of Melville," *Bookman* 69 (April 1929): 184.

42 Andreas Huyssen, "Mass Culture as Woman: Modernism's Other," *After the Great Divide: Modernism, Mass Culture, Postmodernism* (Bloomington: Indiana University Press, 1986), pp. 44–62.

43 Fred Lewis Pattee, *The New American Literature, 1890–1930* (New York: Century, 1930), pp. 373, 379. The chapter is virtually identical to an essay Pattee had earlier published in the *American Mercury* 10 (January 1927): 33–43.

44 Granville Hicks, *The Great Tradition* (New York: Macmillan, 1933), pp. 7–8.

45 V. F. Calverton, *The Liberation of American Literature* (New York: Charles Scribner's Sons, 1932), pp. 272–273.

46 Frank Jewett Mather Jr., "Herman Melville," *Review* 1 (August 9, 1919): 276.

47 Carl Van Vechten, "A Belated Biography," *Literary Review of the New York Evening Post* 2 (December 31, 1921): 316. The Salt article cited by Van Vechten is titled "Marquesan Melville" and appears in the London *Gentleman's Magazine* for March 1892.

48 H. M. Tomlinson, "A Clue to 'Moby Dick,'" *The Literary Review of the New York Evening Post* 2 (November 5, 1921): 142.

49 Mildred Cabell Watkins, *American Literature* (New York: American Book Company, 1894), p. 47. The book is designed to tell "the story of American literature . . . for the benefit of young Americans" (p. 3).

50 "'Moby Dick' and the Years to Come," *New York Tribune,* August 4, 1919.

51 "Melville and Our Sea Literature," *New York Evening Post,* August 2, 1919.

52 Percy H. Boynton, "Harriet Beecher Stowe and Herman Melville," *A History of American Literature* (Boston: Ginn, 1919), p. 307.

53 Paul Lauter, "Race and Gender in the Formation of the American Literary Canon—A Case Study from the Twenties," *Canons and Contexts* (New York:

Oxford University Press, 1991), pp. 22–47. This article was initially published in *Feminist Studies* 9 (fall 1983).

54 Frank Jewett Mather Jr., "Herman Melville," part 2, *Review* 1 (August 16, 1919): 301.

55 Archibald MacMechan, "The Best Sea Story Ever Written," *The Life of a Little College* (Boston: Houghton Mifflin, 1914), p. 190. The article was originally published in 1899. MacMechan goes on: "It is large in idea, expansive; it has an Elizabethan force and freshness and swing, and is, perhaps, more rich in figures than any style but Emerson's. It has the picturesqueness of the New World, and, above all, a free-flowing humour, which is the distinct *cachet* of American literature."

56 William B. Cairns, *A History of American Literature*, rev. ed. (New York: Oxford, 1930), p. 369. Cairns's comments here are virtually identical with those he promulgated in the first, 1912, edition of this book.

57 William P. Trent, *A History of American Literature* (New York: D. Appleton, 1903), p. 390.

58 Carl Van Doren, *The American Novel* (New York: Macmillan, 1921), p. 74. He goes on: if it is "too irregular, too bizarre . . . ever to win the most popular suffrage, the immense originality of *Moby Dick* must warrant the claim of its admirers that it belongs with the greatest sea romances in the whole literature of the world."

59 [Van Wyck Brooks], "A Reviewer's Notebook," *Freeman* 4 (October 26, 1921): 167.

60 Percy Boynton, "Herman Melville," *More Contemporary Americans* (Chicago: University of Chicago Press, 1927), pp. 46–47.

61 John Erskine, "Moby Dick," *The Delight of Great Books* (Indianapolis: Bobbs-Merrill, 1928), p. 230.

62 See, for example, Herschel Brickell, "Herman Melville," *New Republic* 58 (April 3, 1929): 205; John Brooks Moore, "Herman Melville," *American Literature* 1 (May 1929): 215–217; Virginia Woolf, "Phases of Fiction," *Bookman* 69 (June 1929): 407–412.

63 Arthur Johnson, *New Republic* 20 (August 27, 1919): 113–115.

64 Carl Van Vechten, "The Later Works of Herman Melville," *Double Dealer* 3 (January 1922): 12.

65 See, for example, "Herman Melville's 'Pierre,'" *Times Literary Supplement* 1500 (October 30, 1930): 889.

66 Raymond M. Weaver, "Introduction," in Melville, *The Shorter Novels of Herman Melville* (New York: Horace Liveright, 1928).

11. And Now, Ladies and Gentlemen, May I Present Miss Amy Lowell

1 Ezra Pound, "A Few Don'ts by an Imagiste," *Poetry* 1 (March 1913).

2 Amy Lowell to Richard Aldington, Letters of Amy Lowell, Houghton Library, Harvard University, bMS Lowell 19.1 (16). Used by permission of the Houghton Library, Harvard University.

3 *Some Imagist Poets* (Boston: Houghton Mifflin, 1915).

4   Letters of Amy Lowell, bMS Lowell 19.1 (610). Used by permission of the Houghton Library, Harvard University.
5   bMS Lowell 19.1 (607). Used by permission of the Houghton Library, Harvard University.
6   bMS Lowell 19.1 (91). Used by permission of the Houghton Library, Harvard University.
7   bMS Lowell 19.1 (17). Used by permission of the Houghton Library, Harvard University.
8   bMS Lowell 19.1 (607). Used by permission of the Houghton Library, Harvard University.
9   bMS Lowell 19.1 (728). Used by permission of the Houghton Library, Harvard University.
10 Judith Butler, *Gender Trouble: Feminism and the Subversion of Identity* (New York: Routledge, 1990), pp. 24, 25.
11 A section of a longer worked called "Spring Day" from Amy Lowell, *Men, Women, and Ghosts* (Boston: Houghton, Mifflin, 1916).
12 See, for example, Lowell to Margaret Anderson, 29 Nov., 1918, Letters of Amy Lowell, bMS Lowell 19.1. Used by permission of the Houghton Library, Harvard University. "I hate to refuse you anything, but the truth is I am not in sympathy with your paper nowadays, and I think the wisest thing to do is not to appear in its columns. Please forgive me. Should you ever return again to the position you once took in regard to literature, I shall be your most enthusiastic supporter; but there is too little you now and too much Ezra, and much as I admire a great deal of his work, I think his methods in running a magazine are wrong. Forgive me, and believe me. Always affectionately. . . ."
13 Lowell to Winifred Ellerman, Letters of Amy Lowell, bMS 19.1 (180). Used by permission of the Houghton Library, Harvard University.
14 Eve Kosofsky Sedgwick, "The Beast in the Closet: James and the Writing of Homosexual Panic," in *Speaking of Gender*, ed. Elaine Showalter (New York: Routledge, 1989), p. 243.
15 Cf., for example, Bonnie Kime Scott, *Refiguring Modernism* (Bloomington: Indiana University Press, 1995).
16 bMS Lowell 19.1 (180). Used by permission of the Houghton Library, Harvard University.
17 bMS Lowell 19.1 (261). Used by permission of the Houghton Library, Harvard University.
18 Paula Bennett, "Critical Clitoridectomy: Female Sexual Imagery and Feminist Psychoanalytic Theory," *Signs* 18 (winter 1993): 235–259.
19 Paula Bennett, "Late Nineteenth-Century American Women's Nature Poetry and the Evolution of the Imagist Poem," *Legacy* 9 (1992): 94.
20 bMS Lowell 19.1 (867). Used by permission of the Houghton Library, Harvard University.
21 bMS Lowell 19.1 (610). Used by permission of the Houghton Library, Harvard University.

22 bMS Lowell 19.1 (183). Used by permission of the Houghton Library, Harvard University.

23 Amy Lowell, "A Petition," *Sword Blades and Poppy Seed* (Boston: Houghton Mifflin, 1921).

24 Andrew Parker and Eve Kosofsky Sedgwick, "Introduction," *Performativity and Performance* (New York: Routledge, 1995), p. 5.

25 Butler, *Gender Trouble*, p. 339.

26 Letter to Florence Ayscough, May 27, 1922, Letters of Amy Lowell, bMS Lowell 19.1 (56), used by permission of the Houghton Library, Harvard University: "At the moment I am a widow. Ada is staying with her family in Salt Lake City for six weeks."

12. Cold War Culture and the Construction of Modernism

1 See, for example, Sterling Brown, *Negro Poetry and Drama* (Washington: Associates in Negro Folk Education, 1938); Andreas Huyssen, *After the Great Divide: Modernism, Mass Culture, Postmodernism* (Bloomington: Indiana University Press, 1986); Cary Nelson, *Repression and Recovery: Modern American Poetry and the Politics of Cultural Memory, 1910–1945* (Madison: University of Wisconsin Press, 1989); Shari Benstock, "Expatriate Sapphic Modernism: Entering Literary History," *Lesbian Texts and Contexts: Radical Revisions*, ed. Karla Jay and Joanne Glasgow (New York: New York University Press, 1990); Bonnie Kime Scott, ed., *The Gender of Modernism: A Critical Anthology* (Bloomington: Indiana University Press, 1990); and my own "Little White Sheep, or How I Learned to Dress Blue," *Yale Journal of Criticism* 8 (1995): 103–129.

2 Alfred Kreymborg, ed., *Lyric America, An Anthology of American Poetry, 1630–1930* (New York: Coward-McCann, 1930).

3 To some extent, I suppose, this like any such choice of texts is slightly arbitrary and influenced by the distinctive conditions of personal history—in this instance, the fact that I studied both with Eda Lou Walton at New York University and with Cleanth Brooks at the Indiana School of Letters. In other respects, however, these texts are representative of distinct political and cultural tendencies and, at least in the case of *Understanding Poetry*, were powerfully influential in the shaping of critical discourse during the cold war period.

4 Malcolm Cowley, ed., *After the Genteel Tradition; American Writers since 1910* (New York: Norton, 1937). Among the other contributors were Lionel Trilling on Cather and O'Neill, Robert Cantwell on Upton Sinclair and Sinclair Lewis, John Peale Bishop on Hemingway, Hamilton Basso on Thomas Wolfe, and Newton Arvin on Carl Sandburg.

5 Bernard Smith and Malcolm Cowley, eds., *Books That Changed Our Minds* (New York, Doubleday, Doran, 1939).

6 The most comprehensive study of the popular front is undoubtedly that of Michael Denning, *The Cultural Front: the Laboring of American Culture in the Twentieth Century* (London: Verso, 1997).

7   Selden Rodman, ed., *A New Anthology of Modern Poetry* (New York: Random House, 1938; rev. ed. New York: The Modern Library, 1946).

8   William H. Epstein, "Counter-Intelligence: Cold-War Criticism and Eighteenth-Century Studies," *ELH* 57 (1990): 63–99.

9   Among the most useful recent studies of the construction of cold war culture are Robert J. Corber, *In the Name of National Security: Hitchcock, Homophobia, and the Political Construction of Gender in Postwar America* (Durham, N.C.: Duke University Press, 1993); and Alan M. Wald, *The New York Intellectuals: The Rise and Decline of the Anti-Stalinist Left from the 1930s to the 1980s* (Chapel Hill: University of North Carolina Press, 1987).

10 Cleanth Brooks and Robert Penn Warren, eds., *Understanding Fiction* (New York: Crofts, 1943); Brooks and Warren, eds., *Modern Rhetoric* (New York: Harcourt, Brace, 1949) was also issued as *Fundamentals of Good Writing: A Handbook of Modern Rhetoric* in 1950; Brooks and Robert Heilman, eds., *Understanding Drama: Twelve Plays* (New York: Henry Holt, 1945); Brooks, Warren, and John T. Purser, eds., *An Approach to Literature* (New York: Appleton-Century-Crofts, 1952); Brooks and William K. Wimsatt, eds., *Literary Criticism: A Short History* (New York: Knopf, 1957); Brooks, *Modern Poetry and the Tradition* (Chapel Hill: University of North Carolina Press, 1939); Brooks, *The Well-Wrought Urn* (New York: Reynal and Hitchcock, 1947); John Milton, *Poems of Mr. John Milton; the 1645 Edition, with Essays in Analysis*, ed. Brooks and John Edward Hardy (New York: Harcourt, Brace, 1951).

11 Brooks, *Modern Poetry and the Tradition*, pp. 69–109.

12 Brooks, "Metaphysical Poetry and Propaganda Art," in *Modern Poetry and the Tradition*, pp. 39–53.

13 George Core writes in "Agrarianism, Criticism, and the Academy," *A Band of Prophets: The Vanderbilt Agrarians after Fifty Years*, ed. William C. Havard and Walter Sullivan (Baton Rouge: Louisiana State University Press, 1982), p. 129: "The leading Agrarians [e.g., John Crowe Ransom, Allen Tate, and Robert Penn Warren] wrote criticism not only in a positive response to Eliot and the others [e.g., I. A. Richards, William Empson, and F. R. Leavis] but in a negative reaction against Marxism and Marxist criticism (one remembers the alternative title that was proposed for *I'll Take My Stand—Tracts against Communism*)."

14 Lauter, "Little White Sheep," pp. 110–113.

15 Consider, for example, Lionel Trilling's praise of Jane Austen. Her "irony," he writes, "is only secondarily a matter of tone. Primarily it is a method of comprehension. It perceives the world through an awareness of its contradictions, paradoxes, and anomalies. It is by no means detached. It is partisan with generosity of spirit—it is on the side of 'life' and 'affirmation.'" "Mansfield Park," *The Opposing Self* (New York: Harcourt, Brace, Jovanovich, 1955), p. 181.

16 William K. Wimsatt and Cleanth Brooks, *Literary Criticism: A Short History* (New York: Knopf, 1957), p. 665.

17   See, for example, Max Kozloff, "American Painting During the Cold War," *ArtForum* 11 (May 1973): 43–54; and Eva Cockcroft, "Abstract Expressionism: Weapon of the Cold War," *Artforum* 12 (June 1974): 39–41.

18   Leo Marx, "Mr. Eliot, Mr. Trilling, and *Huckleberry Finn*," *The American Scholar* 22 (autumn 1953): 440.

Art (*cont.*)
  American art, 248–49; *War News from Mexico* (Woodville), 120–21, 137
Austen, Jane (*Mansfield Park*), 101, 115, 279 n.15
Authority, cultural: of *Heath Anthology of American Literature*, 184–86, 190–91; media, 79, 186; modernism, 196–97, 247; of universities, 79–80, 184–85, 193, 243

Bodnar, James, 128, 147
Borderlands and boundaries: American studies, 120–21, 133–34, 137–38, 147–48, 253 n.15, 264 n.3; capitalism, 132–33; erosion of national boundaries, 128; ethnicity, 124–28, 134–38, 268 n.38; gender, 130, 221–22, 228–31; Gómez-Peña/Sifuentes performance piece, 129–30, 267 nn.28, 29; literary merit and politics, 195; popular culture vs. elite culture, 22, 103; sexuality, 132, 267 n.32; in *War News from Mexico* (Woodville), 120–21. *See also* Globalization
Bourne, Ralph (*Transnational America*), 122–23
Boy culture, 90–91, 113, 216, 228
Breaking the Social Contract (1997), 35, 39–40, 63
Brooks, Cleanth, 241, 242–43
Budianta, Melani, 26–27, 150

Calavita, Kitty, 269 n.45
California, 39, 45, 60, 62, 138, 269 n.45
Canclini, Néstor Garcia, 128, 253 n.15
Canon: aesthetics vs. politics, 192–93; African Americans in, 23, 178; anthologies of American literature, 176–80, 182; cultural authority of universities, 184–86, 193, 243; men

in the American literary canon, 51, 179–80; and popular culture, 22, 102; women in the American literary canon, 23, 176, 179, 230
Capitalism: acculturation and, 44; in Chesnutt's works, 168–70; culture of, 143–46; globalization and, 21, 124, 132–33; hegemony of, 146, 270 n.8; *Jurassic Park*, 112–14; market reforms, 145–46; Nashville Agrarians, 67–69; science and technology, 112; unions, 54–55
Chesnutt, Charles: assimilation of African Americans, 153–54, 158–64, 271 n.11; capitalism in works of, 168–70; *Colonel's Dream, The*, 157, 158, 167–68; *House behind the Cedars, The*, 157–60, 162, 271 n.11, 272 n.12; illness as metaphor for racism, 165–66; intraracial color prejudice, 161–64, 166, 271 n.11; *Mandy Oxendine*, 162–63; *Marrow of Tradition, The*, 155, 158, 163–64, 167; narration in works of, 155–56, 166–67; passing for White, 160–64, 271 n.11; *Sis' Becky's Pickaninny*, 155–56; strategies for African American advancement, 156–57, 162, 168–69. *See also* Racism
City University of New York, 38, 47–48, 255 n.2
Civil Rights Movement: Congress on Racial Equality (core), 75; Fellowship of Reconciliation (for), 74–75, 261 n.19; James Lawson and, 72–75, 77, 260 n.13, 261 nn.14, 23; Negro Students' Code, 73–75, 261 n.14; nonviolence, philosophy of, 74–77, 261 nn.19, 22; southern blacks and, 72, 260 n.12; Student Nonviolent Coordinating Committee (sncc), 75, 76, 260 n.13. *See also* Racism
Class issues: American studies, 17, 18, 56–58; culture and, 248; economics

research in, 45–46; families and, 42–43, 61–62; in higher education, 44–46; social mobility and, 43; unions and, 52–53, 257 n.18; in the university curriculum, 45–46, 48, 57–58, 60, 63; the working class, 40, 45–46, 48–49, 52–53, 57, 59–60, 63. *See also* Civil Rights movement; Racism

Cold War: American art and, 248; American studies, 15, 23–24; culture and, 84, 142–43; irony, 246–47, 279 n.15; modernism and, 235, 240–41; poetry during, 240–41; values in the academy, 79–80

Colonialism, 106, 143

Commodification, 14, 80, 107–9, 111–12

Community colleges, 45, 47–48

Congress on Racial Equality (CORE), 75

Conservatism (Right), 37–39, 43–48, 62, 69–70, 255 n.2, 256 nn.7, 10

Consumerism, 24–25, 36, 41, 60, 132, 257 n.24

Crichton, Michael, 109–10, 112

Cultural studies, 14, 20–21, 61, 102, 114, 186

Cultural work: of Chesnutt's works, 157; defined, 11–12; individualism and, 50; *Jurassic Park*, 12, 113–14; of World War II era songs, 98

Culture, popular, 22, 26, 102, 189–90

Curriculum: changes in higher education and, 44–45; class studies, 45–46, 48, 57–58; and minority students, 38–39, 44–45; in overseas American studies programs, 27, 149–52; syllabi, 29–33, 70–72, 181–82, 255 n.37; university English departments, 13–14, 114, 251 n.2. *See also* Universities

Denning, Michael, 21, 24, 252 n.13, 278 n.6

Díaz, Junot (*Drown*), 126

Di Leonardo, Micaela, 60, 61, 257 n.18

Dixon, Thomas, 155, 166, 167

Du Bois, W. E. B., 156, 169

Economics: agrarianism and, 69; class issues research in, 45–46; and immigration, 128; of science and technology, 112; and university education, 40, 62

Eliot, T. S., 80, 197, 224–26, 235, 244–48

Ethnicity: borderland scholarship and, 124–28, 134–38, 268 n.38; ethnic identity in America, 133–35; and geographic mobility, 124–29, 132–33, 269 n.45; multiculturalism, 18, 21, 122–27, 265 n.7; transnationalism, 124–27, 266 n.16

Ethnic studies, 120, 136–37

Exceptionalism, American, 18, 49, 112, 121–23

Faculty: adjunct faculty, 34–35, 41–42, 47, 52, 59–60, 66–67; student evaluations, 60, 257 n.24; teaching assistants (TAS), 34–35, 47, 52–56, 59–60; universities and, 35, 41–42, 47

Family issues, 42–43, 61–62, 68–69, 104–5, 113, 264 n.30

Fellowship of Reconciliation (FOR), 74–75, 261 n.19

Feminist Press, 177, 178

Ferguson, Sally Ann, 161, 271 nn.10, 11

Flacks, Richard, 60, 62

Foucault, Michel, 103

Fugitive, The, 70, 260 n.8

Garcia, Cristina (*Dreaming in Cuban*), 126

Gay and lesbian studies, 45, 46, 133–34, 267 n.33

Gender: Amy Lowell on gender identity, 228–32; boundaries of, 130–31,

77, 261 n.22; Congress on Racial Equality, 75; Negro Students' Code, 73–75, 261 nn.14, 23; Student Nonviolent Coordinating Committee (SNCC), 75, 76, 260 n.13. *See also* Nashville movement; Nonviolence: Philosophy of; Racism

Literature, American: aesthetics vs. politics, 192–93; anthologies of, 184–91, 225–27, 235–36, 238; myths and symbols, 18, 212–13; rediscovering works of, 178–80

Lost World, The (movie), 114, 264 n.30

Lowell, Amy: body image, 226; on D. H. Lawrence, 227; and Ezra Pound, 222, 223, 225, 226–27, 277 n.12; gender as performance, 225–26, 232–33; on gender identity, 228–32; Imagism, 222–23, 230–31, 233; imagist anthologies, 223, 225, 227; on James Joyce, 227, 228; poetry as performative medium, 223–24, 229, 232; on self-definition and clothing, 228–29; sexuality, 221, 225, 229–33

Lowell, James Russell, 201–2

Macdonald, Dwight, 99–100, 103, 114
Marketplace, 24, 44, 80–81, 140
Marx, Leo, 16, 248–49, 252 n.6
Marxism, 24, 46, 248, 260 n.9, 270 n.8, 279 n.13
Matthiesson, F. O., 50–51, 257 n.17, 274 n.28
Media, 26, 79, 112–13, 186
Melville, Herman: *Benito Cereno*, 211–12, 274 n.35; boy culture in his works, 216; Carl Van Vechten on, 215; gender in works of, 208, 210–11, 213–14, 216; Henry James and, 217–18; modernism and, 213–16, 218, 219; myth of the misunderstood, 212–13; primitivism, 204, 206–9, 212; race issues, 211–12,

213; Raymond Weaver on, 205, 209–10, 212; readers' reactions to, 200–201, 214–16, 218–19; South Sea Island narratives, 204, 205–6; style of, 216–17

Men: in the American literary canon, 51, 179–80; boy culture, 90–91, 113, 204, 216, 228; cultural identity, 159–60; images of, 16, 109–10, 112, 251 n.5, 264 n.25; social mobility of, 159–60; women and, 130–31

Military, American, 79, 87–90

Miller, Perry (*Errand into the Wilderness*), 15, 16, 22

Mintz, Steven, 27, 28

Modernism: Amy Lowell and, 227–28; anthologies, 235–36; Cold War, 235, 240–41; cultural authority, 196–97, 247; gender and, 213–14; *Heath Anthology of American Literature*, 196–97; Melville, Herman and, 213–16, 218, 219; poetry, 224, 238, 240; *This Generation* (Anderson), 239–40; World War I era, 234–35, 278 n.1

Modern Language Association (MLA), 176, 201

Modern Poet and the Tradition, The (Brooks), 242–43

Morrison, Toni, 106, 122

Multiculturalism, 18, 21, 39, 122–27, 265 n.7

Mumford, Lewis, 210–11

Myths and Symbols, 18, 212–13

Nash, Diane, 72, 261 n.22

Nashville (film), 77–79

Nashville Agrarians, 67–68, 279 n.13

Nashville movement: Congress on Racial Equality (CORE), 75; Fellowship of Reconciliation (FOR), 74–75, 261 n.19; Lawson, James, 72–75, 77, 260 n.13, 261 nn.14, 23; Negro Students' Code, 73–75, 261 n.14; nonviolence, philosophy of, 74–77, 261 nn.19, 22;

media and, 79; minority students, 38, 44, 62; student tracking in, 44–45; working-class students, 48–49, 57

Students for a Democratic Society (SDS), 80

Teaching assistants (TAS), 34–35, 47, 52, 53–54, 59–60
Tenure, 35, 41, 47
Texts and text study, 12–18, 21–22, 103, 251 n.5, 252 n.13
Thomas, Scott, 60, 62
Tompkins, Jane, 103
Trilling, Lionel: high culture, 22, 112, 114, 254 n.25; on *Mansfield Park*, 100–101, 279 n.15; poetry and politics, 241
Turner, Frederick Jackson ("Frontier Thesis"), 49–50

Understanding Poetry (Brooks), 236, 237, 243–44, 245–46
Unions, 34–35, 47–48, 50–56
United States: affluence in, 40; democracy, 36, 81; demographic changes in, 125–26, 265 nn.13, 15; ethnic identity in, 133–35; exceptionalism in, 18, 49, 112, 121–23; immigration, 125–27, 138, 147, 266 n.16, 269 n.45; impact of American policies overseas, 147–48; labor unions, 52–54; multiculturalism, 18, 21, 124–26; nationalism in, 23–24, 90
Universities: access to higher education, 37–39, 43–44, 47–48, 62, 255 n.2, 256 nn.7, 10; adjunct faculty, 34–35, 41–42, 47, 52, 59–60, 66–67; affirmative action, 35, 38–39, 53, 62; American studies, 18–20, 22–23, 25, 253 n.22; California university system, 39, 45, 60; City University of New York, 38, 47–48, 255 n.2;

class issues in, 44–46; community colleges, 45, 47–48; community relations, 48, 58–59; consumerism in, 24–25, 36, 41, 60, 243–44, 257 n.24; cost of higher education, 35, 37, 39–43, 62, 256 nn.4, 6, 258 n.30; cultural authority of, 79–80, 184–86, 193, 243; education as acculturation, 43–44, 85; faculty, 35, 41–42, 47; gay and lesbian studies, 45, 46, 133–34, 267 n.33; gender studies, 45, 46, 133–34; military interests of, 79; social activism in the 1960s, 77, 80; students and, 22, 38, 44–45, 60, 62, 257 n.24; transformations in, 35, 39–40, 54, 66, 186; unions, 34–35, 47–48, 50–56, 59; women in, 38; and the workforce, 38–39, 46–47, 256 nn.4, 6

Van Doren, Carl, 205, 207–8, 217, 273 n.13
Van Vechten, Carl, 215, 218

Walzer, Michael, 128, 266 n.26
Weaver, Raymond, 205, 206, 209–10, 212, 273 n.13
White America: African American assimilation into, 153–54, 158–64, 271 n.11; agrarianism and, 70; immigration restrictions, 203; primitivism and, 206–8, 212
Williams, Raymond, 21, 46, 148
Women: and the American literary canon, 176, 179; in Chesnutt's works, 155–56, 159 62, 271 n.11; images of, 97–98, 226; in Melville's work, 213–14; poetry and, 230, 239; social mobility of, 159–60; women's studies, 20, 39, 45, 57, 182
Woodville, Richard Caton (*War News from Mexico*), 120–21, 137
Workforce: acculturation, 44; the educational workforce, 46–47; social

Workforce (*cont.*)

mobility and, 43; stratification of, 67; unions, 34–35, 47–48, 50–56, 58; university graduates in the, 38–39, 256 nn.4, 6; wages and benefits, 40, 52, 53, 59–60

Working class: students, university, 48–49, 57, 63; in the university curriculum, 45–46; wages and benefits, 40, 52, 53, 59–60

World War I, 70–71, 79, 234–35, 278 n.1

World War II, 83, 84, 87–97

Yale University, 34–35, 47, 48, 54–56, 59–60

PAUL LAUTER is Allen K. and Gwendolyn Miles Smith Professor of Literature at Trinity College, Hartford, Conn. He is the general editor of *The Heath Anthology of American Literature* (D. C. Heath, 1990, 1994; Houghton Mifflin, 1998, 2002). He is the author of *Canons and Contexts* (Oxford, 1991) and (with Florence Howe) *The Conspiracy of the Young* (World Pub., 1970). He is also the editor (with Ann Fitzgerald) of *Literature, Class, and Culture* (Addison, Wesley, Longman, 2000); Henry David Thoreau, *Walden and "Civil Disobedience"* (Houghton Mifflin, 2000); *Reconstructing American Literature: Courses, Syllabi, Issues* (Feminist Press, 1983); (with Louis Kampf) *The Politics of Literature: Dissenting Essays on the Teaching of English* (Pantheon, 1972; Vintage, 1973); *Teaching about Peace Issues* (American Friends Service Committee, 1965); *Theories of Comedy* (Anchor, 1964).

Library of Congress Cataloging-in-Publication Data
Lauter, Paul. From Walden Pond to Jurassic Park:
activism, culture, and American studies / Paul Lauter.
p. cm. — (New Americanists)   Includes index.
ISBN 0-8223-2676-0 (cloth : acid-free paper)
ISBN 0-8223-2671-x (pbk. : acid-free paper)
1. United States—Study and teaching—History—
20th century. 2. United States—Study and teaching—
Political aspects—History—20th century. 3. United
States—Civilization—1945– 4. American literature—
20th century—History and criticism. 5. Social
movements—United States—History—20th century.
I. Title. II. Series.
E175.8. L39 2001   973'.071'073—dc21   00-067208